The
Reference Shelf®

U.S. National Debate Topic 2015-2016
Surveillance

The Reference Shelf
Volume 87 • Number 3
H.W. Wilson
A Division of EBSCO Information Services

Published by
GREY HOUSE PUBLISHING
Amenia, New York
2015

The Reference Shelf

The books in this series contain reprints of articles, excerpts from books, addresses on current issues, and studies of social trends in the United States and other countries. There are six separately bound numbers in each volume, all of which are usually published in the same calendar year. Numbers one through five are each devoted to a single subject, providing background information and discussion from various points of view and concluding with an index and comprehensive bibliography that lists books, pamphlets, and articles on the subject. The final number of each volume is a collection of recent speeches. Books in the series may be purchased individually or on subscription.

Publisher's Cataloging-In-Publication Data
(Prepared by The Donohue Group, Inc.)

Publisher's Cataloging-In-Publication Data
(Prepared by The Donohue Group, Inc.)

U.S. national debate topic, 2015-2016. Surveillance / [compiled by H. W. Wilson].

　　pages : illustrations ; cm. -- (The reference shelf ; volume 87, number 3)

　　Series previously published by H. W. Wilson, a division of EBSCO Information Services.
　　Includes bibliographical references and index.
　　ISBN: 978-1-61925-692-7 (v. 87, no. 3)
　　ISBN: 978-1-61925-689-7 (volume set)

　　1. United States. National Security Agency/Central Security Service. 2. Electronic surveillance--Government policy--United States. 3. Government information--Access control--United States. 4. Privacy, Right of--United States. 5. Police patrol--United States--Surveillance operations. I. H.W. Wilson Company. II. Title: US national debate topic, 2015-2016. Surveillance III. Title: United States national debate topic, 2015-2016. Surveillance IV. Title: Surveillance V. Series: Reference shelf ; v. 87, no. 3.

JK468.S4 U8 2015
352.3/79/0973

Printed in Canada

Contents

2

3

4

Effectiveness of Domestic Surveillance in Fighting Crime and Terror

5

Racial, Ethnic, and Political Profiling

Preface

Surveillance is a key feature of modern American life. Toll booths monitor drivers on the interstate, and social media gather information from users for marketing data. Many people are unaware that when they use websites like Google and Amazon they enter into an agreement that allows retailers to track them for commercial purposes. In the name of national security, the government gathers information on most citizens. Surveillance, particularly government surveillance, constitutes one of the great social and legal tensions of the twenty-first century. How do we embrace technology's magnificent, egalitarian promise of equal access to information for all citizens and use state-of-the-art surveillance tactics that can promote safe communities while also upholding traditional civil liberties and individual privacy?

These concerns are not only philosophical or constitutional conundrums but also practical ethical and legal matters. Cell phone tracking provides a good example of the kind of real-world problems presented by the use of surveillance. Law enforcement agencies commonly use a single cell tower to place a suspect at the scene of a crime, even though defense lawyers have challenged the practice and have shown that it is scientifically unreliable and inaccurate.

If a reporter records a conversation without informing the interviewee (a procedure that is legal in several states), most people would consider this practice unethical or underhanded, or at least a violation of trust. When the government gathers "metadata"[1] from the phone calls of millions of citizens, is this also unethical or a violation of trust?

The articles presented in this volume explore these ideas and how what is done in the name of public safety goes to the core of our country's values.

Surveillance In the Name of Public Policy

In *Olmstead v. United States* (1928), the United States Supreme Court ruled that police could issue warrantless wiretaps on phone conversations. This decision (overturned nearly 40 years later) found that the language of the Fourth Amendment protecting citizens against arbitrary search and seizure did not apply because telephone wires reached well beyond the walls of a private residence. "The intervening wires are not part of his house or office, any more than are the highways along which they are stretched," Chief Justice William H. Taft wrote in the majority opinion.

As with many important court rulings on government surveillance, the case that necessitated the ruling was related to enforcing a major public policy of the time, Prohibition. The government viewed wiretapping as necessary to stamp out bootlegging, which had emerged as a lucrative, and illegal, import and distribution industry.

In the 1960s and 1970s, to counteract civil rights, antiwar activists, and other radicals, the FBI initiated the Counter Intelligence Program (COINTELPRO), which involved massive surveillance, infiltration, and disruption of domestic political groups. Policy makers would later view many of these methods as unnecessary and unconstitutional.

After the attack on the World Trade Center and Pentagon in September 2001, the government, whose case for surveillance was never more forceful, used surveillance on a grander scale than ever before in order to counter faceless enemies and prevent possible repeated terrorist attacks.

Passed in October of 2001, the USA PATRIOT Act became the legislative prototype for preventive surveillance policy in the post-9/11 world and provided the legal tools to advance a national security policy intended to thwart immediate threats to the United States. A key element of the program expanded the federal government's ability to gather data on private citizens and to search telephone, email, and financial records without a court order. Had the act been drafted and considered during a time of peace, it most likely would not have gained much traction but rather would have generated public debate and scrutiny. Instead, in an atmosphere of fear, Congress passed and the president signed a bill with far-reaching and unforeseen consequences.

Big Data in the Private Sector

The expanded use of telephone and Internet surveillance is part of most Americans' daily lives from the moment they wake up and check their smart phones. And as policy makers make the case for increased levels of surveillance as a means toward a safer country, the government has sought to leverage major, private-sector advances in data collection to achieve its national security aims.

Following 9/11, the NSA began working with American telephone companies, which provided access to domestic calling records and company analysis of calling patterns. This was not legal at first, but executive authority made it so in the hope that the information would present a potentially potent tool in the war on terror.

Four Internet and telephone metadata and content collection programs were created under executive authority, deemed the President's Surveillance Program, or PSP. Created during a time of crisis by some of President George W. Bush's top aides, NSA chief General Michael Hayden, and Vice President Dick Cheney, PSP circumvented checks put in place by the Foreign Intelligence Surveillance Act decades before and granted the NSA broad reach into American territories and Americans living overseas. The Foreign Intelligence Surveillance Act (FISA) court wasn't notified of the program at the outset and it would be nearly six years before the PSP would be placed under FISA's jurisdiction.

Ultimately, these programs were halted in 2011 because they did not reach the level of efficacy intended–not because of the prevailing concerns related to privacy, a lack of court orders or, in many cases, the absence of probable cause.

In 2013, Edward Snowden, a government contractor working for the National Security Agency, leaked thousands of classified documents that showed the extent of global surveillance programs, revealing for the first time that the U.S. government was collecting the phone records of most of its own citizens. The documents he leaked fortified the concerns of civil libertarians and intensified the current debate around the balance between national security and information privacy. Since the leaks, two important court rulings have split on the constitutionality of the NSA's bulk collection of telephone metadata, and one recent ruling has stated that the NSA's program, while constitutional, has reached beyond its intended scope.

In December 2013, a federal judge ruled that the government's collection of domestic phone records is unconstitutional. The judge, U.S. District Judge Richard Leon, said the National Security Agency's bulk collection of metadata violates privacy rights. The ruling pushed back at the government's argument that a 1979 Maryland case, *Smith v. Maryland*, provided precedent for the constitutionality of collecting phone metadata, noting that public use of telephones had increased dramatically in the past three decades. In that case, the U.S. Supreme Court ruled that authorities did not need a warrant to install a pen register, or an electronic device that records all numbers called from a particular telephone line, because it did not constitute a "search" as defined by the Fourth Amendment.

However, just days later in December 2013, the NSA scored a victory when a U.S. District Judge William Pauley of New York ruled NSA's bulk collection of phone records under Section 215 of the USA PATRIOT Act was, in fact, legal. Section 215 was among the programs revealed in Snowden's classified leaks.

Striking a Balance

In May 2015, a New York federal appeals court ruled that the NSA's phone record collection program is illegal, signaling a setback for congressional leaders who favored reconstituting the Section 215 statute as its June 1 expiration approached. The ruling, however, did not question the constitutionality of Section 215 or order the program to cease; however, in the years since the act's passage and with the hindsight of a protracted military campaign, there has been increasing political pressure to strike a balance between safeguarding civil liberties and assuring national security.

On June 1, 2015, Section 215 of the USA PATRIOT Act expired, and the May ruling of the New York federal appeals court helped pave the way for a new federal bill designed to rein in government surveillance, the USA Freedom Act. The Freedom Act overwhelmingly passed in the House of Representatives by a vote of 338-88 and, on June 2, after much deliberation also passed in the Senate by a vote of 67-32, despite a strong and vocal opposition led by Senator Mitch McConnell. President Obama signed the bill hours later. Among other things, this act ended the government's bulk collection and storage of phone data, but as the divisive vote in Congress indicates, the act did not end the debate.

Matthew Brian Hersh

Note

1. In this case, metadata is a form of transactional information. It does not specifically document an individual's action as does a wiretap or surveillance video, but, if collected en masse, metadata can paint an accurate picture of someone's daily activities: where she or he goes and whom she or he calls.

1
National Security Versus Personal Privacy

On October 26, 2013, demonstrators march through Washington, DC, toward the National Mall for a rally to demand that U.S. Congress investigate the National Security Agency's mass surveillance programs.

The Digital Invasion: Privacy Versus Secrecy in the Digital Age

The September 11, 2001 (9/11), terrorist attacks on the United States initiated a transformative period in American culture. Given the nature of the threat, the U.S. Government made broad changes to domestic and foreign security policies, including granting increased and often-unregulated powers to security and intelligence organizations to conduct surveillance operations. From 2002 to 2015, federal and state agencies conducted mass surveillance operations that included intercepting mobile telephone calls, text messages and emails, tracking online purchases and browsing, creating databases of images for photo recognition, and conducting widespread video and aerial surveillance operations.

Controversial surveillance operations have raised questions about personal privacy. While federal and state agencies collect and analyze information as part of a broader effort to prevent terrorism, critics argue that mass surveillance violates rights to privacy under the Fourth Amendment. The debate over security versus privacy also raises the question of ownership regarding data shared through private digital networks and whether new regulations are needed to protect the privacy of information given to third-party Internet and communications companies.

History of Domestic Surveillance

Governments have always watched their citizens. In Ancient Rome, emperors created legions of spies to watch over the populace for threats of insurrection. During the "Reign of Terror" of the French Revolution, from 1793 to 1794, Robespierre and his cadre employed surveillance committees to infiltrate and observe the population, eventually targeting as many as 500,000 "suspicious" individuals who were arrested, detained, or interrogated for connections to the former nobility.

The American government began conducting domestic surveillance in the 1920s, with the controversial Black Chamber program created by cryptologist Herbert Yardley. In 1931, Yardley published a book, *The American Black Chamber*, detailing his involvement in the program, which involved collecting and monitoring telegraphs, with the compliance of companies like Western Union. Yardley's surveillance program was disbanded in 1929, with Secretary of State Henry Stimson issuing a statement that reportedly contained the now famous statement "Gentlemen do not read each others' mail."

A similar surveillance program, Operation SHAMROCK, was created during World War II, monitoring communications with the compliance of Western Union, ITT, and RCA Global. This led to the establishment of the National Security Agency (NSA) in 1952, in an effort to counter the perceived threat of Soviet intelligence and spy networks. The "Cold War" lasted from the end of World War II (around 1947–48) to at least the early 1990s, and resulted in a vast escalation of domestic and foreign surveillance programs. In 1975, a series of Senate hearings, the "Church Committee Hearings," were organized to investigate surveillance and privacy. The committee recommended reforms and, in 1978, Congress signed the Foreign Intelligence Surveillance Act (FISA), stipulating that government agencies needed to obtain special warrants before they could spy on American citizens.

In the wake of 9/11, the George W. Bush administration signed laws that gave the NSA and CIA the ability to conduct surveillance without adhering to FISA guidelines.

According to the digital rights group Electronic Future Foundation (EFF), in early 2002 information began to surface indicating that the NSA was engaging in warrantless wiretapping of American citizens. AT&T technician Mark Klein revealed classified data that AT&T was developing a software system that allowed the NSA to capture and analyze cellular communication. The EFF filed suit against AT&T in 2007, charging the company with illegally selling customer data. As a result, Congress passed H.R. 6304 in 2008, an amendment to FISA granting companies that cooperated with the NSA immunity from prosecution.

In 2013, former NSA and CIA analyst Edward Snowden leaked confidential CIA and NSA documents to reporter Glenn Greenwald of the *Guardian* and several American journalists. In June 2013, *The Guardian* and *The Washington Post* published articles revealing details of the NSA PRISM program, which collects stored Internet data from companies like Google Inc. and Yahoo!, for analysis. Snowden was charged with theft and fled the United States.

In October 2013, it was revealed, from the leaked documents, that the NSA collected more than 250 million email views and contact lists from Facebook, Google's Gmail, and Yahoo. In 2014, an article in *The Guardian* revealed that the NSA was also collecting millions of text messages each day in an "untargeted" surveillance sweep. Further revelations in 2014 showed that the NSA was collecting information from webcams and that the NSA's MYSTIC program could record 100 percent of the phone calls coming out of a country. In May 2014, James Risen and Laura Poitras revealed that the NSA was collecting millions of facial images from web images to be used in the creation of facial recognition programs. Journalists Glenn Greenwald and Laura Poitras, who wrote some of the first articles about the Snowden leaks, became editors of the Internet publication *The Intercept,* which continued publishing documents and analysis from Snowden in 2014 and 2015.

Privacy and the Constitution

The United States Constitution does not explicitly and distinctly guarantee a person's right to privacy. However, specific provisions of the Bill of Rights can and have been used to protect personal privacy. The First Amendment, which protects free speech, expression, and the right to "assemble" has been used to protect the privacy to hold beliefs and political views. The Third Amendment, which specifically prohibits the government from forcibly taking property from private owners, has been used to guarantee privacy inside a person's home. The amendment that directly applies to NSA surveillance is the Fourth Amendment, ratified in 1791, which guarantees freedom from "unreasonable searches and seizures."

The Fourth Amendment is the cornerstone of privacy from government intrusion, establishing the legal principle that federal and state authorities must be able to demonstrate compelling cause before searching or confiscating an individual's property, documents, or communication records. While initially applying primarily to written correspondence, digital privacy advocates have argued that Fourth Amendment provisions should apply to digital communications as well. However, the 1979 case of *Smith v. Maryland*, (and similar rulings in the 1960s and 1970s) established that sharing data with a third party, in some situations, relinquished an individual's "expectation of privacy."

As third party sharing is a legal issue regarding the privacy of information, politicians and rights advocates have been struggling to address the issue of ownership with regard to mobile and digital communication. The public telephone system is considered a public trust, and as such, telephone communications are afforded a degree of privacy. Other types of communications, including involvement in social media, email, and other digital transmissions, are not protected under the same provisions. In general, the company providing transmission of the data in question establishes ownership of digital data through corporate policy. A review of Facebook policies, for instance, indicates that any data posted on a person's Facebook site becomes the property, in part, of Facebook. This is the provision that allows Facebook to donate or sell a person's private data to other companies or to government agencies.

In the 2010 case of *U.S. v. Warshak*, the Sixth Circuit Court of Appeals ruled that the government needs a court order to seize email communications, thus effectively extending protections afforded to telephone and U.S. mail to email communications as well. The 2010 case was one of several modern challenges to government surveillance and attempts to establish rules regarding the privacy of digital communications. In the December 2013 case of *Klayman v. Obama*, Federal District Judge Richard J. Leon ruled that NSA surveillance violated the Fourth Amendment, calling the program an "indiscriminate" and "arbitrary invasion." Leon went further, characterizing the NSA program as "almost Orwellian," in reference to the George Orwell novel *1984* about a world under totalitarian government surveillance.

Also in December 2013, District Judge William Pauley delivered a contradicting verdict, in the case of *American Civil Liberties Union v. Clapper*. In sharp contrast to Leon's ruling in *Klayman v. Obama*, Pauley ruled, citing *Smith v. Maryland*, that metadata collected by the NSA, which is already stored by the phone company, is not protected as the customer has no expectation of privacy with regard to data already "given" or "shared" with the phone company. The EFF and ACLU held that Pauley's decision was a major blow against digital privacy and planned to appeal the decision.

The Intelligence Authorization Act of 2015 (H.R. 4681), passed in March, established guidelines for the storage of data collected through government surveillance.

According to the law, data may only be stored for five years unless the agency in possession can demonstrate a link to terrorism or a potential imminent threat to human life. H.R. 4681 also renews and expands research and development of intelligence technology, including a provision to fund the development of intelligence technology that would allow gathering information from space.

Public Opinion

In a November 2014 Pew Research Report, 91 percent of U.S. adults agreed that consumers lack control over digital information used by companies. In addition, 81 percent of respondents felt that their social media data was not secure, while 46 percent felt insecure sharing personal information via cell phone. A Pew report from March 2015, however, indicated that most Americans have mixed feelings about government surveillance. In general, the study indicated that a slight majority of Americans report being "not very" or "not at all" concerned about government surveillance of cell phones, social media, or other digital communications. However, 61 percent of respondents also said they were increasingly skeptical that U.S. surveillance programs served the public interest. In addition, 60 percent of Americans believed it was unacceptable for the government to monitor "ordinary citizens."

In general, though most Americans disapprove of government mass surveillance programs, most also feel that surveillance will not affect them directly and are therefore largely unconcerned. This lack of concern is largely due to the fact that, as of 2015, there have been few widely publicized cases of the government "abusing" the data that it is collecting on citizens. While privacy advocates argue that oversight and regulation are needed now, to preemptively prevent such abuse, many Americans may remain unconcerned until they have direct proof that modern surveillance is not only invasive but also dangerous *to them*. Revelations of mass surveillance have inspired comparisons to "Big Brother," the symbol of the authoritarian police state in George Orwell's book *1984*. Though few would argue that America has become a repressive regime, the level of data collection currently possible and unregulated is a concern to many precisely because it makes this kind of repression possible.

Micah L. Issitt

NSA Spying: It Didn't Start with 9/11

By Jack Kenny
The New American, October 7, 2013

Citizens of the "land of the free and the home of the brave," during the self-advertised "most transparent administration in American history," have learned from a lawbreaker now in exile of the activities of a secret government agency, operating out of a U.S. Army base in Maryland, that collects and stores billions of phone call records and e-mail messages each and every day. The lawbreaker, a fugitive from justice named Edward Snowden, is living in temporary asylum in Russia, home of America's ersatz Cold War enemy, the Union of Soviet Socialist Republics. The U.S. agency and the program conducted at Fort Meade, Maryland, is arguably a Cold War relic that leaves open the question: In the war between freedom and totalitarianism, which side is Washington really on?

For millions of Americans, including many in the news and "in the know," the Snowden revelations and document drop to *The Guardian* and the *Washington Post* were their first brush with knowledge about the activities or even the existence of the super-secret National Security Agency, one of 16 intelligence agencies of the U.S. government. For those with an interest in such matters, however, it was less of a surprise. In 2010, the *Washington Post* alerted readers to the phenomenal growth of the surveillance state in America with a series of articles by leftist reporters Dana Priest and William Arkin, called Top Secret America. The series was published later that year as a book bearing the same title. The revelations by Priest and Arkin dealt entirely with the growth of the security or surveillance state since the terrorist attacks of September 11, 2001, the latter-day Pearl Harbor that shocked the nation into an awareness of the need for enhanced security. Whether all of the security measures adopted since that time, including the vast new bureaucracy known as the Department of Homeland Security, have made the nation and its citizens any safer is a topic of ongoing debate. But most narratives about it begin with the oft-stated premise that "everything changed on 9/11."

Snoops Before 9/11

The change, however dramatic, was of degree, not of nature. The security state growing in America has been ongoing since World War II and even before. The iconic FBI director J. Edgar Hoover, revered by both political parties but especially by the Republicans, began his career with the Department of Justice before the

FBI was even created and was compiling dossiers on suspected subversives even while Woodrow Wilson was in the White House in the waning days of World War I. Hoover became director of the Bureau of Investigation in the 1920s and in the 1930s, when the name "Federal" was added. Hoover was conducting illegal wiretaps and "black bag" operations (break-ins to plant listening devices) to keep President Franklin D. Roosevelt informed and advised on the activities of members of the America First Committee and other political opponents of Roosevelt, his New Deal, and Lend-Lease, the "AAA foreign policy" described by Sen. Burton K. Wheeler (D-Mont.) as a project that would "plow under every fourth American boy," a barb that brought Roosevelt to new levels of fury.

When secret White House tapes threatened to (and eventually did) bring down the Nixon administration in the Watergate scandal, author/journalist Victor Lasky published *It Didn't Start With Watergate*, a 1973 book highlighting the secret snooping activities of Roosevelt's and succeeding administrations.

Similarly, the rogue activities of the NSA did not begin with 9/11. Nor was that agency alone among Washington's clandestine agencies in penetrating the private communications and semi-public activities of the American people. The FBI's COINTELPRO (for counterintelligence program) operations came to light in the mid-1970s when a Senate committee chaired by Idaho Democrat Frank Church began looking into allegations of extra-legal activities by both the FBI and CIA. The FBI had been infiltrating and conducting surveillance activities on pro-communist, antiwar, and other organizations for years by that time, while the CIA, forbidden by law from investigating domestic political activities, had strayed so far from its appointed role of intelligence gathering that its covert activities included assassination attempts on heads of state, most notably Cuban ruler Fidel Castro. The targeting of Castro occurred during the Kennedy administration when Vice President Lyndon Johnson, who was not "in the loop," stumbled upon the project and reportedly exclaimed that the CIA was running "a g**d***ed Murder, Incorporated!"

Certainly, the moral and ethical distinctions between the activities of our democratically elected government and those of organized crime were shrinking to a point that even Lyndon Johnson, no peace-loving disciple of Saint Francis of Assisi, found shocking. On the matter of surveillance, both President John and Attorney General Robert Kennedy approved FBI wiretaps on civil rights leader Martin Luther King, Jr., among others. King's successor and fellow preacher in the Southern Christian Leadership Conference, Ralph Abernathy, was said to have preached a sermon to J. Edgar Hoover through a bug found planted in his pulpit. When the FBI director died, Abernathy observed his passing should remind all that "almighty God conducts the ultimate surveillance."

Since the Church Committee

The result of the Church Committee hearings was an effort by Congress to rein in the antidemocratic activities of government agencies, even when matters of national security were allegedly at stake. The legendary Hoover had died by then, and the Justice Department was expected to reassert its statutory authority over what could fairly be called a "rogue agency." The Foreign Intelligence Surveillance Act established the Foreign Intelligence Surveillance Court, where government officials are required to go to gain warrants for wiretaps and surveillance of al-

> **For years the standing joke in Washington was that NSA stood for "No Such Agency" or "Never Say Anything." Indeed, Congress even made a statutory declaration that if such an agency existed, no one was required to divulge its existence or its activities.**

leged foreign activities within the United States. The FISA "court," of course, hears only the government's argument for placing private citizens under surveillance in connection with an investigation of an alleged foreign operation. The court rarely denies or even modifies a request for authorization of surveillance activity.

Somehow the National Security Agency escaped attention during all that effort at reform. From its beginning the agency has operated without congressional oversight and with hardly any congressional knowledge. While Congress, at least tangentially, created the Bureau of Investigation and authorized the reorganization of the World War II OSS into the Cold War's CIA, the NSA was created entirely by directive of President Harry S. Truman. According to James Bamford, whose 462-page history *The Puzzle Palace* was published in 1982, Truman issued his executive order in October of 1952, effective on a certain date in November. The November 4, 1952, date was not chosen at random. It was reasonably anticipated that the attention of the nation would be occupied by another event that day — the quadrennial election of a president of the United States.

The agency created in secrecy likewise thrived in the shadows of a government that would continue the New Deal tradition in production of "alphabet soup" agencies during the Eisenhower (Health Education and Welfare, aka HEW) and Kennedy (Housing and Urban Development or HUD) administrations. Particularly during the 1960s, the nation's problems appeared to have little to do with secret agencies, given the level of national and international chaos that was played out in each day's general circulation print and telecast news. As debate raged over the Vietnam War and cities went up in flames during race riots, the National Security Agency was not even a blip on the public's radar screen. Yet its growth and influence were enormous. According to Bamford, the CIA's Operations Division reached a personnel peak of eight thousand during the Vietnam War and had been shrunk to four thousand by 1978. The NSA, meanwhile, "controlled 68,203 people" in 1978, "more than all the employees of the rest of the intelligence community put together," Bamford wrote.

Indeed, behind the menacing barbed wire surrounding the NSA headquarters at Fort Meade, the NSA has a city of its own, which, if incorporated as such, would be one of the largest municipalities in the state of Maryland. It includes, Bamford wrote in his 2008 book, *The Shadow Factory*, 32 miles of roads to accommodate more than 37,000 cars and a post office distributing more than 70,000 pieces of mail each day. More than 700 uniformed officers make up the NSA's internal police force, which has its own formidable SWAT team. The NSA's fire department responded to 168 alarms and 44 automobile accidents in one recent year.

They Really Don't Want to Know

Yet few, even among members of the intelligence committees in Congress, have been aware of the agency's size, scope, and influence. "Even a congressional committee was forced to issue a subpoena in order to obtain a copy of the directive that implemented [Truman's] memorandum," Bamford wrote. Nor, apparently, did members of Congress want to know. For years the standing joke in Washington was that NSA stood for "No Such Agency" or "Never Say Anything." Indeed, Congress even made a statutory declaration that if such an agency existed, no one was required to divulge its existence or its activities. In 1959, Congress passed Public Law 86-36, stating in part: "Nothing in this Act or any other law . . . shall be construed to require the disclosure of the organization or any function of the National Security Agency, or any information with respect to the activities thereof, or the names, titles, salaries, or number of persons employed by such agency."

"Never Say Anything," indeed. The congressional head-in-the-sand posture would later bring to mind the comic figure Sergeant Shultz in the TV sitcom *Hogan's Heroes*. "I know nothing! I see nothing!"

While 9/11 was not the origin of the NSA, it did provide a rationale for increased surveillance by it and other government agencies. By the time Priest and Arkin did their study, the U.S. security apparatus was incomprehensible, even to those ostensibly in charge of running it. As the *Washington Post* summarized the findings of the exhaustive study:

> The top-secret world the government created in response to the terrorist attacks of Sept. 11, 2001, has become so large, so unwieldy and so secretive that no one knows how much money it costs, how many people it employs, how many programs exist within it or exactly how many agencies do the same work. . . . After nine years of unprecedented spending and growth, the result is that the system put in place to keep the United States safe is so massive that its effectiveness is impossible to determine.

Security Run Amok

Among the findings disclosed in Top Secret America:

- Some 1,271 government organizations and 1,931 private companies work on programs related to counterterrorism, homeland security, and intelligence in about 10,000 locations across the United States.

- An estimated 854,000 people, nearly 1.5 times as many people as live in Washington, D.C., hold top-secret security clearances.

• In Washington and the surrounding area, 33 building complexes for top-secret intelligence work are under construction or have been built since September 2001. Together they occupy the equivalent of almost three Pentagons or 22 U.S. Capitols — about 17 million square feet of space.

• Many security and intelligence agencies do the same work, creating redundancy and waste. For example, 51 federal organizations and military commands, operating in 15 U.S. cities, track the flow of money to and from terrorist networks.

• Analysts who make sense of documents and conversations obtained by foreign and domestic spying share their judgment by publishing 50,000 intelligence reports each year — a volume so large that many are routinely ignored.

Despite what is, to all appearances, massive overkill, the NSA is building a huge new facility in the desert in Utah to further expand its surveillance operations. And the NSA, recall, is but one — the largest to be sure, but still one — of 16 intelligence agencies of the U.S. government. It's not something the average American would keep track of, so let the late Chalmers Johnson give us the roster from his 2010 book, hopefully entitled *Dismantling the Empire*:

> The sixteen agencies include the intelligence organizations of each military service — the Air Force, Army, Coast Guard, Marine Corps and Navy — and the Defense Intelligence Agency, which reflect interservice rivalries more than national needs or interests; the departments of Energy, Homeland Security, State, Treasury and Drug Enforcement Administration, as well as the FBI and National Security Agency; and the units devoted to satellite and reconnaissance (National Geospatial Intelligence Agency, National Reconnaissance Office).

Nothing Succeeds Like Failure

If that much intelligence could neither detect nor prevent the terrorist attacks of 9/11, why should we believe that more of the same will finally make America safe? In the intelligence industry, as in other areas of government, it appears that nothing succeeds and increases appropriations like failure, even spectacular failure.

Not that there was a complete failure of intelligence leading up to 9/11. While President George W. Bush was clearing brush at his Texas ranch and the government of Vice President Cheney was preoccupied with other things, the Presidential Daily Briefing of August 6, 2001, warned that al-Qaeda was planning a major attack on the United States. Exactly what that meant became clear one month and five days later, as the putative commander in chief was shuttled from one secret bunker to another while the vice president issued orders from the White House basement. The United States of America, which spends more on military defense and employs more people in intelligence than any nation the world has ever known or could even imagine, was struck with four hijacked airplanes that knocked down the twin towers of the World Trade Center and flew into the Pentagon while America's air defenses were elsewhere. Some 3,000 people, Americans and foreign nationals in New York and Washington, were killed, and the land of the free and home of the brave became the nation whose president was in hiding while the vice president was issuing orders to shoot down any civilian plane that strayed into Washington, D.C., airspace.

Now the Congress that for decades saw, heard, and spoke no evil about the NSA is full of indignation over Snowden's revelations, claiming the leaked materials have compromised national security and perhaps even the lives of our intelligence "assets" overseas because the whole world, including our potential enemies, know how the NSA operates. Supposedly, the NSA keeps us safe by discovering the secret plans of terrorists disclosed in e-mails or posted on Facebook.

Gen. Keith Alexander, head of the NSA; former director of the FBI Robert Mueller; and others have said, for example, that a phone call from one of the 9/11 hijackers in San Diego to an al-Qaeda safe house in Yemen might have been detected and the September 11 plot thwarted if the NSA program disclosed by Snowden had been in place in the early months of 2001. Reporters have reported and pundits have repeated that so many times that it begs the question of how intelligent people can overlook something so obvious. If U.S. intelligence could trace the calls to the Yemen safe house, why not simply monitor all calls there, regardless of where they come from, rather than collect the records of all calls from San Diego and everywhere else in the United States? The modus operandi of the NSA apparently is to offset the difficulty of finding a needle in the haystack by ordering more hay — tons and tons of it.

Indeed, the suspect in question, Khalid al-Midhar, had already been targeted by U.S. intelligence, which traced his travels and that of fellow conspirator Nawaf al-Hazmi from an al-Qaeda gathering in Kuala Lumpur to a flight to Los Angeles, where they landed at LA International Airport in January 2001, both with valid U.S. passports. They took up residence in a house in San Diego, where they could be found by name in the greater San Diego phone book.

Yet the Congress of the United States, embroiled decades earlier in debate over who lost China, who knew what at Yalta, and who promoted Peress (an Army dentist with communist connections whose promotion was a key bone of contention in the Army-McCarthy hearings), has shown little interest in who let that hijacker escape detection. Meanwhile, Snowden has been denounced as a traitor, charged with espionage and theft of government property, and has become a bone of contention between the United States, which has demanded his return to stand trial, and Russia, which has granted him asylum.

If, as Priest and Arkin reported in 2010, some 854,000 people have top-secret security clearance, then it is hardly surprising that, given the huge number of them, a few may find it expedient or even patriotic to spill the beans on surveillance operations or covert activities. The danger, of course, is that the government may decide to give every American at birth a top-secret security clearance, eventually making every American guilty of a federal crime for telling what he or she knows. According to investigative journalist Tim Shorrock in *Spies for Hire: The Secret World of*

Intelligence Outsourcing, the number of contractors doing business with the NSA grew from 144 companies in 2001 to 5,400 in 2006. Wrote Shorrock:

> If there's one generalization to be made about the NSA's outsourced IT [information technology] it is this: they haven't worked very well, and some have been spectacular failures. . . . In 2006, the NSA was unable to analyze much of the information it was collecting. . . . As a result more than 90 percent of the information it was gathering was being discarded without being translated into a coherent and understandable format; only about five percent was translated from its digital form into text and then routed to the right division for analysis. The key phrase in the new counterterrorism lexicon is "public-private partnerships.". . . In reality "partnerships" are a convenient cover for the perpetuation of corporate interests.

Defending What?

While we the people are encouraged to believe that the men and women in our armed forces who are sent to fight in foreign lands are always defending our freedoms, we might wonder who and what are the real threats to our liberty. The essence of liberty, the freedom to pursue the "good life," is the ability to stand alone and act in obedience to one's conscience, even when that conscience requires one to try to save his country from his government. The threat to American liberty from Iraq's elusive and illusory "weapons of mass destruction" or Bashar al-Assad's chemical weapons in Syria is remote, perhaps non-existent at a time when the U.S. government has satellites aloft that can detect a whisper from 22,000 miles in space. That has the potential to capture the pillow talk of any one or any number of the 854,000 or so people with top-secret security clearance who may be divulging secrets to their wives or husbands. We can never be too careful in a "post-9/11 world."

It is a world the Founders of this Republic did not know, and ours is a nation they would no longer recognize. The requirements of the Fourth Amendment have gone largely ignored by the FISA "court," as well as by the NSA and other agencies of the federal government. Warrants issued now resemble the Writs of Assistance issued by authority of the British crown, those authorizations of fishing expeditions against which our colonial ancestors rebelled. Those who rebel against such measures in today's America are often accused of having a "pre-9/11 mentality." Former Sen. Russell Feingold once responded to that charge by accusing his accusers of acting on a mindset that is "pre-1776."

Which mindset or vision will ultimately prevail will determine the future — or the end — of freedom in America.

US Privacy Board Dissenters Defend Balancing Act of NSA Surveillance

By Spencer Ackerman
The Guardian, January 23, 2014

Not every member of the US government's independent privacy board signed on to its scathing Thursday report finding that bulk collection of US phone records is illegal and ought to end.

The dissenting minority, who cautiously embraced the practice, presented a defense of mass surveillance that was far more sophisticated and intellectually honest than the one presented until recently by the National Security Agency in the wake of the Edward Snowden revelations.

Accordingly, the difficulty they had in convincing their colleagues of the merits of their narrower defenses of the program speaks to the same difficulty the NSA has had in persuading skeptical members of Congress of its value. It looks to become crucial to the unfolding fight between the agency and Capitol Hill to amend or end the bulk collection outright.

Those two dissenting members of the Privacy and Civil Liberties Oversight Board (PCLOB), Rachel Brand and Elisebeth Collins Cook, both lawyers in the George W. Bush administration, did not endorse bulk metadata collection so much as they were discomfited by the scope of their colleagues' castigation of its legality, propriety, and utility.

The PCLOB majority rested much of its rejection of the mass domestic surveillance on the grounds that it found not one "single instance" in which collecting Americans' phone data in bulk "directly contributed to the discovery of a previously unknown terrorist plot or the disruption of a terrorist attack". It was the strongest government rebuke yet of the root necessity of the 12-year-old surveillance program.

Cook and Brand made a more circumscribed case for what the bulk phone records surveillance can offer—essentially, more than nothing, but less than the visibility into active terrorism links to domestic activity that the NSA has spent months presenting to the public and years presenting to the Hill in secret.

Hypothetical Value over Demonstrated Value

"There is no easy way to calculate the value of this program," Brand conceded during the board's Thursday meeting, echoing a position NSA officials have fallen back on when pressed in congressional hearings. The case she made turned on its hypothetical value, rather than its demonstrated one.

"The test cannot be whether it has already been the key factor in thwarting a previously unknown terrorist attack. Assessing the benefit of a preventive program like this one requires a longer-term view. Most of this data is never used at all. But its immediate availability if it is needed is the program's primary benefit. Its usefulness may not be fully realized until we face another large-scale terrorist plot. But if that happens, analysts' ability to very quickly scan records from multiple service providers at the same time to establish connections or avoid wasting precious time on futile leads could be critical in thwarting a plot."

Cook made a similar argument, comparing the bulk collection to a "triage" mechanism in case of emergency.

"A tool such as the [bulk collection], which allows investigators to triage and focus on those who are more likely to be doing harm to or who are in the United States, or that allows investigators to dismiss potential homeland connections to ongoing terror threats or plots is valuable," Cook contended.

"As the majority has already indicated, section 215 [the bulk phone data collection] has been used in conjunction to other authorities to supply additional leads or supply confirming or supplemental information about our adversaries, which makes it a valuable program."

That is a case intelligence community officials have come to make belatedly and reluctantly.

In the first weeks after Snowden disclosed the phone records mass collection to the *Guardian*, the NSA's leadership publicly portrayed it as a linchpin to stop future terrorist attacks inside the US.

"The intel community failed to connect the dots in 9/11. And much of what we've done since then were to give us the capabilities—and this is the business record FISA, what's sometimes called Section 215 and the FAA 702—two capabilities that help us connect the dots," NSA director Keith Alexander told ABC News in June.

Alexander, rebuffing observations from two Senate intelligence committee members who said NSA was conflating the value of the two programs to protect the bulk domestic phone records collection, continued to say it had sussed out domestic connections to "a little over 10" terrorist plots.

The following month, then-deputy FBI director Sean Joyce and Alexander deputy Chris Inglis conceded to the Senate judiciary committee that there was only one terrorist plot discovered by the bulk phone records program "that comes close to a 'but for' example."

Yet Alexander, the outgoing NSA director, has continued to publicly argue that the program is critical to preventing domestic terrorist attacks.

"Don't drop it, because that's our country, and if you do drop it, the chance of that a terrorist attack gets through increases," Alexander told a Bloomberg forum in Washington on October 30.

Over the years, in classified documents only recently revealed, the NSA has portrayed the program in even starker terms, usually when it required congressional reauthorization for the Patriot Act provisions it cited to justify the bulk collection.

A 2009 secret briefing letter for Congress about bulk phone data collection began: "Since the tragedy of 9/11, the Intelligence Community has developed an array of capabilities to detect, identify and disrupt terrorist plots against the United States and its interests." Only very close readers would notice that it did not claim the bulk phone data collection actually disrupted any such plots within the US.

Inglis has recently backed away from the claim. In an interview with NPR on January 9, he likened the bulk collection to an "insurance policy" for detecting domestic terrorism, rather than a proven, crucial tool. That formulation was echoed days later by Michael Morrell, the former deputy CIA director who advised Obama on surveillance reforms.

During the PCLOB's Thursday press conference, Brand and Cook conceded that the scale of the ongoing data collection "creates at least a risk of a serious privacy intrusion," in Brand's words, and they hoped an alternative could be found. They feared that turning the database into private hands, as President Obama has proposed, would neither satisfy the privacy concerns nor any future counter-terrorism official's security interest.

"It's a value judgment"

All five members of the board demurred when asked if they considered the NSA to have been dishonest about the program's efficacy, despite the majority's harsh rejection of its value and the minority's circumscribed case for it.

But retired federal judge Patricia Wald, a member of the PCLOB majority, argued that the dispute boiled down to a philosophical difference.

"What you have seen is just a different philosophy rather than—at least this is my perception—somebody trying in the intelligence community to mislead people as to the value of the program," Wald said.

"We have heard people inside the intelligence community describe it as like fire insurance: you may never use it, but you ought to have the fire insurance in the one out of a thousand chances that your house is going to go on fire, etcetera. So it is really a notion that if something bad comes on down the line in the one of every 100,000 chances that is—it's a value judgment—worth collecting all the data that some of us think down the line has a risk to privacy. Versus some who think that the so-called One Percent Calculus is just not worth it. It's really a balancing."

Whether Congress accepts that contention, rather than the much-refuted case that the mass phone data collection has stopped terrorism, remains to be seen. It is now, after Obama's surveillance speech last week, his advisors' report and the new PCLOB report, the central question determining the future scope of surveillance policy.

Cook, nodding tacitly at the next phase of the debate, subtly called on the government to come clean.

"I would urge the government to think very seriously about how to evaluate and explain the relative value of its various counter-terrorism authorities and programs," she said.

Privacy Watchdog Says NSA Spying Legal, Effective

By Tom Risen
U.S. News & World Report, July 2, 2014

A federal privacy watchdog unanimously adopted a report Wednesday endorsing a portion of the National Security Agency's surveillance programs, a potential blow for those pressuring Congress and the White House to reshape the government's data collection practices.

The Privacy and Civil Liberties Oversight Board called the controversial collection of Internet data not only legal but effective, contrasting with its report from January that phone data collection by the agency had not made "a concrete difference in the outcome of a terrorism investigation."

"The program has led the government to identify previously unknown individuals who are involved in international terrorism, and it has played a key role in discovering and disrupting specific terrorist plots aimed at the United States and other countries," the new report says.

As part of the report on Section 702 of the Foreign Intelligence Surveillance Act, only two of the five members of the panel backed individual warrants for each time the NSA performs "backdoor" searches of Americans' communications.

The law forbids the targeting of U.S. citizens, but the privacy board's report explains that Americans' communications can be collected when they communicate with or are mentioned in the conversations of non-U.S. citizens. The Foreign Intelligence Surveillance Court reviews and approves efforts by intelligence agencies to request data from phone or Internet companies.

"The Board has seen no trace of any such illegitimate activity associated with the program, or any attempt to intentionally circumvent legal limits," the report says. "But the applicable rules potentially allow a great deal of private information about U.S. persons to be acquired by the government. The Board therefore offers a series of policy recommendations to ensure that the program appropriately balances national security with privacy and civil liberties."

The board's 10 recommendations aim to uncover the extent to which communications involving Americans are being collected, and include a request that the NSA should give written statements explaining why it wants certain data.

This victory for the NSA comes a week after the U.S. Supreme Court decided unanimously that police generally need a warrant before searching people's cellphones, citing that the Fourth Amendment freedom from unreasonable search and seizure applies to digital privacy. The House of Representatives also voted 293–123 on June 19 to ban two types of the NSA's "backdoor" surveillance practices.

Congress should move forward on more reforms to limit warrantless data collection by the NSA, said Kevin Bankston, policy director at the Open Technology Institute.

"In many ways, how the White House responds is beside the point: The real fight now is going to be in Congress, where a majority of the House already supports reforms that are much stronger than the weak sauce being proposed by the board," Bankston said in a statement.

The report lays out in more detail how the NSA is using its authority, but the recommendations are not enough to protect against the privacy risks of its data collection, said a blog post by Cindy Cohn, legal director for the Electronic Frontier Foundation advocacy group.

"The board focuses only on the government's methods for searching and filtering out unwanted information," Cohn wrote. "This ignores the fact that the government is collecting and searching through the content of millions of emails, social networking posts, and other Internet communications, steps that occur before the [board's] analysis starts."

Privacy Advocates Say NSA Reform Doesn't Require "Technological Magic"

By Sara Sorcher
Christian Science Monitor, January 16, 2015

Privacy advocates say a new government study—which found no better technological alternative to intelligence agencies' practice of gathering and storing telephone data en masse—should not become the basis for maintaining the National Security Agency's bulk collection.

"The report doesn't provide justification for continuing mass surveillance programs," says Neema Singh Guliani, the American Civil Liberties Union's legislative counsel.

Last January, President Obama asked intelligence agencies to determine whether there's a way to gather phone data for detecting potential terrorist activity without relying on bulk collection. The request came about after ex-NSA contractor Edward Snowden revealed details of government practices of mass collection of phone metadata—such as the time and length of calls—from millions of Americans.

But the resulting National Academy of Sciences report released Thursday, produced by experts from top technology firms and academia, found no "technological magic" to do this and match the full scale of current intelligence-gathering opportunities.

At a press conference with British Prime Minister David Cameron on Friday, President Obama said the US needs to preserve its capability to track electronic communications of terrorist suspects but is working with companies to ensure the government meets "legitimate privacy concerns."

Obama has already proposed some surveillance reforms, including nixing the government's storage of the phone records and forcing the NSA to gather them from company databases instead. "We just have to work through, in many cases what are technical issues," Obama said Friday.

The press conference took place as Europe is still reeling from the deadly attack on the satirical magazine *Charlie Hebdo* in Paris, which Prime Minister Cameron said heightened the threat level to "severe" in the United Kingdom.

Still, Obama says the US government must not abandon privacy protections in its effort to keep the country secure. "I don't think this is a situation in which because things are so much more dangerous, the pendulum needs to swing," he said. "I think what we have to find is a consistent framework whereby our publics have confidence that their government can both protect them but not abuse our capacity to operate in cyberspace."

But as Obama and Congress attempt to balance security with calls for intelligence reforms, privacy advocates caution that just because the National Academy of Sciences report found no software replacement for the NSA's bulk metadata collection doesn't mean extending that practice is the right policy.

"The report does not discuss whether the program itself is effective," says Harley Geiger, advocacy director and senior counsel at the Center for Democracy and Technology. "The question facing policy makers is whether this program, a domestic mass surveillance program . . . should continue," Geiger continued, "despite its not being supported by the statute and its lack of effectiveness."

After the Snowden leaks, a review board appointed by Obama found this kind of mass collection was not essential to identifying terrorist activity or suspects any more than conventional court orders, and another report from the Privacy and Civil Liberties Oversight Board last year found bulk collection was unlikely to provide significant value in safeguarding the nation in the future. The courts, however, have upheld the practice.

Yet conservatives may still try to use the National Academy of Sciences report's findings to bolster their case to support leaving current surveillance practices in place.

Just this week, House Speaker John Boehner said government surveillance helped foil a terror attack on the Capitol. What's more, the rise of the Islamic State has led some key senators, including now–Majority Leader Mitch McConnell, to argue against curbing the NSA's capabilities at a critical time. Senator McConnell's opposition during the lame duck session last year helped prevent the USA Freedom Act, a bill which would have brought an end to the agency's mass collection of phone data, from moving forward.

If the US moves to targeted collection, intelligence agencies won't have access to a record of past signals intelligence that may be relevant to subsequent investigations, the National Academy of Sciences report said.

"There is no software technique that will fully substitute for bulk collection where it is relied on for queries about the past, after new targets become known," the report states. For instance, it says, "if past events become interesting in the present because of new circumstances, such as the identification of a new target, indications that a nonnuclear nation is now pursuing the development of nuclear weapons, discovery that an individual is a terrorist, or the emergence of new intelligence-gathering priorities, historical events and the data they provide will be available for analysis only if they were previously collected."

But this is not a shocking or even relevant conclusion, privacy advocates say. "All they're saying is there's no software solution to go back in time and look at new targets," says Mark Rumold, a staff attorney at the Electronic Frontier Foundation.

For example, Mr. Rumold says, "there's no way to know 20 years from now who will be in charge in China." Therefore, he said, "if the goal is to collect the future leader of China's communications—and it might be a goal a future intelligence agency has in mind—they might collect everything now because they don't know who the target will actually be. The policy question of whether that policy is useful or valuable is one they don't really weigh into."

The report acknowledges as much: The committee "was not asked to, and did not consider, whether the loss of effectiveness from reducing bulk collection would be too great, or whether the potential gain in privacy from adopting an alternative is worth the potential loss of intelligence information," it states.

Still, some privacy advocates say the report's technological review of bulk collection did not go far enough.

"It failed to consider the risks of bulk collection—misuse on the inside, as well as the vulnerabilities of these large databases enabled by bulk collection," says Marc Rotenberg, executive director of the Electronic Privacy Information Center. "That information in the wrong hands could become very valuable to our enemies."

Collecting records from millions of citizens effectively relies on the idea that the data will be stored securely and immune to compromise or misuse, Mr. Rotenberg said. "But in a post-Snowden world, we know the NSA itself can't protect its own most sensitive information," he said. "A scientific analysis and objective analysis would have acknowledged that . . . potential risk scenario of bulk collection going forward."

Personal Privacy Is Only One of the Costs of NSA Surveillance

By Kim Zetter
Wired, July 29, 2014

There is no doubt the integrity of our communications and the privacy of our online activities have been the biggest casualty of the NSA's unfettered surveillance of our digital lives. But the ongoing revelations of government eavesdropping have had a profound impact on the economy, the security of the Internet and the credibility of the U.S. government's leadership when it comes to online governance.

These are among the many serious costs and consequences the NSA and those who sanctioned its activities—including the White House, the Justice Department and lawmakers like Sen. Dianne Feinstein—apparently have not considered, or acknowledged, according to a report by the New America Foundation's Open Technology Institute.

"Too often, we have discussed the National Security Agency's surveillance programs through the distorting lens of a simplistic 'security versus privacy' narrative," said Danielle Kehl, policy analyst at the Open Technology Institute and primary author of the report. "But if you look closer, the more accurate story is that in the name of security, we're trading away not only privacy, but also the U.S. tech economy, Internet openness, America's foreign policy interests and cybersecurity."

Over the last year, documents leaked by NSA whistleblower Edward Snowden have disclosed numerous NSA spy operations that have gone beyond what many considered acceptable surveillance activity. These included infecting the computers of network administrators working for a Belgian telecom in order to undermine the company's routers and siphon mobile traffic; working with companies to install backdoors in their products or network infrastructure or to devise ways to undermine encryption; intercepting products that U.S. companies send to customers overseas to install spy equipment in them before they reach customers.

The Foundation's report, released today, outlines some of the collateral damage of NSA surveillance in several areas, including:

Economic losses to US businesses due to lost sales and declining customer trust.

The deterioration of Internet security as a result of the NSA stockpiling zero-day vulnerabilities, undermining encryption and installing backdoors in software and hardware products.

Undermining the government's credibility and leadership on "Internet freedom" and governance issues such as censorship.

Economic Costs to U.S. Business

The economic costs of NSA surveillance can be difficult to gauge, given that it can be hard to know when the erosion of a company's business is due solely to anger over government spying. Sometimes, there is little more than anecdotal evidence to go on. But when the German government, for example, specifically cites NSA surveillance as the reason it canceled a lucrative network contract with Verizon, there is little doubt that U.S. spying policies are having a negative impact on business.

"[T]he ties revealed between foreign intelligence agencies and firms in the wake of the U.S. National Security Agency (NSA) affair show that the German government needs a very high level of security for its critical networks," Germany's Interior Ministry said in a statement over the canceled contract.

Could the German government simply be leveraging the surveillance revelations to get a better contract or to put the US on the defensive in foreign policy negotiations? Sure. That may also be part of the agenda behind data localization proposals in Germany and elsewhere that would force telecoms and Internet service providers to route and store the data of their citizens locally, rather than let it pass through the U.S.

But, as the report points out, the Germans have not been alone in making business decisions based on NSA spying. Brazil reportedly scuttled a $4.5 billion fighter jet contract with Boeing and gave it to Saab instead. Sources told Bloomberg News "[t]he NSA problem ruined it" for the US defense contractor.

Governments aren't the only ones shunning US businesses. American firms in the cloud computing sector are feeling the pressure as consumers and corporate clients reconsider using third-party storage companies in the U.S. for their data. Companies like Dropbox and Amazon Web Services reportedly have lost business to overseas competitors like Artmotion, a Swiss hosting provider. The

> The actions are particularly troubling because the insertion of backdoors and vulnerabilities in systems doesn't just undermine them for exploitation by the NSA but makes them more susceptible for exploitation by other governments as well as by criminal hackers.

CEO of the European firm reported that within a month after the first revelations of NSA spying went public, his company's business jumped 45 percent. Similarly, 25 percent of respondents in a survey of 300 British and Canadian businesses earlier this year said they were moving their data outside the US as a result of NSA spying.

The Information Technology and Innovation Foundation has estimated that repercussions from the spying could cost the U.S. cloud computing industry some $22 to $35 billion over the next few years in lost business.

Will the NSA spying revelations have long-term effects? Or will customers return to U.S. companies once the news fades into the background? It's hard to tell.

But German chancellor Angela Merkel has suggested that Europe build a separate permanent internet to keep data local and prevent it from traversing networks the NSA can more easily monitor. Germany also has instituted new data rules that prohibit any company from obtaining a federal contract unless it can guarantee that it will protect data stored in Germany from foreign authorities. These kinds of policies and infrastructure changes tend to remain long after the circumstances that spawned them have passed.

Deterioration of Cybersecurity

Out of all the revelations to come to light in the past year, the most shocking may well be the NSA's persistent campaign to undermine encryption, install backdoors in hardware and software, and amass a stockpile of zero-day vulnerabilities and exploits.

"For the past decade, N.S.A. has led an aggressive, multipronged effort to break widely used Internet encryption technologies," according to a 2010 memo from Government Communications Headquarters, the NSA's counterpart in the UK, leaked by Edward Snowden.

Furthermore, a story from Pro Publica noted the NSA "actively engages the US and foreign IT industries to covertly influence and/or overtly leverage their commercial products' designs" to make them more amenable to the NSA's data collection programs and more susceptible to exploitation by the spy agency.

The NSA, with help from the CIA and FBI, also has intercepted network routers from US manufacturers like Cisco to install spy tools before they're shipped to overseas buyers, further undermining customer trust in US companies. Cisco senior vice president Mark Chandler wrote in a company blog post that his and other companies ought to be able to count on the government not interfering "with the lawful delivery of our products in the form in which we have manufactured them. To do otherwise, and to violate legitimate privacy rights of individuals and institutions around the world, undermines confidence in our industry."

All of these activities are at direct odds with the Obama administration's stated goal of securing the Internet and critical infrastructure and undermine global trust in the Internet and the safety of communications. The actions are particularly troubling because the insertion of backdoors and vulnerabilities in systems doesn't just undermine them for exploitation by the NSA but makes them more susceptible for exploitation by other governments as well as by criminal hackers.

"The existence of these programs, in addition to undermining confidence in the Internet industry, creates real security concerns," the authors of the report note.

Undermining U.S. Support for Internet Freedom

Finally, the NSA's spying activities have greatly undermined the government's policies in support of Internet freedom around the world and its work in advocating for freedom of expression and combating censorship and oppression.

"As the birthplace for so many of these technologies, including the Internet itself, we have a responsibility to see them used for good," then–Secretary of State Hillary Clinton said in a 2010 speech launching a campaign in support of Internet freedom. But while "the US government promotes free expression abroad and aims to prevent repressive governments from monitoring and censoring their citizens," the New American report notes, it is "simultaneously supporting domestic laws that authorize surveillance and bulk data collection." The widespread collection of data, which has a chilling effect on freedom of expression, is precisely the kind of activity for which the U.S. condemns other countries.

This hypocrisy has opened a door for repressive regimes to question the US role in Internet governance bodies and has allowed them to argue in favor of their own governments having greater control over the Internet. At the UN Human Rights Council in September 2013, the report notes, a representative from Pakistan— speaking on behalf of Cuba, Iran, China and other countries—said the surveillance programs highlighted the need for their nations to have a greater role in governing the Internet.

The report makes a number of recommendations to address the problems the NSA's spying has created. These include strengthening privacy protections for Americans and non-Americans, developing clear policies about whether and under what legal standards it is permissible for the government to secretly install malware on a computer or network, and working to restore trust encryption systems and standards.

U.S. Spy Agency Reports Improper Surveillance of Americans

By David Lerman
Bloomberg Business, December 24, 2014

The National Security Agency today released reports on intelligence collection that may have violated the law or U.S. policy over more than a decade, including unauthorized surveillance of Americans' overseas communications.

The NSA, responding to a Freedom of Information Act lawsuit from the American Civil Liberties Union, released a series of required quarterly and annual reports to the President's Intelligence Oversight Board that cover the period from the fourth quarter of 2001 to the second quarter of 2013.

The heavily-redacted reports include examples of data on Americans being e-mailed to unauthorized recipients, stored in unsecured computers, and retained after it was supposed to be destroyed, according to the documents. They were posted on the NSA's website at around 1:30 p.m. on Christmas Eve.

In a 2012 case, for example, an NSA analyst "searched her spouse's personal telephone directory without his knowledge to obtain names and telephone numbers for targeting," according to one report. The analyst "has been advised to cease her activities," it said.

Other unauthorized cases were a matter of human error, not intentional misconduct.

Last year, an analyst "mistakenly requested" surveillance "of his own personal identifier instead of the selector associated with a foreign intelligence target," according to another report.

Unauthorized Surveillance

In 2012, an analyst conducted surveillance "on a U.S. organization in a raw traffic database without formal authorization because the analyst incorrectly believed that he was authorized to query due to a potential threat," according to the fourth-quarter report from 2012. The surveillance yielded nothing.

The NSA's intensified communications surveillance programs initiated after the Sept. 11, 2001, terrorist attacks on New York and Washington unleashed an international uproar after they were disclosed in classified documents leaked by fugitive former contractor Edward Snowden last year.

No New Legislation

Congress has considered but not passed new legislation to curb the NSA's collection of bulk telephone calling and other electronic data.

The Privacy and Civil Liberties Oversight Board, created by lawmakers under post–Sept. 11 anti-terrorism laws, issued a 238-page report in January urging the abolition of the bulk collection of Americans' phone records. The five-member board said the program has provided only "minimal" help in thwarting terrorist attacks.

The ACLU, which filed a lawsuit to access the reports, said the documents shed light on how the surveillance policies of NSA impact Americans and how information has sometimes been misused.

"The government conducts sweeping surveillance under this authority—surveillance that increasingly puts Americans' data in the hands of the NSA," Patrick C. Toomey, staff attorney with the ACLU's National Security Project, said in an e-mail.

No Oversight

"Despite that fact, this spying is conducted almost entirely in secret and without legislative or judicial oversight," he said.

The reports show greater oversight by all three branches of government is needed, Toomey added.

The ACLU filed suit to turn a spotlight on an executive order governing intelligence activities that was first issued by President Ronald Reagan in 1981 and has been modified many times since then.

The order allows the NSA to conduct surveillance outside the U.S. While the NSA by law can't deliberately intercept messages from Americans, it can collect messages that get vacuumed up inadvertently as part of its surveillance of foreigners overseas.

Masking Identities

After foreign intelligence is acquired, "it must be analyzed to remove or mask certain protected categories of information, including U.S. person information, unless specific exceptions apply," the NSA said in a statement before posting the documents.

The extent of that collection has never been clear.

The agency said today it has multiple layers of checks in place to prevent further errors in intelligence gathering and retention.

"The vast majority of compliance incidents involve unintentional technical or human error," NSA said in its executive summary. "NSA goes to great lengths to ensure compliance with the Constitution, laws and regulations."

Report Violations

The intelligence community is required to report potential violations to the oversight board, as well as the Office of the Director of National Intelligence.

In some cases, surveillance of foreign targets continued even when those targets were in the U.S., although such "non-compliant data" were later purged, according to the reports released today.

Some analysts sent intelligence information to other analysts who weren't authorized to receive it, according to the documents. That information was deleted from recipients' files when discovered.

Because of the extensive redactions, the publicly available documents don't make clear how many violations occurred and how many were unlawful. While the reports contain no names or details of specific cases, they show how intelligence analysts sometimes have violated policy to conduct unauthorized surveillance work.

"Intentional Misuse"

The NSA's inspector general last year detailed 12 cases of "intentional misuse" of intelligence authorities from 2003 to 2013 in a letter to Senator Charles Grassley, of Iowa, the top Republican on the Senate Judiciary Committee.

Those cases included a member of a U.S. military intelligence unit who violated policy by obtaining the communications of his wife, who was stationed in another country. After a military proceeding, the violator was punished by a reduction in rank, 45 days of extra duty and forfeiture of half of his pay for two months, according to the letter.

In a 2003 case, a civilian employee ordered intelligence collection "of the telephone number of his foreign-national girlfriend without an authorized purpose for approximately one month" to determine whether she was being faithful to him, according to the letter. The employee retired before an investigation could be completed.

Ignoring Restrictions

The NSA acknowledged last year that some of its analysts deliberately ignored restrictions on their authority to spy on Americans multiple times in the past decade.

"Over the past decade, very rare instances of willful violations of NSA's authorities have been found," the agency said in a statement to *Bloomberg News* in August 2013. "NSA takes very seriously allegations of misconduct, and cooperates fully with any investigations—responding as appropriate."

NSA Sued by Wikimedia, Rights Groups over Mass Surveillance

By David Ingram
Reuters, March 10, 2015

The U.S. National Security Agency was sued on Tuesday by Wikimedia and other groups challenging one of its mass surveillance programs that they said violates Americans' privacy and makes individuals worldwide less likely to share sensitive information.

The lawsuit filed in federal court in Maryland, where the spy agency is based, said the NSA is violating U.S. constitutional protections and the law by tapping into high-capacity cables, switches and routers that move Internet traffic through the United States.

The case is a new potential legal front for privacy advocates who have challenged U.S. spying programs several times since 2013, when documents leaked by former NSA contractor Edward Snowden revealed the long reach of government surveillance.

Other lawsuits have challenged the bulk collection of telephone metadata and are pending in U.S. appeals courts.

The litigation announced on Tuesday takes on what is often called "upstream" collection because it happens along the so-called backbone of the Internet and away from individual users.

Bulk collection there violates the constitution's First Amendment, which protects freedom of speech and association, and the Fourth Amendment, which protects against unreasonable search and seizure, the lawsuit said.

The plaintiffs include the Wikimedia Foundation, which runs the online encyclopedia Wikipedia; the conservative Rutherford Institute; Amnesty International USA and the National Association of Criminal Defense Lawyers, among other groups.

The groups said in the lawsuit that upstream surveillance "reduces the likelihood" that clients, journalists, foreign government officials, victims of human rights abuses and other individuals will share sensitive information with them.

Legal standing, which requires the organizations to show individual, particular harm, is the most significant obstacle for them, said Stephen Vladeck, a professor at American University Washington College of Law.

While it might stand to reason that the plaintiffs' communications are being intercepted, they can only use legally public information, which the government has acknowledged or declassified, to show harm, Vladeck said. It is "not beyond the pale" that the government could make more information public while the lawsuit is pending, he said. For now, the lawsuit is a "longshot" according to Vladeck.

An Obama administration official said: "We've been very clear about what constitutes a valid target of electronic surveillance. The act of innocuously updating or reading an online article does not fall into that category."

> **"By tapping the backbone of the Internet, the NSA is straining the backbone of democracy," Lila Tretikov, executive director of the Wikimedia Foundation, said in a statement.**

The U.S. Department of Justice, which was named as a defendant along with the NSA, said it was reviewing the lawsuit. The NSA did not immediately respond to requests for comment.

"By tapping the backbone of the Internet, the NSA is straining the backbone of democracy," Lila Tretikov, executive director of the Wikimedia Foundation, said in a statement.

State Secrets

Another potential roadblock for the groups is that the government could try to assert what is known as the state secrets privilege, saying that continuing with the lawsuit would expose classified information, said Carrie Cordero, director of national security studies at Georgetown University Law Center.

Tretikov and Wikipedia founder Jimmy Wales wrote in the *New York Times'* opinion pages that they were concerned about where data on their users ends up after it is collected in bulk by the NSA. Citing close intelligence ties between the United States and Egypt, they said a user in Egypt would have reason to fear reprisal if she edited a page about the country's political opposition.

The U.S. Supreme Court in 2013 rejected another challenge to NSA surveillance of email and other communications, ruling that a similar coalition of plaintiffs did not prove they had been spied upon or would be.

The ruling, however, was made just three months before the first of Snowden's revelations. Documents made public by Snowden support the right to sue, said Patrick Toomey, one of the American Civil Liberties Union lawyers working on the lawsuit.

Toomey said that with upstream collection, the NSA systematically taps into Internet message traffic between U.S. and overseas users as it moves in and out of the United States over fiber-optic cables.

The NSA then systematically sweeps through the vast amount of content for anything relating to specific individuals or groups considered by U.S. agencies to be intelligence targets, according to the documents leaked by Snowden.

Consequently, Toomey said, anyone inside the United States who sends or receives messages via the Internet to or from someone outside the country is likely to have had messages examined in some way by NSA.

The case is *Wikimedia Foundation, et al, v. National Security Agency, et al*, U.S. District Court for the District of Maryland, No. 15-662

The New Surveillance Normal: NSA and Corporate Surveillance in the Age of Global Capitalism

By David H. Price
Monthly Review, July–August 2014

The National Security Agency (NSA) document cache released by Edward Snowden reveals a need to re-theorize the role of state and corporate surveillance systems in an age of neoliberal global capitalism. While much remains unknowable to us, we now are in a world where private communications are legible in previously inconceivable ways, ideologies of surveillance are undergoing rapid transformations, and the commodification of metadata (and other surveillance intelligence) transforms privacy. In light of this, we need to consider how the NSA and corporate metadata mining converge to support the interests of capital.

This is an age of converging state and corporate surveillance. Like other features of the political economy, these shifts develop with apparent independence of institutional motivations, yet corporate and spy agencies' practices share common appetites for metadata. Snowden's revelations of the NSA's global surveillance programs raises the possibility that the state intelligence apparatus is used for industrial espionage in ways that could unite governmental intelligence and corporate interests—for which there appears to be historical precedent. The convergence of the interests, incentives, and methods of U.S. intelligence agencies, and the corporate powers they serve, raise questions about the ways that the NSA and CIA fulfill their roles, which have been described by former CIA agent Philip Agee as: "the secret police of U.S. capitalism, plugging up leaks in the political dam night and day so that shareholders of U.S. companies operating in poor countries can continue enjoying the rip-off."[1]

There is a long history in the United States of overwhelming public opposition to new forms of electronic surveillance. Police, prosecutors, and spy agencies have recurrently used public crises—ranging from the Lindbergh baby kidnapping, wars, claimed threats of organized crime and terror attacks, to marshal expanded state surveillance powers.[2] During the two decades preceding the 9/11 terror attacks, Congress periodically considered developing legislation establishing rights of privacy; but even in the pre-Internet age, corporate interests scoffed at the need for any such protections. Pre-2001 critiques of electronic-surveillance focused on privacy rights and threats to boundaries between individuals, corporations, and the state; what would later be known as metadata collection was then broadly understood as violating shared notions of privacy, and as exposing the scaffolding of a police state or a corporate panopticon inhabited by consumers living in a George Tooker painting.

The rapid shifts in U.S. attitudes favoring expanded domestic intelligence powers following 9/11 were significant. In the summer of 2001, distrust of the FBI and other surveillance agencies had reached one of its highest historical levels. Decades of longitudinal survey data collected by the Justice Department establish longstanding U.S. opposition to wiretaps; disapproval levels fluctuated between 70 and 80 percent during the thirty years preceding 2001.[3] But a December 2001 *New York Times* poll suddenly found only 44 percent of respondents believed widespread governmental wiretaps "would violate American's rights."[4]

Public fears in the post-9/11 period reduced concerns of historical abuses by law enforcement and intelligence agencies, and the rapid adoption of the PATRIOT Act precluded public considerations of why the Pike and Church congressional committee findings had ever established limits on intelligence agencies' abilities to spy on Americans. Concurrent with post-9/11 surveillance expansions was the growth of the Internet's ability to track users, collecting metadata in ways that seductively helped socialize all to the normalcy of the loss of privacy.

The depth of this shift in U.S. attitudes away from resisting data collection can be seen in the public's response in the early 1990s to news stories reporting the Lotus Corporation's plans to sell a comprehensive CD-ROM database compiled by Equifax, consisting of Americans' addresses and phone numbers. This news led to broad-based protests by Americans across the country angry about invasions of privacy—protests that lead to the cancellation of the product which produced results less intrusive than a quick Google search would provide today. Similarly, a broad resistance arose in 2003 when Americans learned of the Bush administration's secretive Total Information Awareness (TIA) program. Under the directorship of Admiral John Poindexter, TIA planned to collect metadata on millions of Americans, tracking movements, emails, and economic transactions for use in predictive modeling software with hopes of anticipating terror attacks, and other illegal acts, before they occurred. Congress and the public were outraged at the prospect of such invasive surveillance without warrants or meaningful judicial oversight. These concerns led to TIA's termination, though as the Snowden NSA documents clarify, the NSA now routinely engages in the very activities envisioned by TIA.

Four decades ago broad public outrage followed revelations of Pentagon, FBI, and CIA domestic surveillance campaigns, as news of COINTELPRO, CHAOS, and a host of illegal operations were disclosed by investigative journalists and later the Pike and Church committees. Today, few Americans appear to care about Senator Dianne Feinstein's recent accusations that the CIA hacked her office's computers in order to remove documents her staff was using in investigations of CIA wrongdoing.[5]

Americans now increasingly accept invasive electronic monitoring of their personal lives. Ideologies of surveillance are internalized as shifts in consciousness embedded within political economic formations converge with corporate and state surveillance desires. The rapid expansion of U.S. electronic surveillance programs like Carnivore, NarusInsight, or PRISM is usually understood primarily as an outgrowth of the post-9/11 terror wars. But while post-9/11 security campaigns were a catalyst for these expansions, this growth should also be understood within the context of global capital formations seeking increased legibility of potential consumers, resources, resistance, and competitors.[6]

Convergence of State and Corporate Metadata Dreams

The past two decades brought an accelerated independent growth of corporate and governmental electronic surveillance programs tracking metadata and compiling electronic dossiers. The NSA, FBI, Department of Defense, and CIA's metadata programs developed independently from, and with differing goals from, the consumer surveillance systems that used cookies and consumer discount cards, sniffing Gmail content, compiling consumer profiles, and other means of tracking individual Internet behaviors for marketing purposes. Public acceptance of electronic monitoring and metadata collection transpired incrementally, with increasing acceptance of corporate-based consumer monitoring programs, and reduced resistance to governmental surveillance.

These two surveillance tracks developed with separate motivations, one for security and the other for commerce, but both desire to make individuals and groups legible for reasons of anticipation and control. The collection and use of this metadata finds a synchronic convergence of intrusions, as consumer capitalism and a U.S. national security state leaves Americans vulnerable, and a world open to the probing and control by agents of commerce and security. As Bruce Schneier recently observed, "surveillance is still the business model of the Internet, and every one of those companies wants to access your communications and your metadata."[7]

But this convergence carries its own contradictions. Public trust in (and the economic value of) cloud servers, telecommunications providers, email, and search engine services suffered following revelations that the public statements of Verizon, Google, and others had been less than forthright in declaring their claims of not knowing about the NSA monitoring their customers. A March 2014 *USA Today* survey found 38 percent of respondents believed the NSA violates their privacy, with distrust of Facebook (26 percent) surpassing even the IRS (18 percent) or Google (12 percent)—the significance of these results is that the Snowden NSA revelations damaged the reputations and financial standing of a broad range of technology-based industries.[8] With the assistance of private ISPs, various corporations, and the NSA, our metadata is accessed under a shell game of four distinct sets of legal authorizations. These allow spokespersons from corporate ISPs and the NSA to make misleading statements to the press about not conducting surveillance operations under a particular program such as FISA, when one of the other authorizations is being used.[9]

Snowden's revelations reveal a world where the NSA is dependent on private corporate services for the outsourced collection of data, and where the NSA is increasingly reliant on corporate owned data farms where the storage and analysis of the data occurs. In the neoliberal United States, Amazon and other private firms lease massive cloud server space to the CIA, under an arrangement where it becomes a share cropper on these scattered data farms. These arrangements present nebulous security relationships raising questions of role confusion in shifting patron–client relationships, and whatever resistance corporations like Amazon might have had to assisting NSA, CIA, or intelligence agencies is further compromised by relations of commerce. This creates relationships of culpability, as Norman Solomon suggests, with Amazon's $600 million CIA data farm contract: "if Obama orders the CIA to kill a U.S. Citizen, Amazon will be a partner in assassination."[10] Such arrangements diffuse complicity in ways seldom considered by consumers focused on Amazon Prime's ability to speedily deliver a *My Little Pony* play set for a brony nephew's birthday party, not on the company's links to drone attacks on Pakistani wedding parties.

The Internet developed first as a military-communication system; only later did it evolve the commercial and recreational uses distant from the initial intent of its Pentagon landlords. Snowden's revelations reveal how the Internet's architecture, a compromised judiciary, and duplexed desires of capitalism and the national security state are today converging to track our purchases, queries, movements, associations, allegiances, and desires. The rise of e-commerce, and the soft addictive allure of social media, rapidly transforms U.S. economic and social formations. Shifts in the base are followed by shifts in the superstructure, and new generations of e-consumers are socialized to accept phones that track movements, and game systems that bring cameras into the formerly private refuges of our homes, as part of a "new surveillance normal."[11]

We need to develop critical frameworks considering how NSA and CIA surveillance programs articulate not only with the United States' domestic and international security apparatus but with current international capitalist formations. While secrecy shrouds our understanding of these relationships, CIA history provides examples of some ways that intelligence operations have supported and informed past U.S. economic ventures. When these historical patterns are combined with details from Snowden's disclosures we find continuities of means, motive, and opportunity for neoliberal abuses of state intelligence for private gains. . . .

Theorizing Capitalism's Pervasive Surveillance Culture

. . . We need a theory of surveillance that incorporates the political economy of the U.S. national security state and the corporate interests which it serves and protects. Such analysis needs an economic foundation and a view that looks beyond cultural categories separating commerce and state security systems designed to protect capital. The metadata, valuable private corporate data, and fruits of industrial espionage gathered under PRISM and other NSA programs all produce information of such a high value that it seems likely some of it will be used in a context of global capital.

It matters little what legal restrictions are in place; in a global, high-tech, capitalist economy such information is invariably commodified. It is likely to be used to: facilitate industrial or corporate sabotage operations of the sort inflicted by the Stuxnet worm; steal either corporate secrets for NSA use, or foreign corporate secrets for U.S. corporate use; make investments by intelligence agencies financing their own operations; or secure personal financial gain by individuals working in the intelligence sector.

The rise of new invasive technologies coincides with the decline of ideological resistance to surveillance and the compilation of metadata. The speed of Americans' adoption of ideologies embracing previously unthinkable levels of corporate and state surveillance suggests a continued public acceptance of a new surveillance normal will continue to develop with little resistance. In a world where the CIA can hack the computers of Senator Feinstein—a leader of the one of the three branches of government—with impunity or lack

> **Public acceptance of electronic monitoring and metadata collection transpired incrementally, with increasing acceptance of corporate-based consumer monitoring programs, and reduced resistance to governmental surveillance.**

of public outcry, it is difficult to anticipate a deceleration in the pace at which NSA and CIA expand their surveillance reach. To live a well-adjusted life in contemporary U.S. society requires the development of rapid memory adjustments and shifting acceptance of corporate and state intrusions into what were once protective spheres of private life. Like all things in our society, we can expect these intrusions will themselves be increasingly stratified, as electronic privacy, or illegibility, will increasingly become a commodity available only to elites. Today, expensive technologies like GeeksPhone's Blackphone with enhanced PGP encryption, or Boeing's self-destructing Black Phone, afford special levels of privacy for those who can pay.

While the United States' current state of surveillance acceptance offers little immediate hope of a social movement limiting corporate or government spying, there are enough historical instances of post-crises limits being imposed on government surveillance to offer some hope. Following the Second World War, many European nations reconfigured long-distance billing systems to not record specific numbers called, instead only recording billing zones—because the Nazis used phone billing records as metadata useful for identifying members of resistance movements. Following the Arab Spring, Tunisia now reconfigures its Internet with a new info-packet system known as mesh networks that hinder governmental monitoring—though USAID support for this project naturally undermines trust in this system.[12] Following the Church and Pike committees' congressional investigations of CIA and FBI wrongdoing in the 1970s, the Hughes-Ryan Act brought significant oversight and limits on these groups, limits which decayed over time and whose remaining restraints were undone with the USA PATRIOT Act. Some future crisis may well provide similar opportunities to regain now lost contours of privacies.

Yet hope for immediate change remains limited. It will be difficult for social reform movements striving to protect individual privacy to limit state and corporate surveillance. Today's surveillance complex aligned with an economic base enthralled with the prospects of metadata appears too strong for meaningful reforms without significant shifts in larger economic formations. Whatever inherent contradictions exist within the present surveillance system, and regardless of the objections of privacy advocates of the liberal left and libertarian right, meaningful restrictions appear presently unlikely with surveillance formations so closely tied to the current iteration of global capitalism.

Notes

1. Philip Agee, *Inside the Company: CIA Diary* (New York: Farrar, Straus & Giroux, 1975), 575.

2. David Price, "Memory's Half-Life: A Social History of Wiretaps," *CounterPunch,* August 9–13, 2013, http://counterpunch.org.

3. U.S. Department of Justice, *Sourcebook of Criminal Justice Statistics* (Washington, DC: U.S. Dept. of Justice, Bureau of Justice Statistics, 1994).

4. Robin Toner and Janet Elder, "Public Is Wary but Supportive On Rights Curbs," *New York Times*, December 12, 2001, http://nytimes.com.

5. Mark Mazzetti and Jonathan Weisman, "Conflict Erupts in Public Rebuke on CIA," *New York Times*, March 11, 2014, http://nytimes.com.

6. For more on state legibility, see James Scott, *Seeing Like a State* (New Haven: Yale University Press, 1998).

7. Bruce Schneier, "Don't Listen to Google and Facebook: The Public-Private Surveillance Partnership Is Still Going Strong," *Atlantic*, March 25, 2014, http://theatlantic.com.

8. Jon Swartz, "Consumers Are Souring on Web, Post-NSA, Survey Says," *USA Today,* April 3, 2014, http://usatoday.com.

9. Bruce Schneier, "Don't Listen to Google and Facebook." The four authorizations are the 1978 FISA Act, EO 12333 of 1981, 2004, and 2008, PATRIOT Act of 2001, section 215, and Section 702 of the 2008 FISA Amendment Act.

10. Norman Solomon, "If Obama Orders the CIA to Kill a U.S. citizen, Amazon Will Be a Partner in Assassination," AlterNet, February 12, 2014, http://alternet.org.

11. The phrase "new surveillance normal" is adapted from Catherine Lutz's "the military normal" found in her "The Military Normal," in the Network of Concerned Anthropologists, eds., *Counter-Counterinsurgency Manual* (Chicago: Prickly Paradigm Press, 2009), 23–37.

12. Carlotta Gall and James Glanz, "U.S. Promotes Network to Foil Digital Spying," *New York Times*, April 20, 2014, http://nytimes.com.

2
Legislation and Policy

(Left to right) FBI Director James Comey, Director of National Intelligence James Clapper, and CIA Director John Brennan testify during a hearing on January 29, 2014, before the Senate (Select) Intelligence Committee on Capitol Hill in Washington, DC. The committee held a hearing on current and projected national security threats against the United States.

The Politics of Surveillance: A Brief History

On June 2, 2015, the U.S. government enacted the USA Freedom Act—legislation, based on a House bill, that effectively ended the federal government's program that served as a clearinghouse of phone record data. The law came on the heels of a recent decision handed down from the New York federal appeals court that ruled that the phone record collection program, administered by the National Security Agency (NSA), was illegal because it went beyond the scope of a critical statute, Section 215 or the "Library Records" provision within the sweeping USA PATRIOT Act.

Congress voted to change the PATRIOT Act to prohibit bulk collection by the NSA, which charted domestic-based telephone calls. This maneuver mirrored the court's decision in May, saying the government should still have the authority to access cell phone metadata, but it simply cannot be acquired via Section 215, which expired on June 1, the day before the Freedom Act went into effect. Now, the private sector would need to partner proactively with the NSA for access to those records. So continues the nation's judicial and legislative checks and balances toward providing a safer country without sacrificing an individual's personal liberties. Attempting to arrive at this goal has resulted in a long history of legislative tension arising out of the need both to cater to political demands and to maintain constitutional protections.

The Cold War and Civil Rights Eras

It is not unusual for the United States government to monitor citizens, both domestic and foreign, in the name of national security. But finding a legal path to do so has been thorny indeed and represents one of the great current tensions of our democracy.

In 1971, a group of activists broke into an FBI field office in Media, Pennsylvania, resulting in the revelation of a decades-long surveillance program known as COINTELPRO, or the counterintelligence program. The program, devised by FBI director J. Edgar Hoover, had roots that stretched as far back as the early 1930s, when President Franklin D. Roosevelt instructed Hoover to research domestic fascist and communist movements.

Given *carte blanche* to harass and build files on political leaders and activists alike, Hoover would go on to have a near 40-year run at the FBI, a tenure pockmarked with policies that exceeded the Bureau's reach. As the Cold War escalated in the 1950s, the Hoover-led FBI created COINTELPRO as a response to increasing barriers that prevented prosecution for political beliefs, particularly Communism. Later, the program would focus its attention on exposing and disrupting the

Black nationalist movement, targeting prominent Civil Rights–era leaders like Martin Luther King, Jr., and Huey Newton.

After Hoover's death in 1972 the exposure of the FBI's surveillance efforts paved the way for judicial and legislative maneuvers that created an infrastructure allowing for legal intelligence gathering to thwart and expose public threats while being subject to proper oversight.

United States Senate Select Committee on Intelligence and FISA

Prompted by the revelations from the FBI field office burglary and the fallout from the Watergate scandal,[1] Idaho Sen. Frank Church launched a congressional investigation into intelligence abuses. The findings of that investigation confirmed the FBI's overreach but also revealed that every federal intelligence agency conducted similar campaigns that pushed civil liberties boundaries. These discoveries ultimately led to the creation of the United States Senate Select Committee on Intelligence, a 15-member body that oversees the U.S. intelligence community, including the CIA, the NSA, as well as factions of the FBI and the State, Energy, and Treasury departments.

This period in American politics, marked with a feeling of public distrust following the Vietnam War and Watergate, also led to a piece of legislation called the Foreign Intelligence Surveillance Act, or FISA, introduced in 1977. This bill attempted to provide congressional and judicial oversight of government surveillance programs while still protecting covert information-gathering programs. Under the act, the chief justice of the U.S. Supreme Court would designate seven district court judges from seven of the United States judicial circuits, a FISA court, to consider applications for electronic surveillance anywhere within the United States.

FISA allowed domestic surveillance without a court order for up to one year unless the "surveillance will acquire the contents of any communication to which a United States person is a party." If the surveillance focused on a U.S. citizen, the act required judicial authorization within 72 hours. The FISA Act also allowed the government to obtain a court order to conduct surveillance if there is probable cause that an individual represents another country or non-domestic entity.

Post 9/11, Edward Snowden, Congressional Reins

Whereas in the 1970s Congress responded to public distrust of the federal government by creating new policy to rein in government surveillance, immediately following the terror attacks of September 11, 2001, Congress broadened the intelligence-gathering infrastructure in response to a very different political climate. The USA PATRIOT Act provided the legislative and judicial foundation for the U.S.-led war on terror, making it easier for the government to request private-sector electronic records. But as the nation grew weary of life during wartime and as clues related to the government's widespread dragnet of electronic surveillance data came to light, critics began to question the legality and morality of these programs.

In June 2013, one-time NSA contractor Edward Snowden leaked to several news outlets agency records that exposed the vast extent of government electronic surveillance. Snowden's shocking revelations provided much-needed political cover to advance legislation that would curb the NSA's intelligence-gathering tactics without the threat of lawmakers being characterized as soft on national security.

The courts also provided lawmakers with political cover as Congress sought ways to address overreach in NSA information-gathering techniques. First, U.S. District Judge Richard Leon ruled in December 2013 that the NSA's bulk data collection program violated privacy rights, rebuking the government's argument that there existed legal precedent for the constitutionality of collecting phone metadata. But then, in just a matter of days, a district court judge handed a win to the NSA, this time with a decision that ratified bulk collection of phone records under Section 215 of the USA PATRIOT Act, which, ironically, was among the programs revealed in Snowden's classified leaks.

Now that the courts were beginning to deliberate the legality of key provisions of the PATRIOT Act, Congress began to place a heavier emphasis on establishing probable cause and upholding the Fourth Amendment. In June 2014 the House passed an amendment to the 2015 Defense appropriations bill that ended warrantless searches of government databases for information on U.S. citizens.

In May 2015, a New York federal appeals court ruled that the NSA's phone record collection program was illegal, signaling a setback for congressional leaders who favored reconstituting the Section 215 statute as its June 1 expiration approached. The ruling, however, did not question the constitutionality of Section 215. Moreover, it did not order the program to cease. Legal analysts said that until the statute's expiration date on June 1 the government still could have used it to compel phone companies to turn over customer records.

This decision paved the way to the overwhelming passage of the aforementioned USA Freedom Act in the House of Representatives. The bill prohibits bulk collection of all records under Section 215 of the PATRIOT Act and prohibits large-scale collection, or dragnet-style data collection, that would indiscriminately capture data from an entire state, city, or zip code. Additionally, the bill proposed to close a loophole—one that was a target of critics—that requires the government to stop tracking suspected foreign terrorists when they enter the United States. This provision also gives the government 72 hours to track foreign suspects when they initially enter the United States, which, lawmakers contend, provides ample time for the government to obtain the proper authority under U.S. law. On June 1, 2015, Section 215 of the Patriot Act expired, and on June 2, the Senate, after heated debated over the House-passed USA Freedom Act, finally voted to pass the bill. President Obama signed it a few hours later.

Looking Ahead

Once providing free rein to intelligence apparatuses, Congress now appears to be ready to balance that approach by implementing proactive measures to ensure a citizen's privacy in the new surveillance age. The Secure Data Act, first introduced in December 2014 by Oregon Sen. Ron Wyden, a Democrat, would prohibit government mandates to build backdoors or security vulnerabilities into U.S. software and electronics. "These proposals threaten to undermine the development and deployment of strong data security technologies and the overwhelming economic and national security interest in better data security," Wyden said upon introducing his legislation.

On the opposite end of the political sphere, Kentucky Sen. Rand Paul, a Republican, held the Senate floor in May 2015 as he filibustered the reauthorization of the PATRIOT Act in opposition to the collection of any phone records. The act, he said, "Isn't about the vast majority of good people who work in government. It's about preventing the bad apple. It's about preventing the one bad person that might get into government and decide to abuse the rights of individuals."

The legislative actions and court decisions around government surveillance reflect political maneuverings in an ever-evolving democracy faced with the challenges of a new age. Just how our country will pull through this complicated test remains to be seen.

Matthew Brian Hersh

Note

1. The Watergate scandal revealed the Nixon administration's engagement in covert, illegal activities, including the unauthorized bugging of political opponents' offices. This scandal ultimately led to Nixon's resignation.

The Business of Surveillance

By Heidi Boghosian
Human Rights, May 2013

It is at once revealing and disturbing that the American retailing company Target can learn of a teenager's pregnancy before the family she lives with does. An angry father near Minneapolis found this out firsthand, as reported in the *New York Times,* revealing a modern-day quandary: Communications and information technology have advanced with such speed that privacy safeguards lag far behind. Retailers accumulate and store vast amounts of personal data, and telecommunications and other corporations frequently share this information with government intelligence agencies. Such practices invade privacy and, absent careful interpretation, threaten to render the First Amendment inadequate to protect traditional liberty interests.

U.S. investigators advocating a robust antiterrorism agenda have pressed communications companies to store and, in many cases, turn over an unprecedented amount of information about citizens' telephone calls, Internet communications, and daily movements. Internationally recognized standards of human rights are imperiled by the dual interests of a private sector intent on maximizing profits and a government fixated on preventing future terrorist attacks.

In addition to engaging in data mining, multinational companies are employing sophisticated technology, such as radio frequency identification (RFID) chips, semiconductors, and chips that can be configured to allow law enforcement "back door" access to monitor communications, or that enable location-based services to track citizens' whereabouts. One need only watch an episode of *NCIS, CSI,* or any other police procedural to get an idea of how intrusive such equipment can be. Surveillance has become mainstream as Americans' lives are data driven and uploaded to the Internet, transformed into digital packets, and bared publicly on social media sites. In striving for efficiency and instantaneous communication, consumers have unwittingly impelled retailers and data-mining companies to compete in capturing and reselling shopping habits and related personal information.

Computer Matching—Building Blocks of Mass Surveillance

As the Target example shows, mass surveillance is accomplished in large part by computer matching, the integration and comparing of electronic data records from two or more sources. Software enables computer searches and record-linking based

---

"The Business of Surveillance" was previously published in *Human Rights,* Volume 39, Issue 3, 2013. Reprinted with permission.

on a configuration of common elements and patterns such as names, addresses, or Social Security numbers.

Target devised a pregnancy prediction score to entice prospective parents to become loyal consumers. As Charles Duhigg reported in the *New York Times,* shoppers receive a guest ID number linked to their credit card, name, or e-mail address that retains buying history and demographic information that Target collects or buys from other sources. A Target statistician analyzes purchasing data for women who signed up for Target baby registries for patterns such as unscented lotion purchases, which typically happen around the second trimester. After es-

> **Nearly 2,000 private security companies and over 1,200 government organizations engage in counterterrorism intelligence gathering, according to a two-year** *Washington Post* **investigation.**

timating delivery dates, Target sent coupons tailored to women's different stages of pregnancy. The teenager's father who confronted management at the Target store near Minneapolis did so after receiving coupons for baby clothes.

For decades, the government has labored to reconcile competing interests of law enforcement and privacy in the field of computer matching. After a government program, Project Match, got under way in the 1970s to determine if government employees were inappropriately receiving public benefits, the Carter administration conducted a Privacy Initiative prohibiting the government from gathering information for one purpose and using it for another.

Around that same time the Law Enforcement Assistance Administration of the Department of Justice commissioned the Private Security Advisory Council to study the relationship between private security systems and public law enforcement to create programs and policies concerning private security "consistent with the public interest." A multifaceted working relationship between public and private policing grew over succeeding decades.

Despite early attempts to safeguard individuals' privacy, the executive branch, regardless of the party in power, has asserted that the government has an interest in unfettered access to information in the federal domain. This contention, coupled with national security concerns raised in the aftermath of 9/11, has lessened the protections of private information. Under the Patriot Act, a host of personal records—from medical to magazine subscriptions—are available to the FBI if an agent claims they are sought for an "authorized investigation" related to international terrorism. Since the advent of the Total Information Awareness program, data mining has been the go-to method of domestic spying. In contracting with government agencies, the private sector provides a way for the Department of Justice and the FBI to access a treasure trove of personal information on Americans not suspected of any wrongdoing.

Nearly 2,000 private security companies and over 1,200 government organizations engage in counterterrorism intelligence gathering, according to a two-year *Washington Post* investigation. In exchange for government contracts and funding, corporations amass and store a wealth of personal information on individuals easily retrievable by law enforcement agencies. While data aggregators aggressively collect personal data from hundreds of sources to sell to third parties such as financial services, direct marketing, technology, telecommunications, insurance, retail, health care, and travel companies, the U.S. government is an important client.

ChoicePoint, for example, boasts that it has contracts with at least thirty-five government agencies. An $8 million contract with the Justice Department permits FBI agents to access the company's database of personal information on individuals, as do contracts with the Drug Enforcement Administration; the U.S. Marshals Service; the IRS; the Bureau of Citizenship and Immigration Services; and the Bureau of Alcohol, Tobacco and Firearms.

Several members of Congress have expressed concern that government intelligence agencies are reading the Patriot Act too broadly in permitting vast surveillance of Americans' personal communications. And, in 2012, eight members of Congress called for a wide-ranging investigation of data brokers, seeking information from nine top industry companies—Acxiom, Experian, Equifax, Transunion, Epsilon, Reed Elsevier (Lexis-Nexis), Datalogix, Rapleaf, and Spokeo—about how they amass and sell personal data. Two years earlier the Federal Trade Commission launched an investigation into the practices of more than a dozen data brokers. Spokeo later entered into a settlement over violating federal law by selling consumers' personal information for employment screening. Enforcement actions against several other data brokers are pending. Despite having compiled dossiers on an estimated 500 million individuals, as of late 2012, the companies refused to provide names of data sources to Congress.

Storing aggregated electronic data heightens the potential to compromise individuals' identity and privacy. While the United States has no mandatory data retention law, if providers of public electronic communications or remote computing services store electronic communications or communications records, under the Stored Communications Act (SCA), the government can obtain access. The SCA was enacted as part of the ironically named Electronic Communications Privacy Act in 1986 and requires mandatory data preservation for up to 180 days if the government asks.

The government has applied pressure to lengthen the time data are stored. FBI Director Robert Mueller III and then Attorney General Alberto Gonzales met with industry representatives in 2006 to urge them to keep subscriber and network data for two years, claiming that retention was needed for child pornography and terrorism cases. The United States has also pushed to hold service providers responsible for restructuring systems to allow state agents a way to monitor electronic communications; since 1994, landline phone companies are required to design equipment according to FBI specifications, enabling law enforcement to better wiretap customer communications. The Federal Communications Commission succumbed to pressure from the Department of Justice, the FBI, and the Drug Enforcement Administration and enacted a regulation expanding the Communications Assistance for Law Enforcement Act to build in the ability to conduct surveillance on broadband Internet access services and interconnected voice over Internet protocol (VoIP) providers.

A Potent Partnership Imperils First Amendment–Protected Activities

Surveillance by corporations in the form of obtaining e-mails and phone records not only violates privacy but also dampens First Amendment–protected activities. Corporate spying on reporters who expose government injustices or corporate wrongdoing to uncover confidential sources threatens whistleblowers and the notion of a free press.

The practice of corporate spying was exposed when technology giant Hewlett-Packard (HP) contracted with independent security experts from 2005–06 to investigate journalists to find the source of an information leak. Investigators engaged in pretexting, a spying technique by which company personnel impersonated nine journalists, purportedly from the *New York Times*, the *Wall Street Journal*, and other outlets, to obtain the reporters' telephone records, Social Security numbers, call logs, billing records, dates of birth, and subscriber information—all to determine the reporters' sources.

After learning of HP's use of pretexting, the U.S. House Committee on Energy and Commerce in 2006 announced it was investigating Internet-based data brokers allegedly using fraud and deception to acquire personal information, and allowing anyone who pays a fee to acquire itemized call logs for cellular, VoIP, landline, and unpublished numbers.

The right to free speech and association are affected by the very existence of a wiretapping program, aided by communications companies, in the case of attorneys concerned that their communications may be under surveillance. The American Civil Liberties Union filed a lawsuit in 2006 on behalf of journalists, scholars, attorneys, and nonprofit organizations that communicate by phone and e-mail with people in the Middle East. Suspecting that their communications were intercepted by the National Security Agency (NSA), the plaintiffs claimed this disrupted their ability to advise clients, locate witnesses, conduct scholarship, and engage in advocacy. After the Sixth Circuit Court of Appeals dismissed the case, the Supreme Court declined to hear it.

In a similar case a year later, the Center for Constitutional Rights sued on behalf of twenty-four attorneys representing Guantanamo detainees to find out if the NSA intercepted their attorney-client communications. Several incidents led the lawyers to believe the government had eavesdropped on privileged communications. Tom Wilner, the lead plaintiff in the case, noted: "I have been informed on two occasions by government officials, on the condition that I not disclose their names, that I am probably the subject of government surveillance and should be careful in my electronic communications with others."

Not surprisingly, the NSA and the Department of Justice refused to turn over relevant records and refused to confirm or deny whether the plaintiffs had been subject to surveillance, saying that doing so would compromise the methods of U.S. intelligence communities. It's worth noting that wiretapping also has a chilling effect when lawyers consider the repercussions of taking on national security–related cases.

In addition to targeting members of the media and certain attorneys, corporations regularly spy on activists or individuals with dissenting viewpoints. Especially vulnerable to the dual threat of high-tech spying and surveillance are social justice movements. Surveillance, and infiltration that frequently accompanies it, impedes airing legitimate and important political grievances.

Before 9/11, the United States spent about $500 million annually in counter-terrorism research and development. This sum exploded after the attacks to $4.4 billion in 2006. Surveillance projects, including the Terrorism (Total) Information Awareness System (TIA), MATRIX, and Secure Flight programs, created vast business opportunities for technology corporations. Before Congress halted development of the TIA system in 2003, the Defense Advanced Research Projects Agency was in charge of an approximately $2 billion budget. Total government contracts to data-aggregator companies, including Booz Allen Hamilton Inc., Lockheed Martin, Schafer Corporation, Adroit Systems, CACI Dynamic Systems, Syntek Technologies, ASI International, and SRS Technologies, equaled $88 million from years 1997 through 2002.

It is well known that private "risk mitigation" companies, which help other businesses identify threats to profits, regularly monitor political activists. In 2010, Jeremy Scahill of *The Nation* wrote that biotech giant Monsanto hired subsidiaries of the mercenary firm Blackwater to spy on and infiltrate activists organizing against company practices. Through its Total Intelligence and the Terrorism Research Center, Blackwater served as Monsanto's "acting intel arm" in 2008 and 2009, earning between $100,000 and $500,000.

Another partnership between a corporation and investigative firm came to light after Greenpeace USA filed a lawsuit in 2010 against Dow Chemical and Sasol; their public relations firms, Dezenhall Resources and Ketchum; and Beckett Brown International (BBI). The lawsuit alleged that between 1998 and 2000 these companies conducted surveillance on Greenpeace to thwart its anti-chemical pollution environmental campaigns, relying on subcontractors to access thousands of internal documents, including donor lists, financial reports, campaign strategy memos, personal credit card information, bank statements, and Social Security numbers of agency employees. A federal judge dismissed the suit in 2011, ruling that Greenpeace failed to show injuries or establish a direct connection between corporate espionage and civil racketeering allegations.

Corporations routinely and readily hand over customers' private personal data, absent warrants, to government agencies often without legal justification or beyond what was requested. The NSA has collected records of phone calls of millions of individuals with data provided by AT&T, Verizon, and BellSouth. Despite reports citing abuses of the Patriot Act from the Justice Department Office of the Inspector General, such data collection is authorized by legislation signed by Presidents Bush and Obama. Bush issued an executive order authorizing the NSA to monitor phone calls, e-mails, Internet activity, text messaging, and other communication involving any party believed by the NSA to be outside the United States, even if the other end of the communication lies within the United States, without a warrant or other express approval. This executive order was issued pursuant to congressional passage of the Authorization for Use of Military Force, presumably on the grounds that if the president can order targeted assassinations, there is no reason why lesser intrusions should be limited.

Several former officials and telecommunications workers have indicated that the NSA program extends beyond the surveillance of those suspected to be linked to foreign terrorists. A significant disclosure came in 2005 when former technician Mark Klein revealed that AT&T was cooperating with the NSA. The firm had installed a fiber optic splitter at a San Francisco facility that made copies of Internet traffic to and from AT&T customers, and gave them to the NSA.

In light of Klein's disclosure, the Electronic Frontier Foundation (EFF) filed two lawsuits alleging that the NSA, in violation of federal law and with support from agencies such as AT&T, intercepted the communications and obtained communications records of millions of Americans. *Hepting v. AT&T* was filed in 2006 alleging that AT&T allowed and assisted the NSA in unlawfully monitoring communications of AT&T customers, businesses, and third parties whose communications were routed through the AT&T network and whose VoIP calls were routed through the Internet. The U.S. District Court for the Northern District of California rejected the government's motion to dismiss the case on grounds of state secrets privilege. *Hepting* was appealed to the Ninth Circuit and dismissed in June 2009. The U.S. Supreme Court in 2009 declined to review *Hepting*.

Jewel v. NSA was filed in 2008 on behalf of AT&T customers to stop the NSA and other government agencies from conducting warrantless surveillance of their communications and communications records. A year later, the Obama administration moved to dismiss *Jewel*, again invoking the state secrets privilege. The court dismissed the case on standing grounds, but in December 2011, the Ninth U.S. Circuit Court of Appeals ruled that *Jewel* could proceed in district court. In July 2012, EFF moved to have the court declare that the Foreign Intelligence Surveillance Act (FISA), rather than the state secrets privilege, applied. In September 2012, the government renewed its state secrets claim and the federal district court in San Francisco heard the case in December 2012.

Location-Based Tracking Systems

In addition to being subject to invasion of records privacy, anyone who has cruised through the EZ Pass lane of a toll booth, used a monthly subway swipe card, or searched for locations on a cell phone should know that all movements may be potentially recorded for use by a third party at a later date. Global positioning system (GPS) devices violate what is known as location privacy, the ability to move in public without being tracked or monitored. Associational information, such as establishments visited, can be stored to create a dossier of interactions and personal habits.

RFID chips use electromagnetic energy in the form of radio waves to communicate information from a distance such as with EZ Pass and keyless remote systems for cars and garage door openers. Active tags are read remotely as vehicles drive through toll booths, and the information deducts the toll amount from prepaid accounts. Benefits include increasing the speed with which traffic passes through toll plazas; a downside is the recording of drivers' date and time of travel. Initially invented for retail inventory purposes, the RFID chips are embedded in many articles of clothing.

The Federal Highway Administration hopes to embed RFIDs into all American-manufactured cars, installing a global positioning transmitter that can track vehicles by satellite and a wireless device that uploads location as it passes certain hotspots. Texas students were issued chip-embedded identification cards in 2012 to track their movements on campus. Corporations eager to offer chips for monitoring include AT&T, whose advertising materials say that homeroom teachers no longer need to call roll but can just read the embedded tags.

Many nightclubs use ID scanners to verify patrons' ages. Software on bouncers' smartphones reads information from driver's license barcodes or magnetic strips to extract gender, age, zip code, and time of entry. The information goes to the company's database for aggregation and analysis and is available to bars and marketers. While scanning itself may not pose a problem, record retention implicates privacy concerns. Police in San Francisco, for example, are urging that establishments be required to store information for a period of time so it can be available upon request to aid in crime solving.

GPS is a government-maintained, space-based satellite navigation system that provides information about location and time from any place on earth to anyone with a GPS receiver where an unobstructed line of sight exists to four or more satellites. Most cellular phones are equipped with GPS-receiving capability. Unless the power is turned off, a mobile phone stays in constant communication with the nearest cell towers even

> **Corporations routinely and readily hand over customers' private personal data, absent warrants, to government agencies often without legal justification or beyond what was requested. The NSA has collected records of phone calls of millions of individuals with data provided by AT&T, Verizon, and BellSouth.**

when not being used for a call. Information processed by the cells can be used to precisely locate or track the movements of a phone user.

Some employers use GPS-enabled phones to monitor employees' locations. Other locator phones provide GPS coordinates and can even dial emergency numbers; third parties such as family members or caregivers can track the phone's location and receive alerts when the phone leaves a specified area.

Conclusion

Cloaked in the name of convenience and expediency, electronic technology is literally embedded in most aspects of modern daily life. But for every way in which these systems improve life in our society, more sinister applications undermine privacy and threaten human rights, specifically privacy and First Amendment–protected activities. The impending ubiquity of such devices, irrespective of their original purpose, erodes privacy and endangers a robust participatory democracy: The more we grow to accept that all kinds of information will be transmitted about us in everyday life, the more we accede to the potential abuses of this information. In George Orwell's *1984*, the all-seeing state was represented by a two-way television set. In a more modern adaptation, it would be represented by the devices we carry in our pockets and the very clothes we wear on our backs.

N.S.A. Latest: The Secret History of Domestic Surveillance

By John Cassidy
The New Yorker, June 27, 2013

On a day when President Obama said, "I'm not going to be scrambling any jets to get a twenty-nine-year-old hacker"—thank goodness for that—the *Guardian*'s Glenn Greenwald and Spencer Ackerman have published another set of N.S.A. documents that detail how the agency's domestic-surveillance programs have evolved over the past decade or so. The documents presumably came from Edward Snowden, although the *Guardian* reports don't say so explicitly.

The headline news is that, for two years of the Obama Administration—from 2009 to 2011—the N.S.A. continued a previously undisclosed Bush-era program that enabled the agency to sweep up vast amounts of information about American citizens' Internet use. This included whom they were e-mailing with and which computers they were using. The program, which went under the code name "Stellar Wind," was ended in 2011, and hasn't been restarted, a senior administration official told the newspaper.

For those of us who are concerned about this stuff, it's depressing to think that the administration, in addition to allowing the N.S.A. to collect vast amounts of metadata about Americans' personal phone calls, also preserved a program to track U.S. citizens' Internet usage. (In the case of an e-mail, metadata includes the names of the sender and all of the recipients, plus the I.S.P. address of the device used to access the Internet. The subject line and what the e-mail says are considered "content," and under operation Stellar Wind, at least, they weren't collected.) On the other hand, the online metadata-collection program was ended in 2011, although exactly why that happened isn't clear. Shawn Turner, the Obama administration's director of communications for national intelligence, told the *Guardian* that operation Stellar Wind was stopped for "operational and resource reasons," but he didn't specify what these were.

In a separate story, Greenwald and Ackerman reported that the new documents confirm that the N.S.A., in targeting suspects overseas and those they communicate with, still mines vast amounts of online data from American citizens. Thanks to the previous revelations about Operation Prism, we sort of knew this. But the new documents add some telling details about the scale of the online snooping. For example, by the end of last year, one particular N.S.A. Internet tracking program called ShellTrumpet (there appear to have been many others) had already processed a trillion (1,000,000,000,000) metadata records.

If you, like me, are wondering how things came to this, the documents, which include a top-secret draft of a 2009 historical review by the N.S.A.'s Inspector General, provide some of the answers. Indeed, that may well be their most lasting contribution. As you might have guessed, it all goes back to the immediate aftermath of the 9/11 attacks, when George W. Bush issued an internal order with this title:

AUTHORIZATION FOR SPECIFIED ELECTRONIC SURVEILLANCE ACTIVITIES DURING A LIMITED PERIOD TO DETECT AND PREVENT ACTS OF TERRORISM WITHIN THE UNITED STATES

According to the Inspector General's report, the order was drafted by David Addington, the chief counsel to Vice President Dick Cheney. General Michael Hayden, who was the director of the N.S.A. from 1999 until 2005, "suggested that the ability to collect information with one end in the United States without a court order would increase NSA's speed and agility," the report says. "General Hayden stated that after two additional meetings with the Vice President, the Vice President asked him to work with his counsel, David Addington."

In retrospect, what's most notable about the order President Bush signed are the restrictions it contained. Originally, it lasted for just thirty days and was limited to online communications in which at least one of the communicants was located outside the United States. Moreover, it was explicitly based on "the President's determination that after the 11 September 2001 terrorist attacks in the United States, an extraordinary emergency existed for national defense purposes." Over time, though, the "extraordinary emergency" was deemed a permanent state of affairs, and the scope of the authorization was broadened until, eventually, it came to include even the collection of data from communications between American citizens located inside the United States.

For a few years, the online surveillance didn't have any court approval. "NSA determined that FISA authorization did not allow sufficient flexibility to counter the terrorist threat," the Inspector General's report said. In March 2004, senior officials at the Justice Department, including James Comey, who was then the acting Attorney General, and who has recently been nominated to head the F.B.I., objected to this system, prompting the White House and the N.S.A. to bring Stellar Wind to a halt.

But things didn't end there. As the documents show, and as a must-read piece by Spencer Ackerman explains, the N.S.A. and the White House quickly found a way to bring the online-surveillance operations under the ambit of regular intelligence laws, and barely three months later, in July 2004, the chief judge in the FISA courts, Colleen Kollar-Kotelly, granted the N.S.A. authority to once again begin collecting online metadata. "Although NSA lost access to the bulk metadata from 26 March 2004 until the order was signed, the order essentially gave NSA the same authority to collect bulk Internet metadata that it had," the Inspector General's report says, "except that it specified the datalinks from which NSA could collect, and it limited the number of people that could access the data."

Still, the N.S.A. chafed at the remaining legal restrictions on accessing data from American citizens communicating online with other American citizens. In a November 2007, memorandum, which the *Guardian* has also posted online, a lawyer at the Justice Department, Kenneth Wainstein, told Michael Mukasey, the New York judge who had recently taken over as Attorney General, that the N.S.A. wanted a new set of procedures that would give the agency considerably broader authorization. The memo said:

> The Supplemental Procedures, attached at Tab A, would clarify that the National Security Agency (NSA) may analyze communications metadata associated with United States persons and persons believed to be in the United States. . . . We conclude that the proposed Supplemental Procedures are consistent with the applicable law and we recommend that you approve them.

The memo argued that the new set of procedures, because they covered online metadata rather than actual content, didn't violate the Fourth Amendment's right to privacy, and neither did they need the approval of the FISA courts: "To fall within FISA's definition of 'electronic surveillance,' an action must satisfy one of the four definitions of that term. None of these definitions cover the communications metadata analysis at issue here."

Evidently, Mukasey approved the new procedures, and they formed the legal basis of operation Stellar Wind, which continued until 2011. But it also seems that the FISA courts did, eventually, approve the program. According to the *Guardian's* account, a FISA judge issued a legal order every ninety days approving the collection, in bulk, of online metadata. Why the court did this, and whether it registered any objections to or demanded any changes in the N.S.A.'s actions, we don't know. The FISA court's deliberations, unlike a lot of other things, remain shrouded in secrecy.

Scholars Explain Failures in Oversight of Domestic Spying

By Beth McMurtrie
The Chronicle of Higher Education, August 2, 2013

The revelations from Edward Snowden that the National Security Agency has been tracking the communications of millions of Americans seem to have surprised Congress as much as everyone else.

"Snowden, I don't like him at all," said Rep. Ted Poe, a Texas Republican, during a House Judiciary Committee hearing in July, "but we would have never known what happened if he hadn't told us."

But to scholars who study congressional oversight of the government's intelligence agencies, this is hardly news.

Their analysis is unsparing: Legislators are ill equipped to handle the complexities of the country's fast-growing intelligence industry, turf battles prevent them from carrying out their duties effectively, and the intelligence agencies themselves conspire with the executive branch to limit access to information.

"It's hard not to be cynical," admits Jennifer D. Kibbe, an associate professor of government at Franklin & Marshall College who has written about what she sees as the failures of oversight.

In a 2010 article in the journal *Intelligence and National Security*, Ms. Kibbe lays out a series of interlocking problems that make such failures inevitable. One is jurisdictional complexity. The two main oversight bodies in Congress, the Senate Select Committee on Intelligence and the House Permanent Select Committee on Intelligence, have limited authority. The intelligence community has become so vast, she notes, that it extends into a host of departments, including Energy, Justice, and Treasury.

Moreover, the ability to finance—or kill—particular programs rests with yet another set of committees, further diminishing the ability of legislators ostensibly in charge of oversight to govern the activities of the security agencies.

"No one committee," Ms. Kibbe writes, "has a complete view of the intelligence community to be able to judge priorities and weigh programs against each other."

Then there is the problem of access to information. In short, members of Congress know only what the intelligence agencies and the executive branch tell them. In her article, Ms. Kibbe describes agencies dragging their feet when asked to provide reports by Congress.

Even when legislators get information, it is delivered in a way that is difficult to absorb or share. Briefings are confidential and can be limited to an even smaller "Gang of Eight," who cannot take notes or bring the aides on whom they rely for expertise.

As a result, says Ms. Kibbe, legislators may not know what to look for or what to ask when presented with complicated information.

Those limited briefings have led to controversies in the recent past, including what Congress did or didn't know about the Bush administration's warrantless wiretapping program in 2005 or its use of "enhanced interrogation techniques."

"There's such a huge informational disadvantage," says Ms. Kibbe. "Even when they're briefed, they're briefed in such vague language, and all the time the administration is pushing the terror-terror-terror line, so you feel pressure not to get in the way because if something happens, it's your fault."

In the case of the Internet- and telephone-surveillance programs run by the National Security Agency, which were revealed in June in news-media reports on classified information provided by the former NSA contractor Edward Snowden, it is unclear how many in Congress fully understood the scope of the programs before then.

Sen. Ron Wyden, an Oregon Democrat who sits on the Senate intelligence committee, had been trying to raise alarms about the surveillance programs for a while, Ms. Kibbe says, most recently in March, during a rare public hearing of the committee. There, he asked the director of national intelligence, James R. Clapper, if the NSA had collected "any type of data at all on millions or hundreds of millions of Americans."

Mr. Clapper was not truthful in his response—for which he later apologized—but there was little Senator Wyden could say then without revealing the classified program.

An Attention Deficit

Congress is hardly blameless for this situation, scholars say. Some of the limits it faces in effectively overseeing the complex intelligence community are self-imposed.

Amy B. Zegart, co-director of the Center for International Security and Cooperation at Stanford University and an expert on intelligence, writes in "The Roots of Weak Congressional Intelligence Oversight" that "electoral incentives and institutional prerogatives have led Congress to tie its own hands and block oversight reforms even when the problems are known and the stakes are high."

It's also a challenge for legislators to offer sustained attention to any one issue, says Loch K. Johnson, a professor of public and international affairs at the University of Georgia. "Congress tends to be a reactive institution," he says. "It really takes a shock in the intelligence system in order to have members focus full attention on the issue at hand."

Mr. Johnson, a longtime scholar of national security who has also worked as a congressional aide on intelligence issues, sees historical patterns in how the NSA revelations are playing out on Capitol Hill today. The first meaningful instance of intelligence oversight began in the 1970s, he notes, when a series of scandals prompted a major congressional investigation headed by Sen. Frank Church. (The investigations also led to the creation of the House and Senate intelligence committees.)

Those early scandals, which included domestic spying through such means as mail tampering and wiretapping, gave birth to the Foreign Intelligence Surveillance Act. The law, enacted in 1978, was designed to place limits on—and provide oversight of—domestic spying.

Legislators are ill equipped to handle the complexities of the country's fast-growing intelligence industry, turf battles prevent them from carrying out their duties effectively, and the intelligence agencies themselves conspire with the executive branch to limit access to information.

In the years since the September 11 attacks, the law has been repeatedly amended in ways that complicate efforts at oversight.

Government officials and the public are now attempting to sort out what the law does and should allow with regard to the current surveillance programs.

After that initial flurry of investigations and intelligence reforms, says Mr. Johnson, Congress did not do much until another scandal—Iran-Contra, in the 1980s—brought intelligence oversight back into the spotlight. That same pattern—inactivity, then scandal, then reform—has continued ever since.

"It's an old story of not really being focused enough on accountability until something goes wrong," he says. "Then Congress begins to behave in a more constitutional fashion and holds hearings and takes these matters seriously."

Both Mr. Johnson and Ms. Kibbe think the intelligence committees should demand more informative briefings and could do more to push for public debate about the surveillance programs, without revealing classified information.

Mr. Johnson, for one, says that effective oversight has often rested on the shoulders of particular individuals—people like Senator Church, in the 1970s, and Rep. Lee Hamilton, who headed the House intelligence committee in the 1980s. They acted as true watchdogs, he says, studying the issues carefully and asking tough questions.

Otherwise, the bureaucracy tends to take over, allowing legislators to slip away to focus on the more immediate, and transparent, interests of their constituents.

"Democracy," says Mr. Johnson, "ends up depending on the energy and willingness and commitment not of a whole committee—because that rarely happens—but of at least a few members, who keep the spark of accountability alive."

A New Legal Theory for the Age of Mass Surveillance

By Michael Phillips
The New Yorker, December 17, 2013

Yesterday afternoon, a federal judge ruled that the National Security Agency's collection and storage of all Americans' telephone records was likely unconstitutional. The federal judge, George W. Bush appointee Richard J. Leon, declared that "the author of our Constitution, James Madison," would "be aghast" at the N.S.A.'s "almost Orwellian" surveillance. The ruling is the first public legal setback for the government's surveillance policy since the whistle-blower Edward Snowden's disclosures began in June. It challenges a stale thirty-year-old precedent; undermines a central legal rationale of the secret Foreign Intelligence Surveillance Act court; and nudges the law into the age of Internet-connected smartphones, G.P.S., and Big Data.

The plaintiffs, who included conservative legal activist Larry Klayman, argued that the N.S.A.'s bulk telephony-metadata program violated the Constitution's prohibitions on unreasonable searches and seizures, their First Amendment rights to free speech and association, and their Fifth Amendment due-process rights, and even caused them emotional distress. They asked Leon to order the government to preliminarily halt the collection of phone records while their case progresses. To win that injunction, the plaintiffs had to accomplish three things: First, they had to show that they had the right to challenge the collection and review of the metadata. Then, they had to establish that they would suffer "irreparable harm" if the court did not order the government to stop. Finally, they had to show that they were "substantially likely" eventually to win their case on the merits of their constitutional argument. Leon ruled in the plaintiffs' favor on all three points, but said that, pending the government's appeal, he would not enforce the order to stop the N.S.A. program, because of the "significant national-security interests at stake." Having agreed with the plaintiffs that the program violated the Fourth Amendment, Leon refused to rule preliminarily on their other claims.

In February 2013, the Supreme Court turned away a similar challenge to N.S.A. surveillance, ruling that the parties in that case lacked standing. The plaintiffs were prominent lawyers, journalists, and human-rights activists who represented, interviewed, or otherwise had contact with suspected terrorists. The Supreme Court refused to hear the case, holding that the plaintiffs could not prove that they were

Michael T. Phillips/*The New Yorker*

subject to any surveillance at all. But now, thanks to Snowden's disclosures, Klayman's status as a Verizon customer was all it took. Leon ruled that being a Verizon customer is "strong evidence" that he had been subject to at least seven years of data surveillance and five years of that data's storage by the N.S.A. When the government suggested that Klayman lacked standing because Verizon considers itself immune to N.S.A.-related lawsuits and because its customers are just a small part of the program, Leon scoffed. "Omitting Verizon Wireless, A.T.&T., and Sprint from the collection would be like omitting John, Paul, and George from a historical analysis of the Beatles. A Ringo-only database doesn't make any sense."

Leon left no doubt that he agreed it was "significantly likely" that the N.S.A. had violated the Constitution, and that the "loss of constitutional freedoms" caused Klayman "irreparable harm." "I cannot imagine a more 'indiscriminate' and 'arbitrary' invasion than this systematic and high-tech collection and retention of personal data on virtually every single citizen for purposes of querying and analyzing it without prior judicial approval," he wrote. "Surely, such a program infringes on 'that degree of privacy' that the founders enshrined in the Fourth Amendment." Leon even questioned the efficacy of the program, finding that the government could not show, even with its three strongest examples, any "indication that [the data collected was] immediately useful or that they prevented an impending attack." His footnotes were sharp-elbowed, too, noting sarcastically that the government's concession that the program is only "sometimes" useful was "candor as refreshing as it is rare."

The core of Leon's opinion took aim at the 1979 precedent of *Smith v. Maryland,* which the government has relied upon in the secret FISA court to justify its broader surveillance programs. In *Smith,* the government captured the phone records of one man, a robbery suspect already known to the police, who was also suspected of making threatening calls to the victim of the robbery. The Supreme Court ruled that the government did not need a warrant to collect a list of the phone numbers that he had dialed because the suspect had no reasonable expectation of privacy for his phone records, which were held by the phone company. But as Patrick Di Justo has described (a point cited by Leon in his opinion), the data collected by today's bulk telephony-metadata surveillance is vastly different in scale and scope. Leon noted that, in the age of an Internet-connected smartphone in most citizens' pockets, the government and its computers have access to continuously updated location data and other information that the Supreme Court in 1979 would have looked upon as "the stuff of science fiction." "Put simply, people in 2013 have an entirely different relationship with phones than they did thirty-four years ago," he wrote. "Records that once would have revealed a few scattered tiles of information about a person now reveal an entire mosaic—a vibrant and constantly updating picture of the person's life." In the face of this radical technological change, Leon argued that now is the time to cast this precedent aside. "When do present-day circumstances— the evolutions in the Government's surveillance capabilities, citizens' phone habits, and the relationship between the N.S.A. and telecom companies—become so thoroughly unlike those considered by the Supreme Court thirty-four years ago that a precedent like *Smith* simply does not apply? The answer, unfortunately for the Government, is now."

The "mosaic" language comes from the 2010 circuit-court case *United States v. Maynard*. (As a Washington, D.C., circuit case, *Maynard* is the law of Leon's jurisdiction.) The *Maynard* ruling determined that the government may capture pieces of information that, when reviewed individually, are not invasions of privacy, but may constitute a search subject to a Fourth Amendment review when taken together. With this decision, Leon advanced the "mosaic theory" as a replacement for *Smith*.

The immediate reaction from legal scholars has been mixed. Benjamin Wittes, of the Brookings Institution, wrote that "Leon makes a powerful case that times have changed since the Supreme Court decided *Smith*, which dealt with a pen-register device against a single suspect—and long before the era of Big Data and cell phones," but he suggested that the Supreme Court would be afraid of undermining a national-security program. "Are five justices really ready to shut down a major intelligence program that administrations of both parties have insisted represents a crucial line of defense against terrorism?" Wittes wrote. Wittes' colleague Paul Rosenzweig, of the Lawfare Institute, was similarly skeptical, finding the technological argument for dismissing *Smith* "rather unpersuasive." Fourth Amendment scholar Orin Kerr agreed, finding the attack on *Smith* "deeply unpersuasive," though he later clarified that he would strike down the N.S.A. program on other grounds.

The skepticism toward overturning precedent reflects Supreme Court Chief Justice John Roberts's own relationship with stare decisis, the doctrine that courts should generally follow precedent. In his concurring opinion in the *Citizens United* campaign-finance case, Roberts presented his argument for when it would be appropriate to cast aside precedent: following it is not an "inexorable command" or "mechanical formula of adherence to the latest decision." After all, Roberts wrote, "if it were, segregation would be legal, minimum-wage laws would be unconstitutional, and the Government could wiretap ordinary criminal suspects without first obtaining warrants." Instead, Roberts argued that courts should overturn precedent when "the precedent's validity is so hotly contested that it cannot reliably function as a basis for decision in future cases, when its rationale threatens to upend our settled jurisprudence in related areas of law, and when the precedent's underlying reasoning has become so discredited that the Court cannot keep the precedent alive without jury-rigging new and different justifications to shore up the original mistake." To critics of the opinion such as Rosenzweig, the "passionate" Leon did not find a valid rationale to abandon *Smith*.

But there is reason to believe that at least five Supreme Court justices might agree with Leon that "the time is now" to abandon stare decisis for *Smith*. In the 2012 Supreme Court case *U.S. v. Jones*, an unlikely mix of five justices, including conservative Justice Samuel Alito, suggested that it might be time for the law to change, establishing a reasonable right to privacy for the data and metadata created by our smartphone-charged, increasingly connected lives. In *Jones*, the Supreme Court held that attaching a G.P.S. device to a car to track its movements constitutes a search under the Fourth Amendment. Five of the justices, including

Alito, suggested that the G.P.S. surveillance was a search because it violated citizens' reasonable expectations of privacy in their location, an expectation thrown into question by the new technology. "Technology can change those expectations [of privacy]," Alito wrote. "Dramatic technological change may lead to periods in which popular expectations are in flux and may ultimately produce significant changes in popular attitudes. New technology may provide increased convenience or security at the expense of privacy, and many people may find the trade-off worthwhile. And even if the public does not welcome the diminution of privacy that new technology entails, they may eventually reconcile themselves to this development as inevitable."

Leon's treatment of *Smith* acknowledges our technological reality. We are enmeshed in a twenty-four-seven, cradle-to-grave "mosaic" of digital information. We carry our telephones everywhere. The applications nested within them are tiles of personal data, and we teach those applications more and more about ourselves. The executive branch will take its appeal to the Washington, D.C., circuit court, whose judges have previously shown a willingness to think creatively about our high-tech times. With his decision, Leon may press the N.S.A.—and the law—to come to terms with how we live now.

Newly Revealed NSA Program ICREACH Extends the NSA's Reach Even Further

By Nadia Kayyali
Electronic Frontier Foundation, September 3, 2014

Turns out, the DEA and FBI may know what medical conditions you have, whether you are having an affair, where you were last night, and more—all without any knowing that you have ever broken a law.

That's because the DEA and FBI, as part of over 1000 analysts at 23 U.S. intelligence agencies, have the ability to peer over the NSA's shoulder and see much of the NSA's metadata with ICREACH. Metadata is transactional data about communications, such as numbers dialed, email addresses sent to, and duration of phone calls, and it can be incredibly revealing. ICREACH, exposed by a release of Snowden documents in *The Intercept,*[1] is a system that enables sharing of metadata by "provid[ing] analysts with the ability to perform a one-stop search of information from a wide variety of separate databases." It's the latest in a string of documents that demonstrate how little the intelligence community distinguishes between counter-terrorism and ordinary crime—and just how close to home surveillance may really be.

The documents describe ICREACH as a "one-stop shopping tool for consolidated communications metadata analytic needs." ICREACH brings together various databases with a single search query, allowing analysts to search literally billions of records. The tool allows sharing of "more than 30 different kinds of metadata on emails, phone calls, faxes, Internet chats, and text messages, as well as location information collected from cellphones." It is intended to include data from Five Eyes partners as well. While the program shares data obtained under Executive Order 12333, it includes data from U.S. persons.

ICREACH grew out of CRISSCROSS and PROTON, older tools that allowed the CIA, DEA, FBI, DIA, and NSA to share metadata. Metadata sharing in CRISSCROSS started with only date, time, duration, calling number, and called number. PROTON, which expanded CRISSCROSS, allowed sharing of far more information, including latitude and longitude coordinates, email headers, and travel records like flight numbers. The system had compatibility issues, and NSA never added the additional information PROTON could handle. PROTON also appears to have the capacity for sophisticated data analysis: "PROTON tools find other entities that behave in a similar manner to a specific target."

While data sharing may seem innocuous, and perhaps even necessary, the melding of domestic law enforcement and national security agencies deserves far more attention. The blending of the war on drugs and the war on terror, and domestic and international law enforcement, and the move from targeted to mass, suspicionless surveillance, is leading to a place where everyone is a suspect and can be targeted at any time.

As *The Intercept* article pointed out, one serious concern is that data obtained through ICREACH could be used for parallel construction— the practice through which the DEA obscures the source of tips it receives from the NSA and then passes on to other law enforcement agencies. The DEA will "recreate" investigative trails, and hide the source of the information from defense lawyers, judges, and prosecutors. With parallel construction, NSA data can be used in ordinary criminal investigations, without any way to challenge the collection of that data in court. This runs blatantly counter to notions of due process and the right to a fair trial, to question and confront witnesses, and have competent counsel.

The ICREACH system makes it even easier for law enforcement to use communications data collected by NSA without revealing the source. While domestic law enforcement agencies can already get some of the kinds of data in ICREACH without a warrant, they at least have to serve a subpoena or national security letter on a telecommunications provider. A subpoena requires court approval, and either type of process can be challenged in court. Instead, with ICREACH, any approved analyst at a partner agency can access the data in secret with just a few keystrokes, and with little possibility of judicial review.

That data could then be used in a variety of ways, without revealing the NSA as the original source of the information. With a traffic stop or anonymous informant as pretext, domestic law enforcement could initiate an investigation, conduct physical searches, visit targets, and more.

Even more disturbing: the cops on your block may be getting ICREACH data passed on to them. The information sharing movement goes beyond just big federal agencies. There are myriad channels through which state and local law enforcement agencies can get the information agencies like the FBI and DHS have. The FBI works directly with local law enforcement through Joint Terrorism Task Forces (JTTFs). Through JTTF memoranda of understanding,

> **The blending of the war on drugs and the war on terror, and domestic and international law enforcement, and the move from targeted to mass, suspicionless surveillance, is leading to a place where everyone is a suspect and can be targeted at any time.**

officers from police departments across the country work directly under the FBI's command and agree not to talk about the work they do. Similarly, local agencies and federal agencies share intelligence information through fusion centers, where local law enforcement can access DHS and FBI databases, among others.

The Constitution was intended to constrain the government's investigative authority. The national security state has created a gaping hole in those protections. Although the government has argued that it has bent the rules around surveillance only in the name of national security, the lines of what is appropriate information to share between various agencies continue to get blurrier. Without some safeguards, the same surveillance architecture that targets "terrorists" can be used to target everyday lawbreakers.

The rallying cry from law enforcement is always the need to catch criminals. But constitutional constraints like no unreasonable searches and seizures and the right to the assistance of counsel exist specifically because of the societal agreement that the need to curb government abuse is worth occasionally letting a guilty person go.

Note

1. https://firstlook.org/theintercept/2014/08/25/icreach-nsa-cia-secret-google-criss-cross-proton

Who Can Control N.S.A. Surveillance?

By Mattathias Schwartz
The New Yorker, January 23, 2015

President Obama spent only a few moments of his State of the Union this week talking about the National Security Agency and civil liberties. A year before, he'd promised to "end" Section 215, the N.S.A.'s most controversial surveillance program, "as it currently exists." In his speech last Tuesday, he said almost nothing concrete, aside from mentioning a forthcoming report "on how we're keeping our promise to keep our country safe while strengthening privacy."

Since Edward Snowden revealed the extent of the N.S.A.'s activities in the summer of 2013, there have been a number of official reports on the troubled relationship between surveillance and privacy—one from the President's Review Group, two from the Privacy and Civil Liberties Oversight Board, and another, last week, from the National Academy of Sciences. In August 2013, the Office of the Director of National Intelligence started a Tumblr, on which they've posted many interesting and useful documents, including redacted orders from the secret Foreign Intelligence Surveillance Court (FISA).

But while the government has made some moves toward transparency about its surveillance programs, it has enacted few substantial reforms of them. The N.S.A. continues to use Section 215, named after a part of the Patriot Act, to collect metadata on hundreds of billions of U.S. phone calls. Obama has talked about moving the data to some third party. Congress has talked about more serious reforms, including an independent advocate who would represent privacy concerns before the FISA court. But the most significant reform that has been undertaken as the result of an order from Obama is a reduction in the scope of metadata searches, from three "hops," or degrees of association, to two.

There isn't much evidence to suggest that Section 215 helps catch the most dangerous terrorists, like those who committed the attacks in Paris two weeks ago. It may even slow investigators down, by eating up resources and generating extraneous leads. Nevertheless, opponents of N.S.A. reform continue to claim that Section 215 can stop violent terrorists. Last week, House Speaker John Boehner, of Ohio, said that information collected from phone records helped halt a plot to bomb the U.S. Capitol, despite the fact that, as the *Guardian* reported, the F.B.I. has indicated that the critical information came from a government informant. "The first thing that strikes me is that we would've never known about this had it not been for the FISA program and our ability to collect information for people who pose an imminent threat," Boehner told *Politico*.

When Obama and Congress talk about N.S.A. reform, they're mostly talking about Section 215. But what other classified surveillance programs are out there? The difficulty of answering this question was made clear last week, when the Drug Enforcement Administration revealed in a court filing that it had maintained a database of calls made from U.S. phone numbers to and from overseas callers. The D.E.A. held the database under a law ostensibly related to administrative subpoenas, not metadata, and used it in criminal drug-trafficking investigations, not counterterrorism activities. Despite the apparent lack of a connection to terrorism, all the D.E.A. needed to search the database was a "reasonable articulable suspicion," a lower standard of evidence than probable cause that is most often associated with counterterrorism and counterintelligence programs. According to the D.E.A. filings, the program was suspended in September 2013. All of the information that was contained in the database has since been deleted, a D.E.A. spokesperson told the *Times*.

If Obama and Congress were to undertake serious surveillance reforms, they would have a hard time doing it one authority at a time. The limits on U.S. surveillance were written in an analog age, when "pen registers" and "trap and trace devices" intercepted communications moving on copper wire. The legality of collecting phone metadata rests on a 1979 Supreme Court case, *Smith v. Maryland*, which held that the police did not need a warrant to obtain the phone numbers dialed from a single suspect's land line. It didn't say anything about location tracking, pattern-based analysis, or collecting phone records by the million. The discrepancy between the old guidelines and the new technology they describe has facilitated surprisingly broad interpretations of the ruling, most notably Section 215.

Last October, Senator Patrick Leahy, of Vermont, proposed the U.S.A. Freedom Act, which would curtail some of the N.S.A.'s domestic powers with an independent FISA advocate, more legal authority for a key oversight board, and more stringent legal standards for obtaining phone metadata and other records. It's unclear whether the bill will make it through the Republican-controlled Congress, or what will happen if Congress fails to reform Section 215 before June, when it will expire if it's not renewed. In the end, the branch of government most capable of settling the thorny N.S.A. debate may turn out to be the courts.

Administration Highlights Surveillance Reforms

By Josh Gerstein
Politico, February 3, 2015

With legislation to overhaul a key surveillance program stalled on Capitol Hill, the Obama administration issued a report Tuesday highlighting reforms it has made to the nation's snooping efforts since Edward Snowden jump-started public debate on the issue with a series of unauthorized revelations more than a year ago.

The report, promised by President Barack Obama in his State of the Union address, incorporates previously announced changes to the intelligence-gathering programs as well as some new restrictions imposed as recently as Monday by Director of National Intelligence James Clapper.

The catalog of tweaks to surveillance efforts was released to mark the one-year anniversary of a speech Obama gave last January calling for surveillance reforms. Obama called for legislation to ease one of the key reforms he endorsed—an end to bulk collection of telephone records in the U.S.

Such legislation passed the House last year but died in the Senate. Its prospects for this year are unclear, although the legal authority for the program is set to expire on June 1. Critics of the program have called for Obama to simply shut it down, which he can do. But he wants to replace it with a streamlined system to acquire similar information from phone companies on a case-by-case basis—a system which would likely require legislation to establish.

Among the new surveillance safeguards discussed in Tuesday's report:

—A five-year limit on retention of information about foreigners who don't hold U.S. residency, subject to exceptions to be established by Clapper.

—No dissemination of such information solely because it pertains to a foreigner.

—A written statement of facts will be required before using a U.S. person's name or other identifier to query data produced by the so-called 702 program set up to collect intelligence on foreigners.

—Intelligence about Americans collected in the 702 program must be destroyed if it lacks foreign intelligence value.

Originally published by Politico.com, February 3, 2015.

—Use of 702 information to prosecute a U.S. citizen will require the approval of the attorney general and be available only in national security cases or "other serious crimes."

—Gag orders accompanying National Security Letters used by the FBI to obtain information will end when an investigation ends or three years after it is opened, unless officials take steps to extend the gag in a specific case.

"Our signals intelligence activities must take into account that all persons have legitimate privacy interests in the handling of their personal information. At the same time, we must ensure that our Intelligence Community has the resources and authorities necessary for the United States to advance its national security and foreign policy interests and to protect its citizens and the citizens of its allies and partners from harm," White House Homeland Security and Counterterrorism Adviser Lisa Monaco said in a statement. "As we continue to face threats from terrorism,

> **". . . When it comes to reforming intelligence programs and protecting Americans' privacy, there is much, much more work to be done," [Sen. Ron] Wyden said in a statement.**

proliferation, and cyber-attacks, we must use our intelligence capabilities in a way that optimally protects our national security and supports our foreign policy while keeping the public trust and respecting privacy and civil liberties."

Monaco's statement did not discuss any talks between Congress and the White House about surveillance legislation. She did indicate that an update on the collection of so-called "big data" by private companies is set to be released in the coming days.

Sen. Ron Wyden (D-Ore.), a sharp critic of the phone-records program, said he didn't think much of the administration's update on its surveillance reforms.

"My first impression on reading this report is it's hard to see much 'there' there. When it comes to reforming intelligence programs and protecting Americans' privacy, there is much, much more work to be done," Wyden said in a statement.

Many of the reforms outlined in Clapper's report were urged by the Privacy and Civil Liberties Oversight Board. It issued a statement Tuesday noting the embrace of most of its recommendations, but also observing that Obama hasn't moved unilaterally to end the call-tracking program.

"The Administration has not implemented the Board's recommendation to halt the NSA's bulk telephone records program, which it could do at any time without congressional involvement," the panel noted.

Wyden also called on Obama to halt the program.

One congressman said Tuesday that the White House and the intelligence community could move forward with plans for an overhaul of the phone records program even before a bill addressing the issue passes.

"While legislation may ultimately be necessary and is certainly desirable, the technical work for this change can and should start now. We also need to move forward on further legislative reforms to establish an independent privacy advocate in the FISA Court and to otherwise increase transparency and civil liberties," said Rep. Adam Schiff of California, the top Democrat on the House Intelligence Committee. "Congress should take up reform legislation to accomplish these goals as soon as possible."

How Big Business Is Helping Expand NSA Surveillance, Snowden Be Damned

By Lee Fang
The Intercept, April 1, 2015

Since November 11, 2011, with the introduction of the Cyber Intelligence Sharing and Protection Act, American spy agencies have been pushing laws to encourage corporations to share more customer information. They repeatedly failed, thanks in part to NSA contractor Edward Snowden's revelations of mass government surveillance. Then came Republican victories in last year's midterm congressional elections and a major push by corporate interests in favor of the legislation.

Today, the bill is back, largely unchanged, and if congressional insiders and the bill's sponsors are to believed, the legislation could end up on President Obama's desk as soon as this month. In another boon to the legislation, Obama is expected to reverse his past opposition and sign it, albeit in an amended and renamed form (CISPA is now CISA, the "Cybersecurity Information Sharing Act"). The reversal comes in the wake of high-profile hacks on JPMorgan Chase and Sony Pictures Entertainment. The bill has also benefitted greatly from lobbying by big business, which sees it as a way to cut costs and to shift some anti-hacking defenses onto the government.

For all its appeal to corporations, CISA represents a major new privacy threat to individual citizens. It lays the groundwork for corporations to feed massive amounts of communications to private consortiums and the federal government, a scale of cooperation even greater than that revealed by Snowden. The law also breaks new ground in suppressing pushback against privacy invasions; in exchange for channeling data to the government, businesses are granted broad legal immunity from privacy lawsuits — potentially leaving consumers without protection if companies break privacy promises that would otherwise keep information out of the hands of authorities.

Ostensibly, CISA is supposed to help businesses guard against cyberattacks by sharing information on threats with one another and with the government. Attempts must be made to filter personal information out of the pool of data that is shared. But the legislation — at least as marked up by the Senate Intelligence Committee — provides an expansive definition of what can be construed as a cybersecurity threat, including any information for responding to or mitigating "an imminent threat of death, serious bodily harm, or serious economic harm," or information that is potentially related to threats relating to weapons of mass destruction, threats to minors, identity theft, espionage, protection of trade secrets, and other possible offenses. Asked at a hearing in February how quickly such information could be shared with the FBI, CIA, or NSA, Deputy Undersecretary for Cybersecurity Phyllis Schneck replied, "fractions of a second."

Questions persist on how to more narrowly define a cybersecurity threat, what type of personal data is shared, and which government agencies would retain and store this data. Sen. Ron Wyden, D-Ore., who cast the lone dissenting vote against CISA on the Senate Intelligence Committee, declared the legislation "a surveillance bill by another name." Privacy advocates agree. "The lack of use limitations creates yet another loophole for law enforcement to conduct backdoor searches on Americans," argues a letter sent by a coalition of privacy organizations, including Free Press Action Fund and New America's Open Technology Institute. Critics also argue that CISA would not have prevented the recent spate of high-profile hacking incidents. As the Electronic Frontier Foundation's Mark Jaycox noted in a blog post, the JPMorgan hack occurred because of an "un-updated server" and prevailing evidence about the Sony breach is "increasingly pointing to an inside job."

But the intelligence community and corporate America have this year unified behind the bill. For a look into the breadth of the corporate advocacy campaign to pass CISA, see this letter cosigned by many of the most powerful corporate interests in America and sent to legislators earlier this year. Or another letter, reported in the *Wall Street Journal*, signed by "general counsels of more than 30 different firms, including 3M and Lockheed Martin Corp."

The partnership between leading corporate lobbyists and the intelligence community was on full display at a cybersecurity summit hosted by the U.S. Chamber of Commerce a few days before the midterm election last year, in which NSA director Admiral Mike Rogers asked a room filled with business representatives for support in passing laws like CISA. At one point, Ann Beauchesne, the lead homeland security lobbyist with the U.S. Chamber of Commerce, asked Rogers, "How can the chamber be helpful to you?" — even suggesting a viral marketing campaign akin to the "ALS ice bucket challenge" to build public support.

> **For all its appeal to corporations, CISA represents a major new privacy threat to individual citizens. It lays the groundwork for corporations to feed massive amounts of communications to private consortiums and the federal government, a scale of cooperation even greater than that revealed by Snowden.**

Rogers specifically mentioned during his speech before the Chamber how corporations who partner with agencies like the NSA can shift some of their information security work to the government — a major cost savings. "You have information that I need and I think I have information that can be of value to you," Rogers said.

At the moment, there are multiple versions of CISA, including information sharing proposals from the House Homeland Security Committee and Sen. Tom Carper, D-Del., but momentum has moved behind the Senate Intelligence Committee version, amended under Chairman Sen. Richard Burr, R-N.C., and Ranking Member Sen. Diane Feinstein, D-Calif. "The robust privacy requirements and liability protection make this a balanced bill, and I hope the Senate acts on it quickly," said Feinstein as CISA passed 14–1 in a secret, closed session of the Senate Intelligence Committee.

Reversing course over past opposition to the previous iteration of the bill, CISPA, the White House has demonstrated firm support for information sharing legislation this year. And more importantly, the Senate has drastically changed, helping to create a far more National Security Agency–friendly Congress. Sen. Mark Udall, D-Col., the chief opponent of CISA last session, was defeated in his reelection campaign last November, and the new Senate Majority Leader Sen. Mitch McConnell has made CISA a "priority."

3
Technology

Law enforcement officials monitor surveillance cameras as part of an increased security effort for the Independence Day celebration, the first major public gathering since the Boston Marathon bombings, at the Unified Command Center, Wednesday, July 3, 2013, in Boston. The temporary command center combines the control and management of security by local, state, and federal law enforcement officials in one location.

Big Brother Tech: The Technology of Mass Surveillance and Privacy

In the Information Age, the lives of people can be seen through their digital records, stored in cyberspace by the companies that facilitate and provide digital communications services. High-resolution photos from aerial surveillance and the collective output of millions of mobile cameras have become part of a visual library stored and controlled by communications companies. Mobile phone calls, text messages, emails, and a person's Internet browsing history are similarly recorded, analyzed, and sold for profit. These digital records have increasingly become a tool for surveillance, national security, and law enforcement.

Given the threats of terrorism and cybercrime, government agencies and police increasingly use high-tech surveillance to tap into this digital record. While supporters argue that responsible organizations must stay at pace with or ahead of crime and threats to national security, many around the world feel that modern surveillance technology increasingly poses a threat to personal privacy. The development of surveillance technology has inspired a proliferation of anti-surveillance devices and software. Essentially, in the United States and many other nations, a technological arms race is underway, with law enforcement and intelligence agencies competing with private companies and privacy advocates over the control of digital data.

Security of Digital Data

The unauthorized collection of digital data is one of the major controversies surrounding modern surveillance. In 2013, the American public learned, through leaked government documents, that the National Security Administration (NSA) and Central Intelligence Agency (CIA) were conducting controversial mass surveillance operations that included intercepting and analyzing thousands of emails, texts, mobile phone calls, and web images between 2002 and 2013. NSA and CIA mass surveillance was largely made possible by companies like AT&T and Sprint that provided government agencies with access to consumer data. As most of the information transmitted through private web companies is not protected by privacy laws, the onus for protecting the privacy of digital data falls to the consumer.

In the 1990s, the U.S. Naval Research Laboratories (NRL) developed "onion routing," or "Tor," a system that shifts digital signals through numerous points, making it difficult or impossible to track. In 2004, the NRL released the original code for the Tor routing system, and since then privacy groups, like the Electronic Frontier Foundation (EFF), have supported efforts to create surveillance-resistant browsers and websites for public use. Government and police agencies use Tor to protect the security of official websites and communications, and an organization known as the Tor Project, provides a free Tor-based version of the Firefox browser for consumers.

However, the Tor system has also been controversially used by criminal organizations to set up what has been called the "Dark Net," a collection of hidden Internet sites and users involved in criminal activities such as child pornography, weapons and drug sales, and pirated illegal data.

Security organizations have also found ways to circumvent digital privacy systems, often using techniques similar to those used by "hackers" and cyber criminals. Malware and spyware are programs that can be installed on a computer and then allow another individual to remotely obtain and monitor data from the infected computer. Cyber criminals use malware to commit identity theft or to gain illegal access to a person's online financial accounts. Since at least 2002, the FBI has been using special malware programs, called network investigative techniques (NITs), to obtain data from the computers of targeted individuals and organizations. NITs are installed onto a user's computer by tricking the user into clicking a hyperlink or visiting a certain website. Once installed, the NITs allow the FBI to monitor browsing history and communications, and can access photos and files stored on a computer.

In 2012, the FBI began using "Operation Torpedo," a system designed specifically to infiltrate networks using Tor routing. The specific goal of the program was to infiltrate the networks of the Dark Net, and the operations resulted in the successful arrest of individuals involved in child pornography. However, records of the investigation indicated that FBI malware was also installed on hundreds of computers belonging to users not involved in crime or child pornography. Critics argued that the operation constituted a violation of privacy and that the FBI should only be permitted to conduct operations that violate security measures in cases where legitimate evidence suggests criminal activity.

Another controversial surveillance tool emerging in 2013–2014 is the "Stingray," a tracking device that obtains cell phone data by mimicking a signal coming from a cell phone tower. Police can then track mobile devices that accidentally connect to the Stingray instead of legitimate cell tower signals. While supporters say that police currently use the Stingray only to track known suspects, critics argue that the Stingray is indiscriminate, collecting data from any mobile device in the area, and thus constitutes an illegal search of personal communications.

The Next Generation Identification (NGI) system developed by the FBI became active in 2014. The system creates profiles for individuals that record the individual's fingerprints, voice prints, scans of the individual's iris (a unique identification marker,) and facial recognition photos. By 2015, the FBI estimated that the system would store 51 million images of American citizens to aid in automated photo recognition. Critics argued that the system violated privacy because as millions of Americans will have their personal data recorded in FBI profiles without their consent or knowledge and without having been identified with any illegal or criminal activity. Essentially, the NGI system is a culmination of digital data collection, providing a powerful surveillance tool that, while potentially effective in police and national security operations, also has the potential for abuse.

Drones and Aerial Surveillance

Unmanned aerial vehicles (UAV), also known as "drones," are aircraft designed to function without a human pilot. Modern UAVs developed from the radio-controlled military drones used in World War II and the United States used remote drones to gather data and attack targets during the Vietnam Conflict, the Gulf War, and in the "War on Terror" of the twenty-first century. The emergence of computer technology, coupled with GPS positioning, has allowed the development of "automated" drones that can travel to a location, conduct a surveillance or military operation, and return to a launch site independently.

In February 2012, Congress legalized drones for police and commercial use in the United States. Since then, companies began developing drones for a variety of applications including commercial photography, environmental monitoring, shooting films, and dusting crops. Police agencies also began experimenting with drones for surveillance and search operations.

One of the controversial issues surrounding drones involves the increasing potential to use high-definition aerial photography and video to conduct mass surveillance. Critics argue that the use of drones and aerial cameras represents a violation of the Fourth Amendment, which protects individuals from unlawful "searches." Ryan Calo, from the Center for Internet and Society at Stanford University, explains that U.S. law does not provide citizens with a reasonable expectation of privacy while in public. Therefore, any photos or videos taken by drones of people in public can be legally stored and used by law enforcement.

The Los Angeles County Sheriff's Department incurred controversy for a 2012 operation in which the police conducted surveillance with a Cessna "spy plane" flown over the Compton neighborhood. The plane sent images to the sheriff's department, where officers were able to observe a shooting, several robberies, and a number of car accidents. The LAPD was criticized for not notifying neighborhood residents, which some citizens felt was a violation of privacy. Complicating this issue is the fact that some high-tech cameras and surveillance systems can use heat-sensing technology to watch individuals inside buildings, which some argue constitutes a more invasive violation of privacy rights, including guarantees protecting citizens from unlawful searches.

A December 2014 report from the University of Nevada, Las Vegas, indicated that 93 percent of Americans are opposed to police using drones to monitor activities in or around residential areas. The report also indicates that 77 percent of Americans object to using drones to monitor employees at a work place and 63 percent object to monitoring individuals in public places using the same technology.

By 2015, 42 U.S. states had enacted laws regarding the use of drones. Tennessee, for instance, enacted a law that made flying drones over private property a form of "criminal trespassing." Some states, like North Carolina, have passed laws making it illegal for drones to photograph people without consent, though some exceptions are given in the case of news and police operations. Federal drone regulations are forthcoming, and the Federal Aviation Administration (FAA) released preliminary regulations in 2015 that are not yet official but may prohibit flying drones over pedestrians or out of the line of sight of the remote pilot. It remains to be seen how FAA regulations and state laws will affect the use of drones by police.

Automation and the Human Element

The use of "automated" and "remote" tracking and identification systems has become one of the most controversial issues surrounding surveillance technology. While police are allowed to follow a suspect without a warrant, in some cases for long periods, police officers must justify this decision to various individuals responsible for approving the use of police time. By contrast, automated surveillance technology can track individuals without cause for long periods, and some critics argue that this violates the principles and intention of Fourth Amendment guarantees against unlawful searches.

One manifestation of this debate is the automated license plate readers (ALPRs) that record license plate numbers from passing vehicles and are used in some areas to issue traffic citations. Some object to the fact that individuals identified as "traffic offenders" by ALPRs have been deprived of the ability to question or confront the charges. In cases where a human officer might recognize mitigating circumstances contributing to a violation, ALPRs issue citations based on simple cues, and those identified as "offenders" have little opportunity to address the citation outside of appearing in court. In Virginia, where police were caught using ALPR systems to spy on political rally attendees, the state legislature created an amendment to ban ALPR technology as both indiscriminate and inherently vulnerable to misuse. Similar bans have been proposed in Florida, Indiana, Missouri, New Jersey, and Vermont.

At the core of the surveillance technology issue is the question of whether some actions, decisions, and responsibilities are too nuanced, complex, or sensitive to be effectively translated into automated responses and algorithms. Many citizens have expressed a visceral, if not always logical, objection to the idea of being "watched" or "controlled" by machines, and argue that human judgment is preferable when making decisions that can adversely affect people's lives or violate their rights. Limiting automation does little to prevent the use of technology that might be inherently invasive or indiscriminate, such as in many mass surveillance procedures, but provides, at least, a level of potential understanding, compassion, and wisdom not currently believed to be possible within a purely automated system.

Micah L. Issitt

New Surveillance Technology Can Track Everyone in an Area for Several Hours at a Time

By Craig Timberg
The Washington Post, February 5, 2014

Dayton, Ohio — Shooter and victim were just a pair of pixels, dark specks on a gray streetscape. Hair color, bullet wounds, even the weapon were not visible in the series of pictures taken from an airplane flying two miles above.

But what the images revealed — to a degree impossible just a few years ago — was location, mapped over time. Second by second, they showed a gang assembling, blocking off access points, sending the shooter to meet his target and taking flight after the body hit the pavement. When the report reached police, it included a picture of the blue stucco building into which the killer ultimately retreated, at last beyond the view of the powerful camera overhead.

"I've witnessed 34 of these," said Ross McNutt, the genial president of Persistent Surveillance Systems, which collected the images of the killing in Ciudad Juárez, Mexico, from a specially outfitted Cessna. "It's like opening up a murder mystery in the middle, and you need to figure out what happened before and after."

As Americans have grown increasingly comfortable with traditional surveillance cameras, a new, far more powerful generation is being quietly deployed that can track every vehicle and person across an area the size of a small city, for several hours at a time. Although these cameras can't read license plates or see faces, they provide such a wealth of data that police, businesses and even private individuals can use them to help identify people and track their movements.

Already, the cameras have been flown above major public events such as the Ohio political rally where Sen. John McCain (R-Ariz.) named Sarah Palin as his running mate in 2008, McNutt said. They've been flown above Baltimore; Philadelphia; Compton, Calif.; and Dayton in demonstrations for police. They've also been used for traffic impact studies, for security at NASCAR races and at the request of a Mexican politician, who commissioned the flights over Ciudad Juárez.

A surveillance system designed by a Dayton, Ohio–based company can track crimes in real time, as they occur.

Defense contractors are developing similar technology for the military, but its potential for civilian use is raising novel civil liberties concerns. In Dayton, where

Persistent Surveillance Systems is based, city officials balked last year when police considered paying for 200 hours of flights, in part because of privacy complaints.

"There are an infinite number of surveillance technologies that would help solve crimes ... but there are reasons that we don't do those things, or shouldn't be doing those things," said Joel Pruce, a University of Dayton postdoctoral fellow in human rights who opposed the plan. "You know where there's a lot less crime? There's a lot less crime in China."

The Supreme Court generally has given wide latitude to police using aerial surveillance as long as the photography captures images visible to the naked eye.

McNutt, a retired Air Force officer who once helped design a similar system for the skies above Fallujah, a battleground city in Iraq, hopes to win over officials in Dayton and elsewhere by convincing them that cameras mounted on fixed-wing aircraft can provide far more useful intelligence than police helicopters do, for less money.

A single camera mounted atop the Washington Monument, McNutt boasts, could deter crime all around the Mall. He said regular flights over the most dangerous parts of Washington — combined with publicity about how much police could see — would make a significant dent in the number of burglaries, robberies and murders. His 192-megapixel cameras would spot as many as 50 crimes per six-hour flight, he estimated, providing police with a continuous stream of images covering more than a third of the city.

"We watch 25 square miles, so you see lots of crimes," he said. "And by the way, after people commit crimes, they drive like idiots."

What McNutt is trying to sell is not merely the latest techno-wizardry for police. He envisions such steep drops in crime that they will bring substantial side effects, including rising property values, better schools, increased development and, eventually, lower incarceration rates as the reality of long-term overhead surveillance deters those tempted to commit crimes.

Dayton Police Chief Richard Biehl, a supporter of McNutt's efforts, has proposed inviting the public to visit the operations center to get a glimpse of the technology in action.

"I want them to be worried that we're watching," Biehl said. "I want them to be worried that they never know when we're overhead."

Technology in Action

McNutt, a suburban father of four with a doctorate from the Massachusetts Institute of Technology, is not deaf to concerns about his company's ambitions. Unlike many of the giant defense contractors that are eagerly repurposing wartime surveillance technology for domestic use, he sought advice from the American Civil Liberties Union in writing a privacy policy.

It has rules on how long data can be kept, when images can be accessed and by whom. Police are supposed to begin looking at the pictures only after a crime has been reported. Fishing expeditions are prohibited.

The technology has inherent limitations as well. From the airborne cameras, each person appears as a single pixel indistinguishable from any other person. What people are doing —

> **"If you turn your country into a totalitarian surveillance state, there's always some wrongdoing you can prevent," said Jay Stanley, a privacy expert with the American Civil Liberties Union.**

even whether they are clothed or not — is impossible to see. As technology improves the cameras, McNutt said he intends to increase their range, not the precision of the imagery, so that larger areas can be monitored.

The notion that McNutt and his roughly 40 employees are peeping Toms clearly rankles. The company made a PowerPoint presentation for the ACLU that includes pictures taken to assist the response to Hurricane Sandy and the severe Iowa floods last summer. The section is titled: "Good People Doing Good Things."

"We get a little frustrated when people get so worried about us seeing them in their backyard," McNutt said in his operation center, where the walls are adorned with 120-inch monitors, each showing a different grainy urban scene collected from above. "We can't even see what they are doing in their backyard. And, by the way, we don't care."

Yet in a world of increasingly pervasive surveillance, location and identity are becoming all but inextricable. One quickly leads to the other for those with the right tools.

During one of the company's demonstration flights over Dayton in 2012, police got reports of an attempted robbery at a bookstore and shots fired at a Subway sandwich shop. The cameras revealed a single car moving between the two locations.

By reviewing the images frame by frame, analysts were able to help police piece together a larger story: A man had left a residential neighborhood at midday and attempted to rob the bookstore, but fled when somebody hit an alarm. Then he drove to Subway, where the owner pulled a gun and chased him off. His next stop was a Family Dollar Store, where the man paused for several minutes. He soon returned home, after a short stop at a gas station where a video camera captured an image of his face.

A few hours later, after the surveillance flight ended, the Family Dollar Store was robbed. Police used the detailed map of the man's movements, along with other evidence from the crime scenes, to arrest him for all three crimes.

On another occasion, Dayton police got a report of a burglary in progress. The aerial cameras spotted a white truck driving away from the scene. Police stopped the driver before he got home and found the stolen goods in the back of the truck. A witness identified him soon afterward.

Privacy Concerns

In addition to normal cameras, the planes can carry infrared sensors that permit analysts to track people, vehicles or wildlife at night — even through foliage and into some structures, such as tents.

Courts have put stricter limits on technology that can see things not visible to the naked eye, ruling that they can amount to unconstitutional searches when conducted without a warrant. But the lines remain fuzzy as courts struggle to apply old precedents — from a single overflight carrying an officer equipped with nothing stronger than a telephoto lens, for example — to the rapidly advancing technology.

"If you turn your country into a totalitarian surveillance state, there's always some wrongdoing you can prevent," said Jay Stanley, a privacy expert with the American Civil Liberties Union. "The balance struck in our Constitution tilts toward liberty, and I think we should keep that value."

Police and private businesses have invested heavily in video surveillance since the Sept. 11, 2001, attacks. Although academics debate whether these cameras create significantly lower crime rates, an overwhelming majority of Americans support them. A *Washington Post* poll in November found that only 14 percent of those surveyed wanted fewer cameras in public spaces.

But the latest camera systems raise new issues because of their ability to watch vast areas for long periods of time — something even military-grade aerial cameras have struggled to do well.

The military's most advanced experimental research lab is developing a system that uses hundreds of cellphone cameras to watch 36-square-mile areas. McNutt offers his system — which uses 12 commercially available Canon cameras mounted in an array — as an effective alternative that's cheap enough for local police departments to afford. He typically charges between $1,500 and $2,000 per hour for his services, including flight time, operation of the command center and the time that analysts spend assisting investigations.

Dayton police were enticed by McNutt's offer to fly 200 hours over the city for a home-town discount price of $120,000. The city, with about 140,000 people, saw its police force dwindle from more than 400 officers to about 350 in recent years, and there is little hope of reinforcements.

"We're not going to get those officers back," Biehl, the police chief, said. "We have had to use technology as force multipliers."

Still, the proposed contract, coming during Dayton's campaign season and amid a wave of revelations about National Security Agency surveillance, sparked resistance. Biehl is looking for a chance to revive the matter. But the new mayor, Nan Whaley, has reservations, both because of the cost and the potential loss of privacy.

"Since 2001, we haven't had really healthy conversations about personal liberty. It's starting to bloom about a decade too late," Whaley said. "I think the conversation needs to continue."

To that end, the mayor has another idea: She's encouraging the businesses that own Dayton's tallest buildings to mount rooftop surveillance cameras capable of continuously monitoring the downtown and nearby neighborhoods. Whaley hopes the businesses would provide the video feeds to the police.

McNutt, it turns out, has cameras for those situations, too, capable of spotting individual people from seven miles away.

Domestic Drone Bills Seek to Protect Privacy Rights

By Preston Maddock
The Huffington Post, May 2, 2013

State legislatures nationwide are looking at measures to restrict the use of drones domestically, as privacy and ethical concerns mount among the public about the use of the unmanned vehicles.

The specter of drones surreptitiously hovering over American cities and neighborhoods has not sat well with many state legislators, who fear the technology may open the door to violations of the Fourth Amendment. In 39 state legislatures, 85 bills and resolutions have been proposed to set parameters on the uses of drones. Three states have already passed legislation to restrict their use completely or to limit their use to narrow purposes.

State and local legislators are considering a range of bills: some seek to establish commissions to study the effects of drone use; other legislatures—like those in Montana and Missouri—are proposing a requirement on law enforcement officials to obtain a warrant before using a drone to surveil citizens. The preemptive debate nationwide is being driven by a wariness of the unknown future capabilities of drones to impinge, potentially, on constitutional rights.

"If drones are going to find a place in American life and commerce, then the privacy questions are going to need to be put to rest," Jay Stanley, senior policy analyst at the ACLU, told *The Huffington Post.*

In February, Charlottesville, Va., became the first city government in the nation to make its city a no-drone zone. Subsequently, Gov. Bob McDonnell (R-Va.) signed legislation in April that placed a two-year moratorium on the use of drones throughout the state, allowing for exceptions in the case of emergencies and for military training purposes.

"Our argument was, 'Wait a minute, you know, no one that wrote the Fourth Amendment envisioned a drone parked over your backyard, able to sniff and look and send signals back to home base,'" said state Sen. Donald McEachin (D-Richmond), the moratorium's sponsor. "We need to come up with a 21st-century approach to when these things can be used and when they can't be used."

Little more than a week later, Idaho passed a bill that requires state law enforcement to obtain a warrant before using drones to collect evidence. Allie Bohm, policy strategist at the ACLU, said the legislation would protect "individuals from unfettered surveillance."

"We're trying to prevent high-tech window-peeping," Idaho Senate Assistant Majority Leader Chuck Winder (R), the bill's sponsor, told Reuters while the bill was pending.

Idaho's drone statute is an example of the type of limitations currently being debated in a number of state legislatures and is similar to a bill that Florida Gov. Rick Scott (R) signed into law last week.

"The bill is the right thing to do, because the idea of drones spying on law-abiding citizens is inconsistent with the American experience," state Sen. Rob Bradley (R), co-sponsor of the Florida legislation, told *The Huffington Post*.

Florida's drone bill, which also carries a warrant requirement for law enforcement, passed the state House and Senate unanimously.

"The issue really crosses party lines. It's the one issue that unites hippies and survivalists," Bradley said. "It's amazing that the left and right can come to agreement on this."

In Virginia, McEachin also marveled at the broad support for the drone moratorium. "This is a unique situation where the Tea Party and the ACLU are on the same side," he told *The Huffington Post*. "It was a unique situation where the Republican right and the Democratic left agreed on something. It's a pretty interesting group of people who are interested in this issue."

Still, industry insiders argue that widespread suspicion of domestic drones is completely unfounded.

"The fear that other groups have put into legislators—that they're going to be watching and spying on you—is a bit far stretched," said Mario Mairena, a spokesman for the Association of Unmanned Vehicle Systems International, a drone advocacy organization.

"There is a lot of misinformation out there and a lot of folks scaring state legislators and the community about unmanned aircraft systems," Mairena told *HuffPost*. "This is not revolutionary technology."

According to Steve Gitlin, spokesman for AeroVironment—a leading drone manufacturer and defense industry contractor—drones are "absolutely" capable of being used in situations and environments prohibitive to other, manned aircraft, such as helicopters.

In an urban setting, for example, law enforcement could deploy drones "much more readily where there are buildings and homes and everything around there than you could with a helicopter, just because [a drone is] so much smaller and lighter and quieter," Gitlin told *The Huffington Post*.

It is the rapidly expanding capabilities of drones that have civil libertarians alarmed.

"It's very real, the technology is real. It's happening, and the privacy threats are very real," Stanley told *The Huffington Post*.

In Florida, Bradley said their drone bill was needed to get "ahead of the curve."

In some sense, the state and local debates over the acceptable scope of drone use are not as significant as the passion and bipartisan unanimity might suggest. In 2012, Congress mandated that the FAA prepare for the safe integration of drones into domestic airspace by 2015. So while states and localities can restrict where, on whose orders and for what purposes drones can fly, the regulation of American airspace is ultimately up to the FAA.

Currently, the FAA is accepting applications for six test sites where drones will be flown in a controlled environment, in order to develop a plan for their safe integration by the 2015 deadline. Depending on the results from the test sites, an FAA spokesperson told *HuffPost* that the agency estimates that 7,500 commercial drones could be flying domestic skies by 2018.

More than likely, the thousands of airborne vehicles will not be under the control of law enforcement. Even legislators who are working to limit the government's use of drones concede that the technology has other, less sinister uses—Bradley among them. "There are appropriate applications domestically, for agriculture and surveying lands," he told *HuffPost,* "but when drones are used to spy on law abiding citizens there is a certain creepiness to that."

Most observers agree that drones can have myriad private applications, apart from law enforcement, and can have a positive economic impact. One industry report, published in March by AUVSI, projects that drone manufacturing will create 100,000 jobs and an "economic impact of $82 billion," by 2025.

"There's a whole host of things that drones can do," said the ACLU's Bohm. "And we want to enjoy the benefits of this technology without becoming a surveillance society."

Will Police Body Cameras Usher in a New Surveillance Regime?

By Gerry Bello
Free Press, February 2, 2015

Since the beginning of the recent protest movement around the deaths of multiple unarmed African American men at the hands of police in multiple states, there has been a push for police to wear body cameras. In the Tamir Rice and John Crawford III cases here in Ohio, video exists in the public sphere that clearly shows what happened. Yet in both cases the policeman who pulled the trigger is still free to roam the streets and still feeding at the public trough.

This push has come from within some sectors of the civil rights movement, from private police groups involved in repressing demonstrations, and from the White House itself.[1] A closer look at body cameras, their packaging and companion products, and manufacturers yields a vista of constant public surveillance.

Use of the term "body camera" gives us an image of a small digital camera on a police officer's chest that acts in the fashion of a camcorder, with a record/play buttons and a limited amount of storage. This is a false image. Two of the three leading manufacturers of police body cameras, L-3 Mobile Vision and Motorola, manufacture cameras that are default connected to cellular devices. The third market leader, Taser International, has an option to automatically connect their body camera product to an Android or I-Phone.

A police body camera can constantly record and transmit what is recorded via law enforcement frequencies to a central station for storage. These central stations can also send video back to the officer, and back up their stored data to the cloud. Taser International's body camera offering, AXON, directly uploads GPS tagged data to their own cloud computing service called evidence.com.

This cellular potential also turns the officer into a WiFi hotspot. Motorola's product line includes a police car that is its own WiFi hotspot and also has eight cameras built into the vehicle facing in every direction, constantly recording. The amount of data that can be hoovered up during a single patrol shift is amazing. The processing that happens to that data afterwords is frightening.

Imagine walking down the street and being passed by a police car. You look at it. Your face has been recorded either by the camera on the car or the camera on the officer. That image of your face is uploaded to a central database complete with metadata tracking your exact location and the exact time. Your face can then be scanned in the memory banks by facial recognition software. If, for instance, you are sitting in café talking with a friend as the car drives by, you are both recorded together. Such scenarios would seem to be the stuff of dystopian fiction, but the mechanisms are already in place.

The FBI began a pilot program to incorporate facial recognition software into its Next Generation Identification (NGI) system. Within in this system, there is a special list called the Repository of Individuals of Special Concern (RISC). RISC, as described by the FBI, "enables officers and agents in the field to screen detainees and criminal suspects against a repository of Wanted Persons, Sex Offenders Registry Subjects, Known or appropriately Suspected Terrorists, and other persons of special interest for rapid identification." Thus so-called "appropriately suspected terrorists" and "other persons of special interest" can now be picked out of a crowd. When that crowd is in the cloud the special interest can happen long afterwards. A person with no criminal history or intent can simply walk down the street or have a cup of coffee in public and be of interest later.

Perhaps you sit in the back of the café or face away from the window. Your car gives you away. The constant data streaming from police cameras also vacuums up license plates. The camera on an officer and the cameras on the car constantly view, transmit and record this data, complete with location and time metadata. Both Motorola and L-3 Mobile Vision integrate license plate reading technology into their solution packages for law enforcement.

In Ohio, L-3 Mobile Vision's existing statewide purchasing contract makes them the most likely choice for an integrated solution. L-3 Mobile Vision's parent company, Titan L-3, was one of the government contractors involved in the Abu-Ghraib torture scandal in Iraq. One of the L-3 employees, who was working as a translator, raped at least one male juvenile prisoner. He was not fired.

Once the data has been acquired, it can be processed by MorphoTrak, one of the key contractors for the FBI's NGI system. Before being acquired by a subsidiary of SaFran, MorphoTrack was called L-1 Identity Solutions. It was founded by Robert LaPenta, who also founded Titan L-3. Before founding Titan L-3, LaPenta was an executive at Lockheed Martin, which provides overall integration for the NGI system. A seamless flow of personal data will exist from the police officer's body camera to an FBI database. That seamless flow will further fatten the wallet of a man who directly profited from the rape of child prisoners. It appears that human rights are not central design parameters of this new system.

The sum total of the proposed body camera solution to the problem of police violence is a regime of constant surveillance. This new scheme records everyone for later identification the instant a police officer's device sees them or their car. It creates the basis for a national database that tracks every movement of every single person in the country.

Note

1.   https://www.theoutsidernews.com/articles/2014/12/03/presidents-police-commission-promises-more-repression

It Costs the Government Just 6.5 Cents an Hour to Spy on You

By Drew F. Cohen
Politico, February 10, 2014

Glenn Greenwald, the journalist and activist at the center of the controversy over the National Security Agency's spying operations, launched his new website Monday with a reported look at how the NSA uses tracking technology to hunt down terrorists abroad. He's promising more revelations that will blow the lid off the agency's activities. "We decided to launch now because we believe we have a vital and urgent obligation to this story, to these documents, and to the public," he writes.

In this, he's pushing on an open door. By now, most Americans agree that the NSA surveillance program, brought to light by leaked documents from former NSA contractor Edward Snowden, went "too far." But what Greenwald and many other analysts often miss is that an overzealous security apparatus is not the driving reason behind government overreach. A lot of it has to do with dollars and cents: The price of surveillance technology has dropped so precipitously over the past two decades that once the agency overcame any moral objections, few practical considerations stood in its way of implementing a system that could monitor 315 million Americans every day. Indeed, one estimate tagged the NSA's annual surveillance costs at $574 per taxpayer, a paltry 6.5 cents an hour.

If privacy law experts Kevin S. Bankston and Ashkan Soltani are correct, costs, once a significant check on government spying and police monitoring efforts, have become an afterthought. In a recent study published in the Yale Law Journal Online, Bankston and Soltani found that most technologies deployed for mass surveillance efforts by police departments (e.g., GPS devices and domestic drones) are on cost trajectories similar to the NSA spying program: As the number of subjects increases, the cost of keeping tabs on each target nears zero. Cheaper, more effective tracking devices have been a boon to cash-strapped police departments nationwide, largely to the dismay of civil liberty groups.

Meanwhile, privacy protections afforded to individuals under the Fourth Amendment, which safeguards individuals from unreasonable searches and seizures by the state, have been eroding for years. Whether a particular search or seizure is deemed "reasonable" — thus justifying police action — rests largely on our ephemeral notions of privacy. It's a dicey standard. As we place more of our private lives in the public domain (73 percent of adults online use social media), we, as well as courts, consider fewer acts to be truly private and thus protected by the Constitution. At the height of McCarthyism in the 1950s, for instance, groups fought tooth and nail to keep library lists private; today, we publicize the titles of books we've recently read on sites like Facebook and Goodreads.

We like to think of legal checks on executive power, like the Fourth Amendment, as good enough. But practical considerations, like costs, have long provided structural defenses of our privacy. Imagine, in the 1800s, 10 constables surreptitiously tailing one suspect through the winding streets of Philadelphia; by the 1940s the same task still took eight officers in four police cars to accomplish. Monitoring each suspect was costly. "Only an investigation of unusual importance," according to Justice Samuel Alito, "could have justified such an expenditure of law enforcement resources."

Today, however, diminished privacy expectations coupled with shrinking cost constraints on law enforcement's surveillance activities have emboldened police departments to push the limits of new tracking technologies and techniques with little regard for privacy rights or chances of successful prosecution. A 2012 survey of police chiefs found that 83 percent of departments use GPS devices to track suspects and most respondents "expect to increase the practice of placing GPS devices on crime suspects' vehicles." The same survey found that "89 percent of agencies said they monitor social media to identify investigative leads — for example, reviewing Facebook or Twitter pages." In New York City, of the 4.4 million people questioned by police as part of the department's controversial stop-and-frisk surveillance program, only 11 percent of the encounters resulted in an arrest or a summons, according to an analysis by the New York Civil Liberties Union.

To realign the "equilibrium of power" between police and citizens, Bankston and Soltani propose a bright line, cost-based rule designed to augment the current chimerical "reasonable expectation" standard employed by courts today: If a new technology makes it 10 times cheaper for law enforcement to monitor a target, that technology violates the Fourth Amendment's reasonable expectation of privacy standard and cannot be used without a court-issued warrant. "When new technologies expand law enforcement's capabilities, the law does (and should) respond by placing new limits on government; when new technologies give criminals a leg up, the law does (and should) respond by loosening the government's reins," they write.

In *United States v. Jones*, five Supreme Court justices held that a man's reasonable expectation of privacy was breached after police tracked his movements on public roads for 28 days using a GPS device. The majority in the 2012 opinion, however, stopped short of articulating a clear rule other than Justice Alito's finding that "the line was surely crossed before the 4-week mark."

Using the *Jones* ruling as a baseline, Bankston and Soltani calculated and compared the costs of different location tracking methods used by police. Traditional surveillance methods like covert foot and car pursuits cost $250 and $275, respectively, per hour per target, according to their estimates. Another common method, which the Supreme Court has approved, involves two agents tracking a suspect's movements from their police vehicle through a radio-based transmitter affixed to a target's car or slipped in his bag at a cost of $105 to $113 per hour.

Newer surveillance technologies were significantly cheaper, they found. The total price tag of tracking a suspect

> **As we place more of our private lives in the public domain (73 percent of adults online use social media), we, as well as courts, consider fewer acts to be truly private and thus protected by the Constitution.**

using a GPS device, similar to the one in *Jones,* for instance, came out to $10 an hour over one day, $1.43 per hour over a week and $0.36 per hour over a month. Another relatively new technique, obtaining a suspect's location through his or her cellphone signal with the carrier's assistance, yielded similar results. As of August 2009, fees for obtaining cellphone location data from carriers ranged from $0.04 to $4.17 per hour for one month of surveillance. After tabulating their results, Bankston and Soltani concluded that the total cost of using a GPS device to track a suspect over 28 days (the method rejected in Jones) was roughly 300 times less expensive than the same tracking using a transmitter (technology approved by the Supreme Court) and 775 times less expensive than using the five-car pursuit method (also approved). Meanwhile, the cost of using transmitter-surveillance technology was only 2.5 times less expensive than undercover car pursuit.

As data mining, wiretaps and domestic drones become the new norm for police departments at a cost of a few cents a day, we need to have a frank discussion about where our Fourth Amendment protections are heading. In advocating their cost-based approach for determining the legality of different surveillance technologies, the researchers say they do not "equate police efficiency with unconstitutionality" but rather attempt to preserve the degree of privacy that existed in the Framers' era. As Justice Alito quipped in *Jones,* we must remember that absent "a very tiny constable . . . with [the] incredible fortitude and patience" hiding out in the trunk of a carriage, it would have been impossible for George Washington's colonial law enforcement authorities to have carried out anything near the level of surveillance that today's police forces can do at the drop of a dime.

Visit the Wrong Website, and the FBI Could End Up in Your Computer

By Kevin Poulsen
Wired, August 5, 2014

Security experts call it a "drive-by download": a hacker infiltrates a high-traffic website and then subverts it to deliver malware to every single visitor. It's one of the most powerful tools in the black hat arsenal, capable of delivering thousands of fresh victims into a hacker's clutches within minutes.

Now the technique is being adopted by a different kind of a hacker—the kind with a badge. For the last two years, the FBI has been quietly experimenting with drive-by hacks as a solution to one of law enforcement's knottiest Internet problems: how to identify and prosecute users of criminal websites hiding behind the powerful Tor anonymity system.

The approach has borne fruit—over a dozen alleged users of Tor-based child porn sites are now headed for trial as a result. But it's also engendering controversy, with charges that the Justice Department has glossed over the bulk-hacking technique when describing it to judges, while concealing its use from defendants. Critics also worry about mission creep, the weakening of a technology relied on by human rights workers and activists, and the potential for innocent parties to wind up infected with government malware because they visited the wrong website. "This is such a big leap, there should have been congressional hearings about this," says ACLU technologist Chris Soghoian, an expert on law enforcement's use of hacking tools. "If Congress decides this is a technique that's perfectly appropriate, maybe that's OK. But let's have an informed debate about it."

The FBI's use of malware is not new. The bureau calls the method an NIT, for "network investigative technique," and the FBI has been using it since at least 2002 in cases ranging from computer hacking to bomb threats, child porn to extortion. Depending on the deployment, an NIT can be a bulky full-featured backdoor program that gives the government access to your files, location, web history and webcam for a month at a time, or a slim, fleeting wisp of code that sends the FBI your computer's name and address, and then evaporates.

What's changed is the way the FBI uses its malware capability, deploying it as a driftnet instead of a fishing line. And the shift is a direct response to Tor, the powerful anonymity system endorsed by Edward Snowden and the State Department alike.

Kevin Poulsen/*Wired*

Tor is free, open-source software that lets you surf the web anonymously. It achieves that by accepting connections from the public Internet—the "clearnet"—encrypting the traffic and bouncing it through a winding series of computers before dumping it back on the web through any of over 1,100 "exit nodes."

The system also supports so-called hidden services—special websites, with addresses ending in .onion, whose physical locations are theoretically untraceable. Reachable only over the Tor network, hidden services are used by organizations that want to evade surveillance or protect users' privacy to an extraordinary degree. Some users of such service have legitimate and even noble purposes—including human rights groups and journalists. But hidden services are also a mainstay of the nefarious activities carried out on the so-called Dark Net: the home of drug markets, child porn, murder for hire, and a site that does nothing but stream pirated *My Little Pony* episodes.

Law enforcement and intelligence agencies have a love-hate relationship with Tor. They use it themselves, but when their targets hide behind the system, it poses a serious obstacle. Last month, Russia's government offered a $111,000 bounty for a method to crack Tor.

The FBI debuted its own solution in 2012, in an investigation dubbed "Operation Torpedo," whose contours are only now becoming visible through court filings.

Operation Torpedo began with an investigation in the Netherlands in August 2011. Agents at the National High Tech Crime Unit of the Netherlands' national police force had decided to crack down on online child porn, according to an FBI affidavit. To that end, they wrote a web crawler that scoured the Dark Net, collecting all the Tor onion addresses it could find.

The NHTCU agents systematically visited each of the sites and made a list of those dedicated to child pornography. Then, armed with a search warrant from the Court of Rotterdam, the agents set out to determine where the sites were located.

That, in theory, is a daunting task—Tor hidden services mask their locations behind layers of routing. But when the agents got to a site called "Pedoboard," they discovered that the owner had foolishly left the administrative account open with no password. They logged in and began poking around, eventually finding the server's real Internet IP address in Bellevue, Nebraska.

They provided the information to the FBI, who traced the IP address to 31-year-old Aaron McGrath. It turned out McGrath was hosting not one, but two child porn sites at the server farm where he worked, and a third one at home.

Instead of going for the easy bust, the FBI spent a solid year surveilling McGrath, while working with Justice Department lawyers on the legal framework for what would become Operation Torpedo. Finally, on November 2012, the feds swooped in on McGrath, seized his servers and spirited them away to an FBI office in Omaha.

A federal magistrate signed three separate search warrants: one for each of the three hidden services. The warrants authorized the FBI to modify the code on the servers to deliver the NIT to any computers that accessed the sites. The judge also allowed the FBI to delay notification to the targets for 30 days.

This NIT was purpose-built to identify the computer, and do nothing else—it didn't collect keystrokes or siphon files off to the bureau. And it evidently did its job well. In a two-week period, the FBI collected IP addresses for at least 25 visitors to the sites. Subpoenas to ISPs produced home addresses and subscriber names, and in April 2013, five months after the NIT deployment, the bureau staged coordinated raids around the country.

Today, with 14 of the suspects headed toward trial in Omaha, the FBI is being forced to defend its use of the drive-by download for the first time. Defense attorneys have urged the Nebraska court to throw out the spyware evidence, on the grounds that the bureau concealed its use of the NIT beyond the 30-day blackout period allowed in the search warrant. Some defendants didn't learn about the hack until a year after the fact. "Normally someone who is subject to a search warrant is told virtually immediately," says defense lawyer Joseph Gross Jr. "What I think you have here is an egregious violation of the Fourth Amendment."

But last week U.S. Magistrate Judge Thomas Thalken rejected the defense motion and any implication that the government acted in bad faith. "The affidavits and warrants were not prepared by some rogue federal agent," Thalken wrote, "but with the assistance of legal counsel at various levels of the Department of Justice." The matter will next be considered by U.S. District Judge Joseph Bataillon for a final ruling.

The ACLU's Soghoian says a child porn sting is probably the best possible use of the FBI's drive-by download capability. "It's tough to imagine a legitimate excuse to visit one of those forums: the mere act of looking at child pornography is a crime," he notes. His primary worry is that Operation Torpedo is the first step to the FBI using the tactic much more broadly, skipping any public debate over the possible unintended consequences. "You could easily imagine them using this same technology on everyone who visits a jihadi forum, for example," he says. "And there are lots of legitimate reasons for someone to visit a jihadi forum: research, journalism, lawyers defending a case. ACLU attorneys read *Inspire Magazine*, not because we are particularly interested in the material, but we need to cite stuff in briefs."

Soghoian is also concerned that the judges who considered NIT applications don't fully understand that they're being asked to permit the use of hacking software that takes advantage of software vulnerabilities to breach a machine's defenses. The Operation Torpedo search warrant application, for example, never uses the words "hack," "malware," or "exploit." Instead, the NIT comes across as something you'd be happy to spend 99 cents for in the App Store. "Under the NIT authorized by this warrant, the website would augment [its] content with some additional computer instructions," the warrant reads.

From the perspective of experts in computer security and privacy, the NIT is malware, pure and simple. That was demonstrated last August, when, perhaps buoyed by the success of Operation Torpedo, the FBI launched a second deployment of the NIT targeting more Tor hidden services.

This one—still unacknowledged by the bureau—traveled across the servers of Freedom Hosting, an anonymous provider of turnkey Tor hidden service sites that, by some estimates, powered half of the Dark Net.

This attack had its roots in the July 2013 arrest of Freedom Hosting's alleged operator, one Eric Eoin Marques, in Ireland. Marques faces U.S. charges of facilitating child porn—Freedom Hosting long had a reputation for tolerating child pornography.

Working with French authorities, the FBI got control of Marques' servers at a hosting company in France, according to testimony in Marques' case. Then the bureau appears to have relocated them—or cloned them—in Maryland, where the Marques investigation was centered.

On August 1, 2013, some savvy Tor users began noticing that the Freedom Hosting sites were serving a hidden "iframe"—a kind of website within a website. The iframe contained Javascript code that used a Firefox vulnerability to execute instructions on the victim's computer. The code specifically targeted the version of Firefox used in the Tor Browser Bundle—the easiest way to use Tor.

This was the first Tor browser exploit found in the wild, and it was an alarming development to the Tor community. When security researchers analyzed the code, they found a tiny Windows program hidden in a variable named "Magneto." The code gathered the target's MAC address and the Windows hostname, and then sent it to a server in Virginia in a way that exposed the user's real IP address. In short, the program nullified the anonymity that the Tor browser was designed to enable.

As they dug further, researchers discovered that the security hole the program exploited was already a known vulnerability called CVE-2013-1690—one that had theoretically been patched in Firefox and Tor updates about a month earlier. But there was a problem: Because the Tor browser bundle has no auto-update mechanism, only users who had manually installed the patched version were safe from the attack. "It was really impressive how quickly they took this vulnerability in Firefox and extrapolated it to the Tor browser and planted it on a hidden service," says Andrew Lewman, executive director of the nonprofit Tor Project, which maintains the code.

The Freedom Hosting drive-by has had a lasting impact on the Tor Project, which is now working to engineer a safe, private way for Tor users to automatically install the latest security patches as soon as they're available—a move that would make life more difficult for anyone working to subvert the anonymity system, with or without a court order.

Unlike with Operation Torpedo, the details of the Freedom Hosting drive-by operation remain a mystery a year later, and the FBI has repeatedly declined to comment on the attack, including when contacted by *Wired* for this story. Only one arrest can be clearly tied to the incident—that of a Vermont man named Grant Klein who, according to court records, was raided in November based on an NIT on a child porn site that was installed on July 31, 2013. Klein pleaded guilty to a single count of possession of child pornography in May and is set for sentencing this October.

But according to reports at the time, the malware was seen not just on criminal sites, but on legitimate hidden services that happened to be hosted by Freedom Hosting, including the privacy protecting webmail service Tormail. If true, the FBI's drive-by strategy is already gathering data on innocent victims.

Despite the unanswered questions, it's clear that the Justice Department wants to scale up its use of the drive-by download. It's now asking the Judicial Conference of the United States to tweak the rules governing when and how federal judges issue search warrants. The revision would explicitly allow for warrants to "use remote access to search electronic storage media and to seize or copy electronically stored information" regardless of jurisdiction.

The revision, a conference committee concluded last May, is the only way to confront the use of anonymization software like Tor, "because the target of the search has deliberately disguised the location of the media or information to be searched."

Such dragnet searching needs more scrutiny, Soghoian says. "What needs to happen is a public debate about the use of this technology, and the use of these techniques," he says. "And whether the criminal statutes that the government relies on even permit this kind of searching. It's one thing to say we're going to search a particular computer. It's another thing to say we're going to search every computer that visits this website, without knowing how many there are going to be, without knowing what city, state or countries they're coming from."

"Unfortunately," he says, "we've tiptoed into this area, because the government never gave notice that they were going to start using this technique."

Silicon Valley's Surveillance Cure-All: Transparency

By Joshua Kopstein
The New Yorker, October 1, 2013

Before his trip to Capitol Hill last week, Mark Zuckerberg sat down in front of an audience in Washington, D.C., and answered a few questions about Facebook and online privacy. But, for once, the twenty-nine-year-old C.E.O. wasn't defending some late-night software change that had left millions of Facebook users infuriated. He was talking about the National Security Agency.

When asked by James Bennet, of *The Atlantic*, whether he believed that the N.S.A was respectful of his users' privacy, Zuckerberg declared that "the more transparency the government has, the better folks would feel." He also cryptically explained that, based on his company's internal metrics, tensions over the agency's activities have significantly damaged user trust—not just for Facebook but for its cloud-based competitors as well.

Since the N.S.A.'s mass surveillance programs were exposed, much of the tech industry has become vocally critical of government snooping. Four of the companies named as partners in the N.S.A.'s Prism program—Google, Microsoft, Yahoo, and Facebook—have sued the U.S. government to loosen the legal restraints blocking them from sharing detailed information about their cooperation with government data collection. They hope to combat the perception that the N.S.A. has "direct access" to their servers, language used in one of the Prism slides leaked by Edward Snowden. To them, transparency is a remedy for the recent widespread distrust of the American technology industry.

The group is growing: yesterday, twenty-eight technology companies signed on, through the Center for Democracy and Technology, to support new surveillance legislation, known as the Surveillance Transparency Act in the Senate, and the Surveillance Order Reporting Act in the House. The bills would require the government to annually report on the number of surveillance orders issued by the Foreign Intelligence Surveillance Court, including how many Americans had their data queried or examined by analysts. And they would firmly establish companies' right to disclose the number and type of orders with which they complied.

Part of the reason for the sudden push back on surveillance from tech companies is that that they are seeing new financial incentives for transparency. According to a survey from the Cloud Security Alliance, an industry nonprofit with forty-eight thousand members, 10 percent of two hundred and seven officials at non-U.S. companies cancelled contracts with U.S. service providers after Edward Snowden's

In Facebook's first transparency report, the company said that in the first six months of 2013, it provided at least some data for seventy-nine percent of the U.S. government's requests, which number somewhere between eleven thousand and twelve thousand and affect between twenty thousand and twenty-one thousand accounts.

disclosures about N.S.A. surveillance, in June and July. Fifty-six percent of non-U.S. respondents also indicated that they were hesitant to work with any U.S.-based cloud-computing companies. Researchers have predicted that the cloud-computing industry as a whole stands to lose large sums; estimates range from the tens of billions to around a hundred billion by 2016.

In a significant change for both companies, Facebook and Yahoo have started to release government-request reports, a practice pioneered by Google and Twitter, as "transparency reports." (Until now, Facebook has been notoriously opaque about its operations, and, as recently as 2009, Yahoo used copyright takedown notices to try to mask its compliance with such requests.) The reports list aggregate information about government requests for user data; a typical report will show how many requests were received, how many accounts they affected, who made the requests, and what percentage of the requests resulted in data being disclosed.

But these reports still don't provide a complete picture of the U.S. government's quest for cloud data. In Facebook's first transparency report, the company said that in the first six months of 2013, it provided at least some data for seventy-nine percent of the U.S. government's requests, which number somewhere between eleven thousand and twelve thousand and affect between twenty thousand and twenty-one thousand accounts. (It provides far more specific figures for other countries: for instance, it received a thousand nine hundred and seventy-five requests for user data concerning two thousand three hundred and thirty-seven accounts from the United Kingdom; it provided data in response to 68 percent of the those requests.)

Facebook and other companies are forbidden by the U.S. government from sharing the exact number of orders they receive, which include a mix of requests from different agencies. On Saturday, Microsoft released its latest transparency report, which charts the same period as Facebook's, and shows just under eight thousand U.S. government requests affecting more than twenty-two thousand accounts. Microsoft specifically notes, "We are not currently permitted to report detailed information about the type and volume of any national security orders . . . that we may receive, so any national security orders we may receive are not included in this report." This makes it hard to discern how many demands are for domestic law enforcement and how many relate to national security.

What's still not clear is whether the companies have any interest in surveillance reform beyond what will clear their names. According to the *Guardian*, the first meeting of President Obama's new surveillance-review panel, in mid-September, didn't address N.S.A. reform; instead, attendees said, the tech industry's concerns dominated the session. In many cases, those concerns have stopped short of taking a hard stance on the nature of the government's activities. Eric Schmidt, the executive chairman of Google, recently stated, "There's been spying for years, there's been surveillance for years, and so forth, I'm not going to pass judgment on that, it's the nature of our society."

Still, tech firms' recent interest in surveillance transparency is contrasted by the silence of another important group: phone companies. Recently declassified documents show that the telecoms have not challenged any of the orders that compel them to provide all of their customers' calling records to the government. The biggest carrier, Verizon, has even argued in court that it has a right to share customer data with the N.S.A.

Conversely, there's evidence that some Internet companies are striving to be better stewards of user data. The Electronic Frontier Foundation, a digital-rights advocacy group based in San Francisco, issues an annual report, called "Who Has Your Back," that grades over a dozen cloud services, phone companies, and Internet service providers. The report awards merits not just for publishing privacy reports but for also categories such as proactively sticking up for users in Congress and the courts and sharing law-enforcement guidelines. Twitter and the Internet service provider Sonic.net lead the pack, followed by Google, Dropbox, LinkedIn and SpiderOak, a privacy-oriented cloud-storage company.

Parker Higgins, the co-author of the most recent "Who Has Your Back" report, noted that, unlike with the telecoms, there's been notable improvement among Internet companies since the first report was published, in 2011. "E.F.F. has been around longer than a lot of these Silicon Valley companies, and I think as a result we've established a credibility with them," he said during a phone interview. The group frequently spars with tech companies on issues ranging from privacy and transparency to patents and copyright, but Higgins said that the N.S.A. leaks have catalyzed a closer collaboration between the two sides.

Other than policy, the most obvious way that tech companies can act is through engineering. Google recently announced that it would begin encrypting data as it traverses its internal network. Facebook has followed Google in implementing an effective but rarely used encryption technique called Perfect Forward Secrecy, which makes private Web traffic less susceptible to eavesdroppers. It works by establishing connections in such a way that even if a private encryption key is compromised, the attacker won't be able to use it to decipher and snoop on all of the site's traffic. "The effect is that instead of being able to collect information passively and decrypt it later, when you get a key, this requires that you're active in the middle," Higgins explained. "It changes the incentive structure from 'let's just collect everything and do surveillance retroactively' to 'lets make sure we have some legitimate reason to collect from this person, because it's expensive.' " This protection is especially crucial in light of reports that the N.S.A. has been secretly intercepting Internet traffic en masse, weakening cryptographic standards, and making companies hand over their encryption keys.

"I can tell you from firsthand experience that privacy is now at the forefront of how all these companies are thinking about their strategies moving forward," Ethan Oberman, the C.E.O. of SpiderOak, told me. His company is one of many whose notoriety has spiked since the Snowden leaks. Its latest project, Crypton, is an open-source framework for "zero knowledge" privacy systems—that is, systems where user data is encrypted locally before travelling to cloud servers, leaving the company with nothing to hand over to authorities but jumbled ciphertext and the tiniest fragments of metadata. "It makes it so that users don't have to trust the company in the middle," said Higgins. "In the long run, that leads to a better relationship with that company, and, ultimately, I think it does lead to trust."

Both Higgins and Oberman said that demanding transparency is an important first step in a much longer process, and they admit that many companies may not be willing to go the extra mile just yet. But Oberman said that once transparency measures are in place, users can start to make more informed decisions about how much they value their privacy and what information is important to them. He predicts that this could create an incentive for services to offer multiple levels of privacy, storing sensitive data in secure containers while allowing less-sensitive bits to be available for ad-targeting purposes. "We're engaged with a lot of companies that are starting to think about data along those terms," he said. "I think they're all now taking a deep breath and considering what they can do to rebuild trust."

In Surveillance Debate, White House Turns Its Focus to Silicon Valley

By David E. Sanger
The New York Times, May 2, 2014

Nearly a year after the first disclosures about the National Security Agency's surveillance practices at home and abroad, the agency is emerging with mandates to make only modest changes: some new limits on what kind of data about Americans it can hold, and White House oversight of which foreign leaders' cellphones it can tap and when it can conduct cyberoperations against adversaries.

The big question now is whether Silicon Valley will get off as easily. It was the subject of a new White House report about how technology and the crunching of big data about the lives of Americans—from which websites they visit to where they drive their newly networked cars—are enlarging the problem.

At their core, the questions about the N.S.A. are strikingly similar to those about how Google, Yahoo, Facebook and thousands of application makers crunch their numbers. The difference is over the question of how far the government will go to restrain the growth of its own post–Sept. 11 abilities, and whether it will decide the time has come to intrude on what private industry collects, in the name of protecting privacy or preventing new forms of discrimination.

President Obama alluded to that at the White House on Friday, when he was forced to take up the issue at a news conference with one of the N.S.A.'s most prominent targets: Chancellor Angela Merkel of Germany, who said she was still not satisfied with America's responses to the revelations that her phone — and her country — were under blanket surveillance for a dozen years.

"The United States historically has been concerned about privacy," Mr. Obama said, trying to seize some high ground in the debate. His string of assurances along that line rang a bit hollow last year, as the administration reacted to each disclosure by Edward J. Snowden, the former N.S.A. contractor, with assurances that the programs were among the most closely monitored in the intelligence world and that they were necessary to protect the country.

But by January, Mr. Obama had arrived in a different place. After approving, for five years, a government program to collect telephone metadata—the information about telephone numbers dialed and the duration of calls—he acceded to recommendations to leave that information in the hands of telecommunications companies. Quietly, the White House ended the wiretapping of dozens of foreign leaders.

Now, by expanding the debate to what America's digital titans collect, Mr. Obama gains a few political advantages. He is hoping to reinvigorate legislative proposals that went nowhere in his first term. And now that the revelations about the N.S.A. have tapered off, at least for a while, his aides seem to sense that Americans are at least as concerned about the information they entrust to Google and Yahoo.

In Silicon Valley, there is a suspicion that the report issued on Thursday by John D. Podesta, a presidential adviser, is an effort to change the subject from government surveillance. Mr. Podesta insists it is about expanding the discussion about how information is used.

"It's a good time to revisit both public and private data collection and handling," said Jonathan Zittrain, a founder of the Berkman Center for Internet and Society at Harvard. He noted that the last time the government looked at how private companies collected data online, "it regulated lightly," asking companies to disclose their privacy policies and little else. Since then, he noted, "the scope of what both private companies and public authorities can collect from us has increased enormously."

The question is whether restrictions placed on the N.S.A. — and public resistance — will spill over to regulation of the private sector, and conversely whether new norms of what companies can collect will begin to affect the intelligence world.

At the N.S.A., there is grumbling about the continuing disclosures of material stolen by Mr. Snowden, but comparatively little complaint on the new limits Mr. Obama has proposed. In some cases, the N.S.A. gained some access to data even as it lost some autonomy. For example, its program to collect metadata missed a large percentage of cellphone calls. Under Mr. Obama's plan, if it becomes law, the N.S.A. would have to leave that data in private hands, but when the N.S.A. does get it, under court order, the agency should have access to a lot more than it does today.

"It's a pretty good trade," said one senior intelligence official who has been working on the issue. "All told, if you are an N.S.A. analyst, you will probably get more of what you wanted to see, even if it's more cumbersome."

In other cases, the N.S.A. is clearly giving up authority. Decisions about whether to exploit flaws in software to allow for surveillance or cyberattacks will be made at the National Security Council, not at the agency's headquarters in Fort Meade, Md. That list of leaders being wiretapped now gets high-level scrutiny. But more oversight does not necessarily mean operations will end.

While Mr. Obama has a lot of latitude in intelligence collection, the area pushed in the Podesta report will run headlong into considerable resistance in the country's most innovative companies. Most turned out statements on Thursday embracing the idea of enhancing individual privacy; Microsoft said that it supported the effort and "will keep working with lawmakers to make these tougher privacy protections a reality."

The argument will be over what constitutes "effective use." The report discussed a range of potential abuses: algorithms so effective that they could be used to create subtle, hard-to-detect biases in decisions about who can get a loan or whom to hire for a job. It even took a shot at metadata, the N.S.A.'s favorite tool, noting that it can reveal a lot about personal habits.

That is information that most Americans say they do not want intelligence agencies to have. But whether they are willing, as the price for joining an interconnected world, to put it in the hands of private firms, and whether the government should intervene to set the rules is not clear.

Obama Heads to Tech Security Talks Amid Tensions

By David E. Sanger and Nicole Perlroth
The New York Times, February 12, 2015

President Obama will meet [in Palo Alto California] on Friday with the nation's top technologists on a host of cybersecurity issues and the threats posed by increasingly sophisticated hackers. But nowhere on the agenda is the real issue for the chief executives and tech company officials who will gather on the Stanford campus: the deepening estrangement between Silicon Valley and the government.

The long history of quiet cooperation between Washington and America's top technology companies — first to win the Cold War, then to combat terrorism — was founded on the assumption of mutual interest. Edward J. Snowden's revelations shattered that. Now, the Obama administration's efforts to prevent companies from greatly strengthening encryption in commercial products like Apple's iPhone and Google's Android phones has set off a new battle, as the companies resist government efforts to make sure police and intelligence agencies can crack the systems.

And there is continuing tension over the government's desire to stockpile flaws in software — known as zero days — to develop weapons that the United States can reserve for future use against adversaries.

"What has struck me is the enormous degree of hostility between Silicon Valley and the government," said Herb Lin, who spent 20 years working on cyberissues at the National Academy of Sciences before moving to Stanford several months ago. "The relationship has been poisoned, and it's not going to recover anytime soon."

Mr. Obama's cybersecurity coordinator, Michael Daniel, concedes there are tensions. American firms, he says, are increasingly concerned about international competitiveness, and that means making a very public show of their efforts to defeat American intelligence-gathering by installing newer, harder-to-break encryption systems and demonstrating their distance from the United States government.

The F.B.I., the intelligence agencies and David Cameron, the British prime minister, have all tried to stop Google, Apple and other companies from using encryption technology that the firms themselves cannot break into — meaning they cannot turn over emails or pictures, even if served with a court order. The firms have vociferously opposed government requests for such information as an intrusion on the privacy of their customers and a risk to their businesses.

"In some cases that is driving them to resistance to Washington," Mr. Daniel said in an interview. "But it's not that simple. In other cases, with what's going on in China," where Beijing is insisting that companies turn over the software that is their lifeblood, "they are very interested in getting Washington's help."

Mr. Daniel's reference was to Silicon Valley's argument that keeping a key to unlocking terrorists' secret communications, as the government wants them to do, may sound reasonable in theory but in fact would create an opening for others. It would also create a precedent that the Chinese, among others, could adopt to ensure they can get into American communications, especially as companies like Alibaba, the Chinese Internet giant, become a larger force in the American market.

"A stupid approach" is the assessment of one technology executive who will be seeing Mr. Obama on Friday, and who asked to speak anonymously.

That tension—between companies' insistence that they cannot install "back doors" or provide "keys" giving access to law enforcement or intelligence agencies and their desire for Washington's protection from foreign nations seeking to exploit those same products—will be the subtext of the meeting.

That is hardly the only point of contention. A year after Mr. Obama announced that the government would get out of the business of maintaining a huge database of every call made inside the United States but would instead ask the nation's telecommunications companies to store that data in case the government needs it, the companies are slow-walking the effort.

They will not take on the job of "bulk collection" of the nation's communications, they say, unless Congress forces

> "The government is realizing they can't just blow into town and let bygones be bygones," Eric Grosse, Google's vice president of security and privacy, said in an interview. "Our business depends on trust. If you lose it, it takes years to regain."

them to. And some executives whisper it will be at a price that may make the National Security Administration's once-secret program look like a bargain.

The stated purpose of Friday's meeting is trying to prevent the kinds of hackings that have struck millions of credit card holders at Home Depot and Target. A similar breach revealed the names, Social Security numbers and other information of about 80 million people insured by Anthem, the nation's second-largest health insurer.

Mr. Obama has made online security a major theme, making the case in his State of the Union address that the huge increase in attacks during his presidency called for far greater protection. Lisa Monaco, Mr. Obama's homeland security adviser, said this week that attacks have increased fivefold since the president came to office; some, like the Sony Pictures attack, had a clear political agenda.

The image of Kim Jong-un, the North Korean leader, shown in the Sony Pictures comedy "The Interview" has been emblazoned in the minds of those who downloaded the film. But the one fixed in the minds of many Silicon Valley executives is the image revealed in photographs and documents released from the Snowden trove of N.S.A. employees slicing open a box containing a Cisco Systems server and placing "beacons" in it that could tap into a foreign computer network. Or the reports of how the N.S.A. intercepted email traffic moving between Google and Yahoo servers.

"The government is realizing they can't just blow into town and let bygones be bygones," Eric Grosse, Google's vice president of security and privacy, said in an interview. "Our business depends on trust. If you lose it, it takes years to regain."

When it comes to matters of security, Mr. Grosse said, "Their mission is clearly different than ours. It's a source of continuing tension. It's not like if they just wait, it will go away."

And while Silicon Valley executives have made a very public argument over encryption, they have been fuming quietly over the government's use of zero-day flaws. Intelligence agencies are intent on finding or buying information about those flaws in widely used hardware and software, and information about the flaws often sells for hundreds of thousands of dollars on the black market. N.S.A. keeps a potent stockpile, without revealing the flaws to manufacturers.

Companies like Google, Facebook, Microsoft and Twitter are fighting back by paying "bug bounties" to friendly hackers who alert them to serious bugs in their systems so they can be fixed. And last July, Google took the effort to another level. That month, Mr. Grosse began recruiting some of the world's best bug hunters to track down and neuter the very bugs that intelligence agencies and military contractors have been paying top dollar for to add to their arsenals.

They called the effort "Project Zero," Mr. Grosse says, because the ultimate goal is to bring the number of bugs down to zero. He said that "Project Zero" would never get the number of bugs down to zero "but we're going to get close."

The White House is expected to make a series of decisions on encryption in the coming weeks. Silicon Valley executives say encrypting their products has long been a priority, even before the revelations by Mr. Snowden, the former N.S.A. analyst, about N.S.A.'s surveillance, and they have no plans to slow down.

In an interview last month, Timothy D. Cook, Apple's chief executive, said the N.S.A. "would have to cart us out in a box" before the company would provide the government a back door to its products. Apple recently began encrypting phones and tablets using a scheme that would force the government to go directly to the user for their information. And intelligence agencies are bracing for another wave of encryption.

4

Effectiveness of Domestic Surveillance in Fighting Crime and Terror

The security entrance to the NSA's new spy data collection center is seen south of Salt Lake City on May 7, 2015, in Bluffdale, Utah. Reportedly, the center is the largest of its kind, with massive computer power for processing data. A New York Court of appeals ruled that the NSA's bulk collection of phone data is illegal.

Evaluating Federal Surveillance Programs: A Difficult Task

Evaluating the effectiveness of intelligence programs—surveillance or any other kind—is inherently difficult. As with the evaluation of any policy, it requires the measurement of results in comparison with goals. The overall goals of surveillance are to uncover information about criminal activity, catch perpetrators, and thwart serious threats to national security and public safety. While the federal government has used domestic surveillance to gather information on crimes as varied as child pornography, drug trafficking, and money laundering, in the contemporary world, the greatest public attention has focused on how intelligence is used to prevent terrorist attacks.

Historically, it was the memory of the attack on Pearl Harbor that triggered the rise of the massive U.S. intelligence bureaucracy in the years following World War II. Likewise, it was the terrorist attacks of September 11, 2001, that turned a portion of that bureaucracy inward in the form of a massive, domestic electronic surveillance program: intelligence fusion centers in locations throughout the country that bring together federal, state, and local agencies with intelligence or law enforcement responsibilities; and intelligence-sharing databases under the Nationwide Suspicious Activity Reporting Initiative. Still, the task of preventing surprise attacks is difficult to evaluate. Many are content to conclude that if no attack has occurred, then the preventive measures, whatever they are, must be successful. Yet if no one has attempted an attack in that period, the final outcome would be the same.

An ever present problem in intelligence analysis is the task of distinguishing signals from noise.[1] Some bits of information may be valuable clues to impending events. Others—most, nearly all—are irrelevant distractions. The problem is that it is nearly impossible before the event to know which is which. That is why nonroutine political occurrences are so hard to predict and why the element of surprise is so easy to achieve. Of course, after an attack such as Pearl Harbor or 9/11, congressional committees can go through old records that in retrospect seem to provide clear clues to the event. But, as they say, hindsight is 20/20.

Former naval intelligence officer Erik Dahl points out that in addition to the difficulty of distinguishing signals from noise, most of the relevant signals are too vague, too imprecise to be meaningful in advance of the event. He argues that most intelligence breakthroughs do not come from analysts "connecting the dots" of disparate bits of information, but rather from (1) the chance discovery of specific, precise information and (2) finding a policy maker who is willing to listen and take the discovery seriously. Policy makers, as much as some of them may talk of the importance of big data, really respond only to specific, concrete information, not "hunches" based on connecting vague "dots."[2]

With regard to mass surveillance, pressure to amass larger and larger quantities of information may exacerbate the signals/noise problem by leading to a reduction in the quality of the information gathered. For example, law-enforcement officers file Suspicious Activity Reports (SARs) about people observed doing things that could—conceivably—have a nefarious purpose but almost always do not. Some of these activities can be as mundane as: using binoculars, taking photographs, or writing notes. Those SARs are then added to the databases of the Nationwide Suspicious Activity Reporting Initiative. They could end up in the Terrorist Identities Datamart Environment (TIDE) or the FBI's Terrorist Screening Database (TSDB). As of August 2013, the TSDB contained 680,000 names, 40 percent of which—according to government figures—had "no recognized terrorist group affiliation."[3] That suggests that the database contains a considerable amount of noise.

When most people speak of mass surveillance, however, they mean the National Security Agency's bulk-surveillance programs. The short answer regarding the effectiveness of these NSA programs is that the results appear to be meager, especially regarding the collection of domestic landline telephone metadata under Section 215 of the USA PATRIOT Act. In 2013 General Keith Alexander, the director of the NSA at the time, claimed that bulk surveillance had allowed the United States to thwart 54 "potential terrorist events." People loosely paraphrasing his words quickly elevated his claim to the thwarting of 54 "terrorist attacks." It turned out, however, that only 13 of those cases involved activity or potential activity within the United States, and only one of those cases (resulting in four arrests) had been initiated by the Section 215 telephone metadata program. Furthermore, that case did not concern a planned terrorist attack, but rather a group of Somalis living in San Diego who had, two years earlier, raised just under $8,500 for al-Shabaab militants. (According to the defendants, they had supported what they saw as al-Shabaab's fight against an Ethiopian invasion of Somalia, but they stopped when they realized the nature of al-Shabaab's rule.)[4]

A task force set up by President Barack Obama in 2013, the President's Review Group on Intelligence and Communications Technologies, which had access to classified reports, was particularly dismissive of the effectiveness of bulk surveillance under Section 215:

> NSA believes that on at least a few occasions, information derived from the section 215 bulk telephony meta-data program has contributed to its efforts to prevent possible terrorist attacks, either in the United States or somewhere else in the world. More often, negative results from section 215 queries have helped to alleviate concern that particular terrorist suspects are in contact with co-conspirators in the United States. Our review suggests that the information contributed to terrorist investigations by the use of section 215 telephony meta-data was not essential to preventing attacks and could readily have been obtained in a timely manner using conventional section 215 orders. Moreover, there is reason for caution about the view that the program is efficacious in alleviating concern about possible terrorist connections, given the fact that the meta-data captured by the program covers only a portion of the records of only a few telephone service providers.[5]

Note that the President's Review Group is making a distinction between the "bulk" collection of metadata (the attempt to sweep up the telephone records of all customers) and "conventional" warrants (aimed at the telephone records or other evidence of specified, individual suspects), which are also secret and issued under the same law. Although the bulk program is closely identified with Section 215, many legal experts (now including the U.S. Court of Appeals for the Second Circuit) consider it to exceed the statute's provisions. It is also worth noting that while computers can process and analyze vast quantities of records in order to map out the connections between customers, the connections are not useful unless you can identify at least one of those customers as a suspect. If you can identify one as a suspect, then you do not need the bulk collection; you can start with the suspect's calls and work outward.

Other studies have come to similar conclusions. Peter Bergin and his associates at the New America Foundation, for example, studied 225 terrorism-related court cases on which public information was available. They found that bulk telephone metadata collected under Section 215 played some identifiable role in just 1.8 percent of the cases. Information from the Internet communications of foreigners based abroad (collected under Section 702 of the FISA Amendments Act of 2008) played a role in 4.4 percent. Unidentifiable NSA sources (perhaps bulk collection, perhaps not) played a role in 1.3 percent. On the other hand, conventional, targeted surveillance warrants issued by the Foreign Intelligence Surveillance Court (FISC) played a role in 21 percent. Thus they concluded that conventional law-enforcement techniques appeared to be more effective than the expensive and elaborate bulk-intelligence-gathering operations of the NSA, while posing less threat to privacy and civil liberties.[6] The evident limitations of the study's sources, of course, mean that the conclusions cannot be considered definitive, but they are nonetheless suggestive.

At the same time, some critics have raised questions about the very law-enforcement techniques that Bergen argues we should rely on. One study found that of 508 defendants tried on terrorism-related charges, 243 (48 percent) involved an FBI informant; of those, 158 (31 percent) were caught in sting operations. In a number of cases, the defendants would not have been able to carry out their alleged plots without materials provided by the informant. The study concludes that for 49 of the defendants (10 percent), the informant actually led the plot.[7] The investigations are based in part on tips from the public and in part on the data-mining of immigration records and demographic information to locate communities of a certain ethnic makeup. The aim is to catch perpetrators before they have a chance to carry out the act and hopefully, to deter others from even trying. Yet if there really are cases in which the defendants are incapable of engineering a plot or of obtaining the necessary materials without the help of FBI informants, then the terrorist threat is being overstated.

In the spring of 2015, as Congress debated whether to revise the mass-surveillance programs or to continue them as they were, evidence began to emerge that even the intelligence community did not find them terribly effective. A declassified 2009 report on an early, especially expansive and intrusive surveillance program (codenamed Stellarwind) written by the inspectors general of five intelligence and law enforcement agencies relayed that the very secrecy surrounding the program (even CIA analysts had been kept in the dark) made them less useful. It also reported that an FBI review of the tips produced by Stellarwind between 2001 and 2004 had concluded that only 1.2 percent of them had made a "significant contribution" to identifying a terrorist, deporting a terrorism suspect, or developing a confidential informant about terrorists. A separate FBI review of warrantless wiretaps conducted as part of Stellarwind found that, between August 2004 and January 2006, they had produced no useful leads.[8] Unattributed comments from NSA employees suggest that the expensive, cumbersome, and controversial collection of landline telephone metadata is now considered more troublesome than it is worth. The NSA expected that, even without direct collection, it would still have access to the telephone companies' metadata for specific suspects under targeted FISC warrants and, in that case, would probably gain access to cell phone metadata and possibly billing addresses as well.[9]

If the effectiveness of federal surveillance programs corresponds to how many serious threats the programs have uncovered and prevented, they have been of dubious value. To date, they have not come up with much. Neither has the CIA's detention and interrogation program.[10] No major terrorist attacks have occurred since 9/11, but that is not because any plots have been discovered through mass surveillance. For the most part, there have been a few independent, or "lone wolf," operations, which by their very nature are difficult to detect through the surveillance of communications because "lone wolves" do not communicate much. It is possible that the U.S. attacks on al-Qa'ida in Afghanistan and Pakistan disrupted the terrorist threat that appeared so pervasive after 9/11, or it may be that the perceived threat was exaggerated from the beginning. Some domestic terrorism plots have been thwarted since 9/11, but the evidence shows that traditional law enforcement methods have been responsible, not mass surveillance. The threat of terrorism, whether of foreign or domestic origin, may not have diminished in the past decade and a half, but it seems the federal surveillance programs have yet to prove their effectiveness in detecting those threats.

Scott C. Monje

Notes

1. On the question of signals and noise, the classic study is Roberta Wohlstetter, *Pearl Harbor: Warning and Decision* (Stanford, CA: Stanford University Press, 1962).
2. "Transcript of Erik Dahl," interviewed by Mike German on June 2, 2014, http://www.brennancenter.org/transcript-erik-dahl.
3. Hina Shamsi and Matthew Harwood, "Uncle Sam's Databases of Suspicion," Speak Freely [ACLU blog] (Nov. 6, 2014), https://www.aclu.org/blog/speakeasy/uncle-sams-databases-suspicion.

4. Mattathias Schwartz, "The Whole Haystack," *The New Yorker* 90:45 (Jan. 26, 2015); Peter Bergin et al., *Do NSA's Surveillance Programs Stop Terrorists? A National Security Program Report* (Washington, DC: New America Foundation, January 2014).

5. *Liberty and Security in a Changing World: Report and Recommendations of the President's Review Group on Intelligence and Communications Technologies* (Washington, DC, Dec. 12, 2013), 104, https://s3.amazonaws.com/s3.documentcloud.org/documents/929267/review-group-exec-summary-and-recs.pdf. The last part of the quote reminds us that NSA surveillance is not as comprehensive as some news reports suggest. See also Lauren Fox, "Sen. Bob Corker Is 'Shocked' by How Little Data the NSA Is Collecting," *National Journal* (May 13, 2015), http://www.nationaljournal.com/congress/sen-bob-corker-is-shocked-by-how-little-data-the-nsa-is-collecting-20150513.

6. Bergin et al., *Do NSA's Surveillance Programs Stop Terrorists?* See also Schwartz, "The Whole Haystack."

7. Trevor Aaronson, "The Informants," *Mother Jones* (Sept.–Oct. 2011); John Knefel, "The FBI Keeps Arresting Hapless Jihadi Fanboys and Calling Them ISIS Recruits," *New Republic* (March 24, 2015).

8. Charlie Savage, "Declassified Report Shows Doubts about Value of N.S.A.'s Warrantless Spying," *New York Times*, April 25, 2015; http://www.nytimes.com/2015/04/25/us/politics/value-of-nsa-warrantless-spying-is-doubted-in-declassified-reports.html.

9. Shane Harris, "'Big Win' for Big Brother: NSA Celebrates the Bill That's Designed to Cuff Them," *The Daily Beast*, May 14, 2015; http://www.thedailybeast.com/articles/2015/05/14/nsa-loves-the-nothing-burger-spying-reform-bill.html; Peter Baker and David E. Sanger, "Why the N.S.A. Isn't Howling over Restrictions," *New York Times*, May 1, 2015; http://www.nytimes.com/2015/05/02/us/politics/giving-in-a-little-on-national-security-agency-data-collection.html?ref=us. Note that this applies primarily to the Section 215 metadata program. The NSA insists that the Section 702 program surveilling Internet communications outside the United States is much more effective, and it would probably fight harder to keep it.

10. US Senate Select Committee on Intelligence, Committee Study of the Central Intelligence Agency's Detention and Interrogation Program, 113th Cong., 2d sess. (Washington, DC, released Dec. 9, 2014), http://www.intelligence.senate.gov/study2014.html.

The Whole Haystack

By Mattathias Schwartz
The New Yorker, January 26, 2015

Almost every major terrorist attack on Western soil in the past fifteen years has been committed by people who were already known to law enforcement. One of the gunmen in the attack on *Charlie Hebdo*, in Paris, had been sent to prison for recruiting jihadist fighters. The other had reportedly studied in Yemen with Umar Farouk Abdulmutallab, the underwear bomber, who was arrested and interrogated by the F.B.I. in 2009. The leader of the 7/7 London suicide bombings, in 2005, had been observed by British intelligence meeting with a suspected terrorist, though MI5 later said that the bombers were "not on our radar." The men who planned the Mumbai attacks, in 2008, were under electronic surveillance by the United States, the United Kingdom, and India, and one had been an informant for the Drug Enforcement Administration. One of the brothers accused of bombing the Boston Marathon was the subject of an F.B.I. threat assessment and a warning from Russian intelligence.

In each of these cases, the authorities were not wanting for data. What they failed to do was appreciate the significance of the data they already had. Nevertheless, since 9/11, the National Security Agency has sought to acquire every possible scrap of digital information—what General Keith Alexander, the agency's former head, has called "the whole haystack." The size of the haystack was revealed in June 2013, by Edward Snowden. The N.S.A. vacuums up Internet searches, social-media content, and, most controversially, the records (known as metadata) of United States phone calls—who called whom, for how long, and from where. The agency stores the metadata for five years, possibly longer.

The metadata program remains the point of greatest apparent friction between the N.S.A. and the Constitution. It is carried out under Section 215 of the Patriot Act, which allows the government to collect "books, records, papers, documents, and other items" that are "relevant" to "an authorized investigation." While debating the Patriot Act in 2001, Senator Russ Feingold worried about the government's powers to collect "the personal records of anyone—perhaps someone who worked with, or lived next door to . . . the target of the investigation." Snowden revealed that the N.S.A. goes much further. Metadata for every domestic phone call from Verizon and other carriers, hundreds of billions of records in all, are considered "relevant" under Section 215. The N.S.A. collects them on an "ongoing, daily basis."

The N.S.A. asserts that it uses the metadata to learn whether anyone inside the U.S. is in contact with high-priority terrorism suspects, colloquially referred to as "known bad guys." Michael Hayden, the former C.I.A. and N.S.A. director, has said, "We kill people based on metadata." He then added, "But that's not what we do with *this* metadata," referring to Section 215.

Soon after Snowden's revelations, Alexander said that the N.S.A.'s surveillance programs have stopped "fifty-four different terrorist-related activities." Most of these were "terrorist plots." Thirteen involved the United States. Credit for foiling these plots, he continued, was partly due to the metadata program, intended to "find the terrorist that walks among us."

President Obama also quantified the benefits of the metadata program. That June, in a press conference with Angela Merkel, the German Chancellor, Obama said, "We know of at least fifty threats that have been averted because of this information." He continued, "Lives have been saved."

Section 215 is just one of many legal authorities that govern U.S. spy programs. These authorities are jumbled together in a way that makes it difficult to separate their individual efficacy. Early in the metadata debate, the fifty-four cases were sometimes attributed to Section 215 and sometimes to other sections of other laws. At a Senate Judiciary Committee hearing in October 2013, Senator Patrick Leahy, of Vermont, called the fifty-four-plots statistic "plainly wrong . . . these weren't all plots, and they weren't all thwarted." He cited a statement by Alexander's deputy that "there's only really one example of a case where, but for the use of Section 215 bulk phone-records collection, terrorist activity was stopped." "He's right," Alexander said.

The case was that of Basaaly Moalin, a Somali-born U.S. citizen living in San Diego. In July 2013, Sean Joyce, the F.B.I.'s deputy director at the time, said in Senate-committee testimony that Moalin's phone number had been in contact with an "Al Qaeda East Africa member" in Somalia. The N.S.A., Joyce said, was able to make this connection and notify the F.B.I. thanks to Section 215. That February, Moalin was found guilty of sending eighty-five hundred dollars to the Shabaab, an extremist Somali militia with ties to Al Qaeda. "Moalin and three other individuals have been convicted," Joyce continued. "I go back to what we need to remember, what happened in 9/11." At the same hearing, Senator Dianne Feinstein, of California, talked about "how little information we had" before 9/11. "I support this program," she said, referring to Section 215. "They will come after us, and I think we need to prevent an attack wherever we can."

In the thirteen years that have passed since 9/11, the N.S.A. has used Section 215 of the Patriot Act to take in records from hundreds of billions of domestic phone calls. Congress was explicit about why it

> **Michael Hayden, the former C.I.A. and N.S.A. director, has said, "We kill people based on metadata." He then added, "But that's not what we do with this metadata," referring to Section 215.**

passed the Patriot Act—despite concerns about potential effects on civil liberties, it believed that the law was necessary to prevent another attack on the scale of 9/11. The government has not shown any instance besides Moalin's in which the law's metadata provision has directly led to a conviction in a terrorism case. Is it worth it?

Before 9/11, the intelligence community was already struggling to evolve. The technology of surveillance was changing, from satellites to fibre-optic cable. The targets were also changing, from the embassies and nuclear arsenals of the Cold War era to scattered networks of violent extremists. The law still drew lines between foreign and domestic surveillance, but the increasingly global nature of communications was complicating this distinction.

In Washington, many people blamed 9/11 on a "wall" between intelligence gathering and criminal investigations. In a report on pre-9/11 failures, the Department of Justice criticized the F.B.I.'s San Diego field office for not making counterterrorism a higher priority. Two of the hijackers—Nawaf al-Hazmi and Khalid al-Mihdhar—took flying lessons in San Diego and attended a mosque where the imam, Anwar al-Awlaki, had been the target of an F.B.I. investigation. They lived for a time in an apartment that they rented from an F.B.I. informant, and Mihdhar made phone calls to a known Al Qaeda safe house in Yemen. But the F.B.I. wasn't solely at fault. The C.I.A. knew that Mihdhar had a visa to travel to the U.S., and that Hazmi had arrived in Los Angeles in January 2000. The agency failed to forward this information to the F.B.I.

Three years after 9/11, the size of San Diego's Joint Terrorism Task Force had tripled. In California, hundreds of local police became "terrorism liaison officers," trained to observe anomalous activity that could presage an attack. The San Diego "fusion center" spent hundreds of thousands of dollars on computers and monitors, including fifty-five flat-screen televisions, which officials said were for "watching the news." This was one of seventy-seven such centers nationwide, at a cost of several hundred million dollars. The F.B.I. office established a "field-intelligence group," a special unit that gathered information about domestic terrorism threats. . . .

. . . I met General Keith Alexander one morning last spring, in midtown Manhattan. He had retired from the N.S.A. a few weeks earlier and was soon to announce the launch of IronNet Cybersecurity, a new private venture. . . . "You might ask, 'What's the best way to figure out who the bad guys are?'" he said. "What would you start with? You'd say, 'Well, I need to know who his network of friends are, because chances are many of them are bad, too.'"

It's possible that Moalin would have been caught without Section 215. His phone number was "a common link among pending F.B.I. investigations," according to a report from the Privacy and Civil Liberties Oversight Board (PCLOB), an independent agency created in 2004 at the suggestion of the 9/11 Commission, which Obama had tasked with assessing Section 215. Later, in a congressional budget request, the Department of Justice said that the Moalin case was part of a broader investigation into Shabaab funding. Senator Ron Wyden, of Oregon, who, like Leahy, has pressured the N.S.A. to justify bulk surveillance, said, "To suggest that the government needed to spy on millions of law-abiding people in order to catch this individual is simply not true." He continued, "I still haven't seen any evidence that the dragnet surveillance of Americans' personal information has done a single thing to improve U.S. national security." Representative James Sensenbrenner, of Wisconsin, who introduced the Patriot Act in the House, agreed. "The intelligence community has never made a compelling case that bulk collection stops terrorism," he told me.

Khalid al-Mihdhar's phone calls to Yemen months before he helped hijack American Airlines Flight 77, on 9/11, led Obama, Alexander, Feinstein, and others to suggest that Section 215 could have prevented the attacks. "We know that we didn't stop 9/11," Alexander told me last spring. "People were trying, but they didn't have the tools. This tool, we believed, would help them."

But the PCLOB found that "it was not necessary to collect the entire nation's calling records" to find Mihdhar. I asked William Gore, who was running the F.B.I.'s San Diego office at the time, if the Patriot Act would have made a difference. "Could we have prevented 9/11? I don't know," he said. "You can't find somebody if you're not looking for them."

Last year, as evidence of the fifty-four disrupted plots came apart, many people in Washington shifted their rhetoric on Section 215 away from specific cases and toward hypotheticals and analogies. "I have a fire-insurance policy on my house," Robert Litt, the general counsel of the Office of the Director of National Intelligence, said. "I don't determine whether I want to keep that fire-insurance policy by the number of times it's paid off." James Clapper, the director of National Intelligence, has called this "the peace-of-mind metric."

Michael Leiter, who led the National Counterterrorism Center under George W. Bush and Obama, told me that Section 215 was useful but not indispensable: "Could we live without Section 215? Yes. It's not the most essential piece. But it would increase risk and make some things harder."

In addition to phone metadata, the N.S.A. has used Section 215 to collect records from hotels, car-rental agencies, state D.M.V.s, landlords, credit-card companies, "and the like," according to Justice Department reports. Once the N.S.A. has the phone metadata, it can circulate them through a shared database called "the corporate store."

To some, this sounds less like fire insurance and more like a live-in fire marshal, authorized to root through the sock drawer in search of flammable material. "The open abuse is how they use that data," Mike German, a former F.B.I. agent and lobbyist for the A.C.L.U., who is now a fellow at the Brennan Center, said. "It's no longer about investigating a particular suspect."

In 2013, *Le Monde* published documents from Edward Snowden's archive showing that the N.S.A. obtained seventy million French phone-metadata records in one month. It is unknown whether any of these calls could be retrospectively associated with the Paris attacks. "The interesting thing to know would be whether these brothers made phone calls to Yemen in a way that would have been collected by a program like Section 215 or another signals intelligence program," Leiter told me last week. "I don't know the answer to that question."

Philip Mudd, a former C.I.A. and senior F.B.I. official, told me that tallying up individual cases did not capture the full value of Section 215. "Try to imagine a quicker way to understand a human being in 2015," he said. "Take this woman in Paris. Who is she? How are you going to figure that out? You need historical data on everything she ever touched, to accelerate the investigation. Now, do we want to do that in America? That's a different question, a political question."

Documents released by Snowden and published by the *Washington Post* show that the N.S.A. accounted for $10.5 billion of the $52.6 billion "black budget," the top-secret budget for U.S. intelligence spending, in 2013. About $17 billion of the black budget goes to counterterrorism each year, plus billions more through the unclassified budgets of the Pentagon, the State Department, and other agencies, plus a special $5-billion-dollar fund proposed by Obama last year to fight the Islamic State in Iraq and al-Sham (ISIS).

The maximalist approach to intelligence is not limited to the N.S.A. or to Section 215. A central terrorist watch list is called the Terrorist Identities Datamart Environment, or TIDE. According to a classified report released by the Web site the Intercept, TIDE, which is kept by the National Counterterrorism Center, lists more than a million people. The C.I.A., the N.S.A., and the F.B.I. can all "nominate" new individuals. In the weeks before the 2013 Chicago Marathon, analysts performed "due diligence" on "all of the records in TIDE of people who held a drivers license in Illinois, Indiana, and Wisconsin." This was "based on the lessons learned from the Boston Marathon."

In retrospect, every terrorist attack leaves a data trail that appears to be dotted with missed opportunities. In the case of 9/11, there was Mihdhar's landlord, the airport clerk who sold Mihdhar his one-way ticket for cash, and the state trooper who pulled over another hijacker on September 9. In August 2001, F.B.I. headquarters failed to issue a search warrant for one of the conspirators' laptops, despite a warning from the Minneapolis field office that he was "engaged in preparing to seize a Boeing 747-400 in commission of a terrorist act."

There was plenty of material in the haystack. The government had adequate tools to collect even more. The problem was the tendency of intelligence agencies to hoard information, as well as the cognitive difficulty of anticipating a spectacular and unprecedented attack. The 9/11 Commission called this a "failure of the imagination." Finding needles, the commission wrote in its report, is easy when you're looking backward, deceptively so. They quoted the historian Roberta Wohlstetter writing about Pearl Harbor:

> It is much easier *after* the event to sort the relevant from the irrelevant signals. After the event, of course, a signal is always crystal clear; we can now see what disaster it was signaling since the disaster has occurred. But before the event it is obscure and pregnant with conflicting meanings.

Before the event, every bit of hay is potentially relevant. "The most dangerous adversaries will be the ones who most successfully disguise their individual trans-actions to appear normal, reasonable, and legitimate," Ted Senator, a data scientist who worked on an early post-9/11 program called Total Information Awareness, said, in 2002. Since then, intelligence officials have often referred to "lone-wolf terrorists," "cells," and, as Alexander has put it, the "terrorist who walks among us," as though Al Qaeda were a fifth column, capable of camouflaging itself within civil society. Patrick Skinner, a former C.I.A. case officer who works with the Soufan Group, a security company, told me that this image is wrong. "We knew about these networks," he said, speaking of the *Charlie Hebdo* attacks. Mass surveillance, he continued, "gives a false sense of security. It sounds great when you say you're monitoring every phone call in the United States. You can put that in a PowerPoint. But, actually, you have no idea what's going on."

By flooding the system with false positives, big-data approaches to counterterrorism might actually make it harder to identify real terrorists before they act. Two years before the Boston Marathon bombing, Tamerlan Tsarnaev, the older of the two brothers alleged to have committed the attack, was assessed by the city's Joint Terrorism Task Force. They determined that he was not a threat. This was one of about a thousand assessments that the Boston J.T.T.F. conducted that year, a number that had nearly doubled in the previous two years, according to the Boston F.B.I. As of 2013, the Justice Department has trained nearly three hundred thousand law-enforcement officers in how to file "suspicious-activity reports." In 2010, a central database held about three thousand of these reports; by 2012 it had grown to almost twenty-eight thousand. "The bigger haystack makes it harder to find the needle," Sensenbrenner told me. Thomas Drake, a former N.S.A. executive and whistle-blower who has become one of the agency's most vocal critics, told me, "If you target everything, there's no target." Drake favors what he calls "a traditional law-enforcement" approach to terrorism, gathering more intelligence on a smaller set of targets. Decisions about which targets matter, he said, should be driven by human expertise, not by a database.

One alternative to data-driven counterterrorism is already being used by the F.B.I. and other agencies. Known as "countering violent extremism," this approach bears some resemblance to the community-policing programs of the 1990s, in which law enforcement builds a listening relationship with local leaders. "The kinds of people you want to look for, someone in the community might have seen them first," Mudd said. After the Moalin arrests, the U.S. Attorney's office in San Diego began hosting a bimonthly "Somali roundtable" with representatives from the F.B.I., the Department of Homeland Security, the sheriff's office, local police, and many Somali organizations. "They've done a lot of work to reach out and explain what they're about," Abdi Mohamoud, the Somali nonprofit director, who has attended the meetings, said.

Does the Moalin case justify putting the phone records of hundreds of millions of U.S. citizens into the hands of the federal government? "Stopping the money is a big deal," Joel Brenner, the N.S.A.'s former inspector general, told me. Alexander called Moalin's actions "the seed of a future terrorist attack or set of attacks."

But Senator Leahy contends that stopping a few thousand dollars, in one instance, over thirteen years, is a weak track record. The program "invades Americans' privacy" and "has not been proven to be effective," he said last week. The Moalin case, he continued, "was not a 'plot' but, rather, a material-support prosecution for sending a few thousand dollars to Somalia."

> **But Senator Leahy contends that stopping a few thousand dollars, in one instance, over thirteen years, is a weak track record. The program "invades Americans' privacy" and "has not been proven to be effective," he said last week.**

On June 1st, Section 215 and the "roving wiretap" provision of the Patriot Act will expire. Sensenbrenner told me that he doesn't expect Congress to renew either unless Section 215 is revised. "If Congress knew in 2001 how the FISA court was going to interpret it, I don't think the Patriot Act would have passed," he told me. In 2013, Leahy and Sensenbrenner introduced the U.S.A. Freedom Act, which would scale back the N.S.A.'s powers; the act would grant subpoena power for the PCLOB and create an advocate charged with representing privacy interests before the secret FISA court. The bill was watered down and passed by the House, but it failed to reach the Senate floor. Mitch McConnell, the Senate's top Republican, said that the N.S.A. needed every available tool for the fight against ISIS. "This is the worst possible time to be tying our hands behind our back," he said.

The Paris attacks offered yet another opportunity to argue for the value of Section 215. Senator Bob Corker, of Tennessee, said that his priority was "insuring we don't overly hamstring the N.S.A.'s ability to collect this kind of information." Senator Chuck Grassley, of Iowa, said, "If it can happen in Paris, it can happen in New York again, or Washington, D.C." The senators focused on attacks that Section 215 had not stopped and imagined attacks that it could theoretically stop. There was no mention of what it had actually stopped, or of Basaaly Moalin.

The Militarization of Domestic Surveillance Is Everyone's Problem

By Michael German
Brennan Center for Justice, December 18, 2014

Many Americans were shocked to see the militarized police response to public protests this summer in Ferguson, Missouri. Of course, many working on police reform issues have identified the growing militarization of police tactics and equipment as a problem for over two decades. What is less observable but equally dangerous to American civil liberties is the increasing militarization of domestic law enforcement intelligence operations.

The American tradition of prohibiting military involvement in domestic policing is designed to ensure that we maintain democratic and civilian control over an extraordinarily powerful fighting force. An army designed and equipped to protect Americans should never be turned against Americans except to quell active rebellion. But just as the drug war fueled increased military participation and militarization in domestic policing, the war on terrorism is driving the militarization of domestic intelligence operations. Unlike the purchases of armored vehicles, military weapons, and SWAT gear, domestic intelligence activities take place mostly in the dark and neither the public nor policymakers really know what is happening.

Military intelligence officials are trained for war against hostile enemies. Their tools, tactics, and attitudes reflect that mission, and are completely inappropriate to a domestic application.

In a recent interview, Dr. Erik Dahl, a former Navy intelligence officer and now a professor at the Naval Postgraduate School, explains why someone who trained to spy on the Soviet Navy shouldn't be involved in domestic intelligence gathering.

Despite such warnings, domestic intelligence programs have become militarized in three ways.

First, military agencies are conducting domestic intelligence collection against Americans and providing that information to law enforcement officials. The National Security Agency scoops up domestic telephone calling data, as well as the content of U.S. international communications ("inadvertently" grabbing tens of thousands of purely domestic calls each year in the process). The FBI has direct access to this material and can use it for general criminal purposes through so-called back-door searches.

Military officials also collect domestic intelligence for "force protection." A military unit that was caught spying on anti-war protesters under this authority was disbanded in 2008, but the Defense Intelligence Agency picked up its "offensive counterintelligence" duties and re-established an intelligence database in 2010. National Guard units and civilians working at military agencies have been caught illegally spying on domestic protesters and, more recently, engaging in undercover law enforcement activities in violation of the Posse Comitatus Act, a law prohibiting U.S. military personnel from enforcing criminal laws.

Second, military agencies and personnel participate in formal and informal information sharing programs on the federal and state level, including between FBI Joint Terrorism Task Forces, state and local law enforcement intelligence fusion centers, and information sharing networks like the Navy's Law Enforcement Information Exchange (LInX), and the FBI's eGuardian program. Though there are legal limits to the type of work military officials can do within these programs and the information they can share, there is little to no oversight conducted to ensure they follow the law.

Third, military intelligence tactics and attitudes rub off on law enforcement personnel assigned to intelligence matters. Most nations outlaw espionage, so foreign intelligence activities have to be carried out through stealth and deception. Avoidance of the law and contempt for the truth can become habitual among intelligence officials, but they simply have no place in a democratic government's interactions with its own citizens. Yet throughout the history of domestic intelligence operations in the U.S., law enforcement officials have gone to the military intelligence toolbox in selecting their methods.

> **Though there are legal limits to the type of work military officials can do within these programs and the information they can share, there is little to no oversight conducted to ensure they follow the law.**

In 1976, the Church Committee called the tactics J. Edgar Hoover brought to bear against civil rights and peace activists in the United States "techniques of wartime" better suited for use against agents of hostile foreign nations like the Soviet Union. The Attorney General issued guidelines to ensure future FBI intelligence activities would focus on criminal activity. The Justice Department imposed similar regulations restricting state and local law enforcement criminal intelligence systems.

Restricting domestic intelligence collection to suspected criminal activity is essential to the concepts of limited government and individual liberty, whose foundation lies in what Supreme Court Justice Louis Brandeis called "the right to be left alone." It also reinforces the rule of law. Methods used in criminal intelligence gathering tend to get exposed in the prosecutions that follow their effective use. Defendants can then challenge their legality, while judges, juries and the public can weigh whether the government tactics are appropriate. Law enforcers can't be law breakers.

Unfortunately, the federal government has loosened or ignored law enforcement guidelines restricting intelligence gathering in the years since 9/11, removing or weakening the criminal predicates necessary to ensure a proper focus on illegal activity. The results were predictable—increased police spying on minorities and political dissidents and increased efforts to escape judicial and public oversight. Federal law enforcement agencies have adopted policies of "parallel construction" to mask the surveillance methods they use to gather evidence, misleading courts and depriving defendants of their right to challenge their constitutionality. Where evidence of improper FBI surveillance has leaked to the public, the Justice Department invoked "state secrets" to shut down litigation. And at the request of the State Police and FBI, the Virginia legislature exempted its intelligence fusion center from open government laws.

Trained by the military to spy on hostile foreign nations, Dahl cautioned that "you wouldn't want to hire me to conduct domestic surveillance." His statement should serve as a warning to those in Congress who authorized the NSA to play a major role in seizing Americans' electronic communications (and want to give it more authority over U.S. cyber security) and sat silent as the FBI has transitioned into a domestic intelligence agency.

It should also serve as a warning to federal, state and local law enforcement officials. As these agencies have increasingly claimed a role in intelligence collection, they've looked to the military and foreign intelligence agencies for tactics, expertise and personnel, without sufficiently recognizing the important distinctions between domestic and foreign intelligence.

The negative public reaction to recent militarized police tactics and equipment is an indication of the unease Americans will feel with militarized law enforcement intelligence efforts. Americans trust the NSA far less than their local police. But when the local police begin adopting intelligence methods used by the NSA and other foreign intelligence agencies, they will begin to lose that essential public support.

No one disputes that there are violent criminals, spies, and terrorists within our country and that our law enforcement officials need adequate intelligence tools to catch them. Requiring that police focus on illegal activity doesn't impair their mission; it puts these threats squarely in their cross-hairs. It is no surprise that Dahl's research on successfully prevented terrorist attacks show that traditional law enforcement techniques are far more effective than NSA mass surveillance programs:

Q: You also, for the book, compiled a database of successfully thwarted or prevented terrorist attacks. What did you learn from studying those incidents?

Dahl: I found really two major, major points. One is that the nature of the domestic terrorism threat in the United States today is actually more serious, more severe than many believe it is—especially when you consider that there are a number of plots that have been thwarted since 9/11 from domestic right-wing or other sorts of organizations. It's certainly not just international terrorist groups. It's certainly not just Muslim groups. That's the nature of the threat. But then the most important question I thought that we need to look at is how are these threats thwarted? How do we stop these things from happening? And here I found that for the most part, the tools and techniques that are used to stop these would-be terrorists are usually very similar, the same tools and techniques that law enforcement has been using for many years. It's tips from the public, it's undercover officers, it's the use of informants. It's not so much when we're talking domestic homeland security threats, it's not so much the national intelligence assets such as spies overseas or satellites or even signals intelligence efforts.

Q: And so over the course of the last year, there were some intelligence leaks, and many Americans were shocked about the scope of the domestic electronic surveillance that's going on. What did you find about the role of that type of electronic surveillance in stopping terrorist attacks?

Dahl: I think that what we're finding is that the domestic plots that have been foiled—I found over 100 domestic terrorism plots that have been prevented since 9/11—at least from what I can tell, and from what we've seen from a number of the official studies into the National Security Agency programs for instance. We aren't finding that it's that sort of program that stops domestic plots and homeland security plots. Those sorts of programs may certainly be effective overseas, we don't have the information on that, but domestically it's mostly this low level, much more of a law enforcement approach that seems to be effective.

As Dr. Dahl suggests, we need to have a "much better public discussion about intelligence."

Uncle Sam's Databases of Suspicion

By Hina Shamsi and Matthew Harwood
American Civil Liberties Union, November 6, 2014

It began with an unexpected rapping on the front door.

When Wiley Gill opened up, no one was there. Suddenly, two police officers appeared, their guns drawn, yelling, "Chico Police Department."

"I had tunnel vision," Gill said, "The only thing I could see was their guns."

After telling him to step outside with his hands in the air, the officers lowered their guns and explained. They had received a report—later determined to be unfounded—that a suspect in a domestic disturbance had fled into Gill's house. The police officers asked the then-26-year-old if one of them could do a sweep of the premises. Afraid and feeling he had no alternative, Gill agreed. One officer remained with him, while the other conducted the search. After that they took down Gill's identification information. Then they were gone—but not out of his life.

Instead, Gill became the subject of a "suspicious activity report," or SAR, which police officers fill out when they believe they're encountering a person or situation that "reasonably" might be connected in some way to terrorism. The one-page report, filed shortly after the May 2012 incident, offered no hint of terrorism. It did, however, suggest that the two officers had focused on Gill's religion, noting that his "full conversion to Islam as a young [white male] and pious demeanor is [sic] rare."

The report also indicated that the officer who entered the house had looked at Gill's computer screen and recalled something "similar to 'Games that fly under the radar'" on it. According to the SAR, this meant Gill "had potential access to flight simulators via the Internet." Gill suspects that he was probably looking at a website about video games. The SAR also noted earlier police encounters with Gill, in his mosque and on the street. It recorded his "full beard and traditional garb" and claimed that he avoided "eye contact."

In short, the Chico Police Department was secretly keeping tabs on Gill as a suspected terrorist. Yet nowhere in the SAR was there a scintilla of evidence that he was engaged in any kind of criminal activity whatsoever. Nevertheless, that report was uploaded to the Central California Intelligence Center, one of a network of Department of Homeland Security–approved domestic intelligence fusion centers. It was then disseminated through the federal government's domestic intelligence-sharing network as well as uploaded into an FBI database known as e-Guardian, after which the Bureau opened a file on Gill.

We do not know how many government agencies now associate Wiley Gill's good name with terrorism. We do know that the nation's domestic-intelligence network is massive, including at least 59 federal agencies, over 300 Defense Department units, and approximately 78 state-based fusion centers, as well as the multitude of law enforcement agencies they serve. We also know that local law enforcement agencies have themselves raised concerns about the system's lack of privacy protections.

And it wouldn't end there for Gill.

The Architecture of Mass Suspicion

The SAR database is part of an ever-expanding domestic surveillance system established after 9/11 to gather intelligence on potential terrorism threats. At an abstract level, such a system may seem sensible: far better to prevent terrorism before it happens than to investigate and prosecute after a tragedy. Based on that reasoning, the government exhorts Americans to "see something, say something"—the SAR program's slogan.

Indeed, just this week at a conference in New York City, FBI Director James Comey asked the public to report any suspicions they have to authorities. "When the hair on the back of your neck stands, listen to that instinct and just tell somebody," said Comey. And seeking to reassure those who do not want to get their fellow Americans in trouble based on instinct alone, the FBI director added, "We investigate in secret for a very good reason: we don't want to smear innocent people."

> **What we have here isn't just a failure to communicate genuine threat information, but the transformation of suspicion into pernicious ideological, racial, and religious profiling, often disproportionately targeting activists and American Muslims.**

There are any number of problems with this approach, starting with its premise. Predicting who exactly is a future threat before a person has done anything wrong is a perilous undertaking. That's especially the case if the public is encouraged to report suspicions of neighbors, colleagues, and community members based on a "hair-on-the-back-of-your-neck" threshold. Nor is it any comfort that the FBI promises to protect the innocent by investigating "suspicious" people in secret. The civil liberties and privacy implications are, in fact, truly hair-raising, particularly when the Bureau engages in abusive and discriminatory sting operations and other rights violations.

At a fundamental level, suspicious activity reporting, as well as the digital and physical infrastructure of networked computer servers and fusion centers built around it, depends on what the government defines as suspicious. As it happens, this turns out to include innocuous, First Amendment–protected behavior.

As a start, a little history: the Nationwide Suspicious Activity Reporting Initiative was established in 2008 as a way for federal agencies, law enforcement, and the public to report and share potential terrorism-related information. The federal government then developed a list of 16 behaviors that it considered "reasonably indicative of criminal activity associated with terrorism." Nine of those 16 behaviors, as the government acknowledges, could have nothing to do with criminal activity and are constitutionally protected, including snapping photographs, taking notes, and "observation through binoculars."

Under federal regulations, the government can only collect and maintain criminal intelligence information on an individual if there is a "reasonable suspicion" that he or she is "involved in criminal conduct or activity and the information is relevant to that criminal conduct or activity." The SAR program officially lowered that bar significantly, violating the federal government's own guidelines for maintaining a "criminal intelligence system."

There's good reason for, at a minimum, using a reasonable suspicion standard. Anything less and it's garbage in, garbage out, meaning counterterrorism "intelligence" databases become anything but intelligent.

When the Mundane Looks Suspicious

The SAR program provides striking evidence of this.

In 2013, the ACLU of Northern California obtained nearly 2,000 SARs from two state fusion centers, which collect, store, and analyze such reports, and then share those their intelligence analysts find worthwhile across what the federal government calls its Information Sharing Environment. This connects the fusion centers and other federal agencies into an information-sharing network, or directly with the FBI. Their contents proved revealing.

A number of reports were concerned with "ME"—Middle Eastern—males. One headline proclaimed, "Suspicious ME Males Buy Several Large Pallets of Water at REDACTED." Another read, "Suspicious Activities by a ME Male in Lodi, CA." And just what was so suspicious about this male? Read into the document and you discover that a sergeant at the Elk Grove Police Department had long been "concerned about a residence in his neighborhood occupied by a Middle Eastern male adult physician who is very unfriendly." And it's not just "Middle Eastern males" who provoke such suspicion. Get involved in a civil rights protest against the police and California law enforcement might report you, too. A June 2012 SAR was headlined "Demonstration Against Law Enforcement Use of Excessive Force" and reported that "a scheduled protest" by demonstrators "concerned about the use of excessive force by law enforcement officers" was about to occur.

What we have here isn't just a failure to communicate genuine threat information, but the transformation of suspicion into pernicious ideological, racial, and religious profiling, often disproportionately targeting activists and American Muslims. Again, that's not surprising. Throughout our history, in times of real or perceived fear of amorphously defined threats, government suspicion focuses on those who dissent or look or act differently.

Counterterrorism Accounting

Law enforcement officials, including the Los Angeles Police Department's top counterterrorism officer, have themselves exhibited skepticism about suspicious activity reporting (out of concern with the possibility of overloading the system).

In 2012, George Washington University's Homeland Security Policy Institute surveyed counterterrorism personnel working in fusion centers and in a report generally accepting of SARs noted that the program had "flooded fusion centers, law enforcement, and other security outfits with white noise," complicating "the intelligence process" and distorting "resource allocation and deployment decisions." In other words, it was wasting time and sending personnel off on wild goose chases.

A few months later, a scathing report from the Senate subcommittee on homeland security described similar intelligence problems in state-based fusion centers. It found that Department of Homeland Security (DHS) personnel assigned to the centers "forwarded 'intelligence' of uneven quality—oftentimes shoddy, rarely timely, sometimes endangering citizens' civil liberties and Privacy Act protections . . . and more often than not unrelated to terrorism."

Effectiveness doesn't exactly turn out to be one of the SAR program's strong suits, though the government has obscured this by citing the growing number of SARs that have triggered FBI investigations. However, according to a report from the Government Accountability Office (GAO), the FBI doesn't track whether SARs uploaded into the domestic intelligence network actually help thwart terrorism or lead to arrests or convictions.

You are, of course, what you measure—in this case, not much; and yet, despite its dubious record, the SAR program is alive and kicking. According to the GAO, the number of reports in the system exploded by 750%, from 3,256 in January 2010 to 27,855 in October 2012.

And being entered in such a system, as Wiley Gill found out, can prove just the beginning of your problems. Several months after his home was searched, his telephone rang. It was a Chico police officer who told Gill to shut down his Facebook page. Gill refused, responding that there was only one reason he thought the police wanted his account deleted: its references to Islam. The phone call ended ominously with the officer warning Gill that he was on a "watchlist."

The officer may have been referring to yet another burgeoning secret database that the federal government calls its "consolidated terrorism watchlist." Inclusion in this database—and on government blacklists that are generated from it—can bring more severe repercussions than unwarranted law enforcement attention. It can devastate lives.

Twenty-First-Century Blacklists

When small business owner Abe Mashal reached the ticket counter at Chicago's Midway Airport on April 20, 2010, an airline representative informed him that he was on the no-fly list and could not travel to Spokane, Washington, on business. Suddenly, the former Marine found himself surrounded by TSA agents and Chicago police. Later, FBI agents questioned him at the airport and at home about his Muslim faith and his family members.

The humiliation and intimidation didn't end there. A few months later, FBI agents returned to interview Mashal, focusing again on his faith and family. Only this time they had an offer to make: if he became an FBI informant, his name would be deleted from the no-fly list and he would be paid for his services. Such manipulative quid pro quos have been made to others.

Mashal refused. The meeting ended abruptly, and he wasn't able to fly for four years.

As of August 2013, there were approximately 47,000 people, including 800 U.S. citizens and legal permanent residents like Mashal, on that secretive no-fly list, all branded as "known or suspected terrorists." All were barred from flying to, from, or over the United States without ever being given a reason why. On 9/11, just 16 names had been on the predecessor "no transport" list. The resulting increase of 293,650 percent—perhaps more since 2013—isn't an accurate gauge of danger, especially given that names are added to the list based on vague, broad, and error-prone standards.

The harm of being stigmatized as a suspected terrorist and barred from flying is further compounded when innocent people try to get their names removed from the list.

In 2007, the Department of Homeland Security established the Traveler Redress Inquiry Program through which those who believe they are wrongly blacklisted can theoretically attempt to correct the government's error. But banned flyers quickly find themselves frustrated because they have to guess what evidence they must produce to refute the government's unrevealed basis for watchlisting them in the first place. Redress then becomes a grim bureaucratic wonderland. In response to queries, blacklisted people receive a letter from the DHS that gives no explanation for why they were not allowed to board a plane, no confirmation of whether they are actually on the no-fly list, and no certainty about whether they can fly in the future. In the end, the only recourse for such victims is to roll the dice by buying a ticket, going to the airport, and hoping for the best.

Being unable to board a plane can have devastating consequences, as Abe Mashal can attest. He lost business opportunities and the ability to mark life's milestones with friends and family.

> ... [L]aw enforcement personnel across the country are given access to a database of people who have secretly been labeled terrorism suspects with little or no actual evidence, based on virtually meaningless criteria.

There is hope, however. In August, four years after the ACLU filed a lawsuit on behalf of 13 people on the no-fly list, a judge ruled that the government's redress system is unconstitutional. In early October, the government notified Mashal and six others that they were no longer on the list. Six of the ACLU's clients remain unable to fly, but at least the government now has to disclose just why they have been put in that category, so that they can contest their blacklisting. Soon, others should have the same opportunity.

Suspicion First, Innocence Later . . . Maybe

The no-fly list is only the best known of the government's web of terrorism watchlists. Many more exist, derived from the same master list. Currently, there are more than one million names in the Terrorist Identities Datamart Environment, a database maintained by the National Counterterrorism Center. This classified source feeds the Terrorist Screening Database (TSDB), operated by the FBI's Terrorist Screening Center. The TSDB is an unclassified but still secret list known as the "master watchlist." containing what the government describes as "known or suspected terrorists," or KSTs.

According to documents recently leaked to the *Intercept,* as of August 2013 that master watchlist contained 680,000 people, including 5,000 U.S. citizens and legal permanent residents. The government can add people's names to it according to a shaky "reasonable suspicion" standard. There is, however, growing evidence that what's "reasonable" to the government may only remotely resemble what that word means in everyday usage. Information from a single source, even an uncorroborated Facebook post, can allow a government agent to watchlist an individual with virtually no outside scrutiny. Perhaps that's why 40% of those on the master watchlist have "no recognized terrorist group affiliation," according to the government's own records.

Nothing encapsulates the post-9/11, Alice-in-Wonderland inversion of American notions of due process more strikingly than this "blacklist first, innocence later . . . maybe" mindset.

The Terrorist Screening Database is then used to fill other lists. In the context of aviation, this means the no-fly list, as well as the selectee and expanded selectee lists. Transportation security agents subject travelers on the latter two lists to extra screenings, which can include prolonged and invasive interrogation and searches of laptops, phones, and other electronic devices. Around the border, there's the State Department's Consular Lookout and Support System, which it uses to flag people it thinks shouldn't get a visa, and the TECS System, which Customs and Border Protection uses to determine whether someone can enter the country.

Inside the United States, no watchlist may be as consequential as the one that goes by the moniker of the Known or Appropriately Suspected Terrorist File. The names on this blacklist are shared with more than 17,000 state, local, and tribal police departments nationwide through the FBI's National Crime Information Center (NCIC). Unlike any other information disseminated through the NCIC, the KST File reflects mere suspicion of involvement with criminal activity, so law enforcement personnel across the country are given access to a database of people who have secretly been labeled terrorism suspects with little or no actual evidence, based on virtually meaningless criteria.

This opens up the possibility of increased surveillance and tense encounters with the police, not to speak of outright harassment, for a large but undivulged number of people. When a police officer stops a person for a driving infraction, for instance, information about his or her KST status will pop up as soon a driver's license is checked. According to FBI documents, police officers who get a KST hit are warned to "approach with caution" and "ask probing questions."

When officers believe they're about to go face to face with a terrorist, bad things can happen. It's hardly a stretch of the imagination, particularly after a summer of police shootings of unarmed men, to suspect that an officer approaching a driver whom he believes to be a terrorist will be quicker to go for his gun. Meanwhile, the watchlisted person may never even know why his encounters with police have taken such a peculiar and menacing turn. According to the FBI's instructions, under no circumstances is a cop to tell a suspect that he or she is on a watchlist.

And once someone is on this watchlist, good luck getting off it. According to the government's watchlist rulebook, even a jury can't help you. "An individual who is acquitted or against whom charges are dismissed for a crime related to terrorism," it reads, "may nevertheless meet the reasonable standard and appropriately remain on, or be nominated to, the Terrorist Watchlist."

No matter the verdict, suspicion lasts forever.

Shadow ID

The SARs program and the consolidated terrorism watchlist are just two domestic government databases of suspicion. Many more exist. Taken together, they should be seen as a new form of national ID for a growing group of people accused of no crime, who may have done nothing wrong, but are nevertheless secretly labeled by the government as suspicious or worse. Innocent until proven guilty has been replaced with suspicious until determined otherwise.

Think of it as a new shadow system of national identification for a shadow government that is increasingly averse to operating in the light. It's an ID its "owners" don't carry around with them, yet it's imposed on them whenever they interact with government agents or agencies. It can alter their lives in disastrous ways, often without their knowledge.

And they could be you.

If this sounds dystopian, that's because it is.

ISIS Online: A Pretext for Cyber COINTELPRO?

By Eric Draitser
Global Research, February 27, 2015

In its ever expanding war against Syria, now under the broader pretext of "fighting ISIS," the US government has employed a variety of tactics. From arming terrorists whom it dishonestly labels "moderates," to encouraging Turkey and Jordan to host jihadi training centers, to the CIA working with the Muslim Brotherhood to funnel weapons and fighters into Syria, the US and its allies have demonstrated the multi-faceted approach they're taking to fighting ISIS, extremism, and the Syrian government.

The war, once believed to be relegated solely to Syria and Iraq, has now been broadened to a regional, and indeed, a global war with no geographical boundaries or time limits. And now, the Obama administration has announced that its war will also be waged in cyberspace. As the *NY Times* reported:

> At the heart of the plan is expanding a tiny State Department agency, the Center for Strategic Counterterrorism Communications, to harness all the existing attempts at countermessaging by much larger federal departments, including the Pentagon, Homeland Security and intelligence agencies. The center would also coordinate and amplify similar messaging by foreign allies and nongovernment agencies, as well as by prominent Muslim academics, community leaders and religious scholars who oppose the Islamic State.

While the use of social media and other online platforms is nothing new, the coordinated nature of the program demonstrates the broader capacity the US State Department and intelligence agencies are going to employ in penetrating cyberspace to, in theory, counter ISIS and other extremists groups' propaganda. But is this all they'll be doing? There is good reason to doubt the seemingly innocuous sounding mission of the Center for Strategic Counterterrorism Communications (CSCC).

Eric Draitser, Independent Political Analyst, Founder, StopImperialism.org. Reprinted with permission.

Countermessaging or Counterintelligence?

It is clear that the US government is actively going to expand its social media and cyberspace presence vis-à-vis online extremism. According to the expressly stated goal, the CSCC is intended to:

> . . . coordinate, orient, and inform government-wide foreign communications activities targeted against terrorism and violent extremism . . . CSCC is comprised of three inter-active components. The integrated analysis component leverages the Intelligence Community and other substantive experts to ensure CSCC communicators benefit from the best information and analysis available. The plans and operations component draws on this input to devise effective ways to counter the terrorist narrative. The Digital Outreach Team actively and openly engages in Arabic, Urdu, Punjabi, and Somali.

Although the description makes the program seem harmless enough, a close reading should raise very serious questions about just what exactly the CSCC will be involved in. The so called "integrated analysis" and "plans and operations" components provide an ambiguously worded description of collaboration with US intelligence agencies—CIA, DIA, DHS, and NSA undoubtedly among them. These agencies, aside from gathering intelligence and performing surveillance in every corner of the globe, are also involved in everything from espionage to "black ops" and "dirty ops" and other shadowy activities.

In effect, the CSCC will act in concert with these agencies both in the realm of information and activity. Does anyone seriously doubt, especially in light of the Snowden revelations about the all-encompassing nature of US surveillance and counterintelligence capabilities, that ultimately part of the CSCC's responsibilities will be to act as a de facto arm of US intelligence in the cyberspace realm, with specific attention to global hotspots such as Syria, Iran, Pakistan, Libya, etc.?

As for the so called "Digital Outreach Team," it could rightly be described as a cyberwar unit, one that will be able to operate both openly and anonymously in a variety of capacities online. And therein lay the danger. As Richard Stengel, Under Secretary of State for Public Diplomacy and Public Affairs, told the *Times,* "[CSCC] would use more than 350 State Department Twitter accounts, combining embassies, consulates, media hubs, bureaus and individuals, as well as similar accounts operated by the Pentagon, the Homeland Security Department and foreign allies." Now, of course, if this much has been admitted publicly, there is undoubtedly a much larger cyber capacity being developed covertly. The question then becomes: how will this capacity be used?

If history is any indicator, then activists, political radicals, dissidents, and many others will be targeted online. The revelations about COINTELPRO documented by the Church Committee demonstrated the way in which "intelligence gathering" becomes counterintelligence with all the attendant repression, subversion, entrapment, and more. As William C. Sullivan, former head of the FBI's intelligence operations was quoted in the Church Committee report:

> This is a rough, tough, dirty business, and dangerous. It was dangerous at times. No holds were barred . . . We have used [these techniques] against Soviet agents. They have used [them] against us . . . [The same methods were] brought home against any organization against which we were targeted. We did not differentiate. This is a rough, tough business.

Sullivan quite bluntly explained how the line between foreign and domestic counterintelligence became completely blurred as the repression of political radicals became equated with fighting the Cold War. Of course, anyone seriously examining today's world cannot help but draw parallels between the aggressive rhetoric about the Soviet threat during the Cold War and that around the "terrorist threat" of "radical Islam" today. It would be folly to think that, in light of the exponentially more powerful and all-encompassing surveillance architecture (to say nothing of the draconian laws such as the PATRIOT Act, National Defense Authorization Act, etc.), the government would not employ similar, and perhaps more severe and repressive, tactics today against any individuals and groups challenging dominant narratives, organizing antiwar/anti-imperialist activities, building economic and political alternatives, and much more.

It's Happened Before; It'll Happen Again

It should come as no surprise that there is a voluminous documented record of online information manipulation and propaganda designed to achieve political ends. Recent examples specific to the war on Syria are endlessly instructive about some of the tactics one should be prepared for.

A recent example of the sort of social media disinformation that has been (and will continue to be) employed in the war on Syria/ISIS came in December 2014 when a prominent "ISIS twitter propagandist" known as Shami Witness (@ShamiWitness) was exposed as a man named "Mehdi," described as "an advertising executive" based in Bangalore, India. @ShamiWitness had been cited as an authoritative source—a veritable "wealth of information"—about ISIS and Syria by corporate media outfits, as well as ostensibly "reliable and independent" bloggers such as the ubiquitous Eliot Higgins (aka Brown Moses) who cited Shami repeatedly. Conveniently enough, once exposed, Mehdi's identity has been withheld from investigators, and he has since disappeared from public view. While it is impossible to say for certain exactly who Mehdi is, the significant point here is that this is a prime example of how social media is used to manipulate and frame false narratives, and to bolster threats and propaganda that serves particular interests.

> **The point is not to allege some grand conspiracy, but rather to illustrate the documented history of manipulation and fabrication of threats – both real and imagined – for the purposes of justifying the military-industrial-intelligence-surveillance complex**

In early 2011, as the war on Syria was just beginning, and many in the West especially were still harboring the delusion of an "Arab Spring uprising," a blogger then known only as the "Gay Girl in Damascus" rose to prominence as a key source of information and analysis about the situation in Syria. Corporate news outlets such as *The Guardian* lauded her as "an unlikely hero of revolt" who "is capturing the imagination of the Syrian opposition with a blog that has shot to prominence as the protest movement struggles in the face of a brutal government crackdown." However, by June of 2011, the "brutally honest Gay Girl" was exposed as a hoax, a complete fabrication concocted by one Tom MacMaster. Naturally, the same outlets that had been touting the "Gay Girl" as a legitimate source of information on Syria immediately backtracked and disavowed the blog. However, the one-sided narrative of brutal and criminal repression of peace-loving activists in Syria stuck. While the source was discredited, the narrative remained entrenched.

There are many other examples specific to the war in Syria, as was the case in Libya where dozens of Twitter accounts purportedly from anti-Gaddafi Libyans mysteriously emerged in the lead-up to the war that toppled the Libyan government, providing much of the "intelligence" relayed on western media including CNN, NBC, and all the rest. It was at precisely that same moment (February 2011) that PC World ran a story headlined "Army of Fake Social Media Friends to Promote Propaganda," which noted that:

> . . . the U.S. government contracted HBGary Federal for the development of software which could create multiple fake social media profiles to manipulate and sway public opinion on controversial issues by promoting propaganda. It could also be used as surveillance to find public opinions with points of view the powers-that-be didn't like. It could then potentially have their "fake" people run smear campaigns against those "real" people.

Of course, if the story had already been broken by that point, one could rest assured that such programs were already long since being employed by US and other intelligence agencies for the purposes of achieving precisely what they achieved in Libya: the dissemination of disinformation for the purposes of constructing a false narrative to sway public opinion to support Washington's agenda.

So, we know that US intelligence has the ability to create an endless supply of Facebook, Twitter, and other social media accounts. In light of this information, it is not terribly difficult to see the danger of allowing a centralized, intergovernmental "counterterrorism center" from engaging in an online spook war with the alleged threat of ISIS online. It is entirely plausible that this is yet another manufactured pretext for still further penetration of social media by US intelligence for the purposes of infiltrating and subverting online activists, independent journalists, and others.

Indeed, such activities would fit perfectly into the broader strategic imperative infamously articulated by Obama confidant, friend, and former head of the Office of Information and Regulatory Affairs, Cass Sunstein. As Glenn Greenwald wrote in 2010:

[Sunstein] is responsible for "overseeing policies relating to privacy, information quality, and statistical programs." In 2008, while at Harvard Law School, Sunstein co-wrote a truly pernicious paper proposing that the U.S. Government employ teams of covert agents and pseudo-"independent" advocates to "cognitively infiltrate" online groups and websites . . . Sunstein advocates that the Government's stealth infiltration should be accomplished by sending covert agents into "chat rooms, online social networks, or even real-space groups." He also proposes that the Government make secret payments to so-called "independent" credible voices to bolster the Government's messaging.

This sort of "cognitive infiltration" is undoubtedly happening in myriad ways that still remain largely unknown. What can be said for certain though is that US intelligence agencies have both the tools and strategic vision to manufacture online threats such as the meme of "ISIS social media recruiting" in order to bolster their failing propaganda war and to justify yet another unpopular war to the American people.

This wouldn't be the first time that intelligence and law enforcement agencies have manufactured threats and/or entrapped alleged "terrorists" for the purposes of justifying the repressive apparatus of the police state, not to mention their own jobs.

State Sponsored Terror at Home

Just looking at the recent historical record, one begins to see an unmistakable pattern of terror plots concocted by the FBI and other agencies which they then portray themselves as having thwarted. In September 2011, the FBI allegedly foiled an "aerial bombing plot and attempts to deliver bomb-making materials for use against US troops in Iraq." However, as the AFP article casually noted:

During the alleged plot, undercover FBI agents posed as accomplices who supplied Ferdaus with one remote-controlled plane, C4 explosives, and small arms that he allegedly envisioned using in a simultaneous ground assault in Washington. However, "the public was never in danger from the explosive devices, which were controlled by undercover FBI employees," the FBI said. Ferdaus was arrested in Framingham, near Boston, immediately after putting the newly delivered weapons into a storage container, the FBI said.

So, this alleged "terrorist" had neither the means nor the opportunity to carry out any plot at all, until the FBI became involved, supplying him with everything he needed, including actual explosives. They then high-fived each other for a job well done, foiling this dastardly plot. It would be comical if it weren't so utterly repugnant.

Similarly, in 2010 the FBI claimed to have stopped a terrorist operation in Oregon—the insidious "Christmas Tree Bomber"—who likewise was supplied with the explosives, not to mention training, by the FBI themselves. In 2012, the FBI claimed to have thwarted a suicide bomb attack on the US Capitol. Conveniently buried in the story, however, is the fact that the explosives and technical expertise were all provided by the bureau's undercover operatives.

There are literally a dozen or more other incidents that one could point to where US government agencies have been intimately involved in planning, and then "foiling," terrorist operations. The point is not to allege some grand conspiracy, but rather to illustrate the documented history of manipulation and fabrication of threats—both real and imagined—for the purposes of justifying the military-indus-trial-intelligence-surveillance complex.

If such agencies have proven countless times that they have the wherewithal and determination to carry out such operations, why should we believe that today is any different?

It is clear that the government has hyped threats against the US for a variety of reasons. So too is this story of ISIS and social media being hyped for a specific agenda—to legitimize the creation of yet another shadowy COINTELPRO-style interagency unit that will further entrench US intelligence in cyberspace, especially in social media.

How will you know if that Instagram picture of an ISIS member holding a cute kitten is authentic, or is simply a government-controlled troll, a fake identity created by some guy in a room in Virgina? How will you know if those young British-Saudis holding jars of Nutella in front of an ISIS flag are who they are alleged to be? How will you know if any of what you're seeing on Twitter, Facebook, or anywhere else is real at all?

You won't know for sure. And that is precisely the point.

The FBI Keeps Arresting Hapless Jihadi Fanboys and Calling Them ISIS Recruits

By John Knefel
The New Republic, March 24, 2015

On August 8, 2013, Jordan Nicole Furr met with someone she almost certainly thought was a friend, most likely somewhere near Austin, Texas. The subject at hand was her husband, Michael Wolfe, who also went by the name Faruq. "[H]e just wants to hop into Syria. He's just ready to die for his deen," Furr said—using an Arabic word for faith or religion—according to a criminal complaint filed by the FBI. "He's ready to die for someone. For something."

Unwittingly, Furr was speaking with an undercover FBI agent, one of two involved in a sting operation against her and her husband. During the next ten months, Wolfe and Furr repeatedly talked to the two agents in person and over the phone, concocting a plan to travel to Syria and fight jihad. By July 2014, Michael Wolfe would be arrested for material support of terrorism: specifically, attempting to go to Syria to join the Islamic State (ISIS).

James Clapper, the director of national intelligence, recently said that around 180 people have attempted or succeeded in traveling from the United States to Syria, though not all have joined militant groups. Wolfe is among the failed attempts: at least 26 Muslims who have been arrested in the United States for trying to travel abroad to join a militant group in recent years, according a report from the Triangle Center on Terrorism and Homeland Security. Most of them were allegedly attempting to get to Syria to join ISIS; others, to join Al Qaeda affiliates in Syria or Yemen.

U.S. officials regularly tout the dangers of domestic terrorists and lone wolves. "Homegrown violent extremists continue to pose the most likely threat to the homeland," Clapper told a Senate committee in February. FBI director James Comey echoed that line when addressing another congressional committee: "The threat from homegrown violent extremists is of particular concern." Media tend to repeat those claims on face value. An ABC report on Wolfe's paraphrases unnamed law enforcement officials who posit that "young men and women could possibly return home [from Syria], freshly trained in deadly operations, and unleash havoc on the homeland."

Homegrown. Homeland. The FBI wants you to remember where it's fighting this battle. The Bureau has evolved from an agency focused on law enforcement to one focused on counterterrorism, which now commands $3.3 billion annually, or

40 percent of the total operating budget, according to a 2014 report from Human Rights Watch. Busts like Wolfe's help the Bureau justify the billions spent on preventing terrorist attacks.

Yet a close examination of Wolfe's case, as well as numerous similar cases, call into question the threat posed by homegrown extremists. The recent cases, taken as a whole, describe an intelligence agency indulging in borderline entrapment. The FBI is conflating jihadi fanboys on social media with serious threats to national security; to make cases, the FBI relies heavily on paid informants acting in their own self-interest. The feds are flexing to show they can prevent terror attacks—a mission only made more difficult when the Bureau overreaches, sowing suspicion in communities it is tasked with protecting.

Prior to his departure, Wolfe waffled about his decision to make the trip, and at times in the complaint he comes across as unsure of his plan. "It's not that I don't want to go, it's just that I need to figure out the best situation," he tells one of the undercover agents. Later, the complaint states: "Wolfe indicated he had struggled with whether to stay or go." Getting the money together for the tickets was a major obstacle for him as well. The second coming of Ramzi Yousef, he wasn't. He is, however, facing up to 15 years in prison after pleading guilty to attempting to join ISIS.

Since 9/11 the FBI has repeatedly used informants to manufacture plots for targets who would never have been capable of carrying them out on their own. "Of 508 defendants prosecuted in federal terrorism-related cases in the decade after 9/11, 243 were involved with an FBI informant, while 158 were the targets of sting operations," writes Trevor Aaronson, a journalist who has studied the FBI's use of informants. As the enemy du jour has shifted from Al Qaeda to ISIS, the practice still appears to be common in FBI terrorism arrests.

In at least a dozen recent terrorism busts, confidential informants or undercover FBI agents were intimately involved in crafting travel plans or violent plots that the suspects would later be arrested for. In many cases, the suspect's illegal conduct took place only after an informant or undercover agent appeared. An analysis of court documents in more than a dozen cases shows the arrest of three bumbling Brooklyn would-be jihadis in February is only the most recent example of the FBI overhyping a threat that was largely of its own making. And though the practice of using informants and undercover officers to ensnare unsuspecting Muslims is widely criticized by civil liberties groups, the FBI hasn't faced any official sanctions for its reliance on the practice.

"What the FBI can't do is treat terrorism cases as fundamentally different [from other cases]—to use their own agents and informants to manufacture reasonable suspicion for a crime," says Naureen Shah, director of the security and human rights program at Amnesty International USA. "They've got a hunch, or a suspicion, and so they send in an informant in some of these cases to produce the evidence that in another case would be the evidence they were waiting for."

Social media seems to be the FBI's preferred way into the latest batch of would-be jihadis. Many of the criminal complaints list Facebook or Twitter entries that tip off the Bureau and evince a criminal disposition, thus hampering any future entrapment defense. The FBI's heavy scrutiny of social media tracks with a broader phenomenon of law enforcement trolling Facebook and Twitter for perceived threats that range from anti-gang initiatives to surreptitiously befriending activists for illegally questionable surveillance. ISIS's savvy on social media only increases the FBI's interest in monitoring those platforms. The group "has proven dangerously competent at employing such tools for its nefarious strategy," FBI Director James Comey said at the congressional hearing.

But investigating online loudmouths can result in cases with more smoke than fire. Take the case of Mufid Elfgeeh. Elfgeeh was arrested in September 2014 for allegedly sending money to a Yemeni man to help him travel to Syria, for attempting to facilitate travel of two New York men—both FBI informants—to fight alongside ISIS, and plotting to kill U.S. veterans. But he only took those actions after one of the two FBI informants had been working him for about a year.

In early 2013, that informant—who has been working with the Bureau since 2000—told the FBI about Elfgeeh's inflammatory Twitter posts and was ultimately paid more than $21,000 for his work on the case. Additionally the FBI "made an informal request to Immigration and Customs Enforcement (ICE) for visitor visas for five of CS-1's family members." Just how hard the informant pressed Elfgeeh in evolution from Twitter warrior to low-level ISIS recruiter isn't clear, but he had strong incentives to make sure Elfgeeh ended up in handcuffs.

A second FBI informant in the case was paid $7,000, and repeatedly pressed Elfgeeh to provide proof that killing U.S. soldiers returning from war overseas was religiously permissible. Neither informant knew the other was working with the FBI.

Chris Cornell, the Ohio man who made headlines for his alleged plot to bomb the U.S. Capitol, was similarly pulled into the FBI's orbit by an informant "who began cooperating with the FBI in order to obtain favorable treatment with respect to his criminal exposure on an unrelated case," according to the criminal complaint. The FBI paid an informant to ensnare Nicholas Teausant after he posted on Instagram and other social media that (all sic) he "despise[d] america and want its down fall." Teausant repeatedly told the informant that, although he wanted to fight in Syria, he had no idea how to get there. When the informant asked Teausant what group he wanted to join, Teausant responded, "I like ISIS," though he forgot what the name stood for. "Islamic state of um crap . . . I forget. Islamic State of Al Sham," he said, according to the criminal complaint.

Another recent arrestee, Basit Javed Sheikh, has said in court that he believed he was traveling to Syria to marry a nurse with Jabat Al Nusra, who was in fact an FBI informant. In subsequent pre-trial hearings, Sheikh was found to be incompetent to stand trial and ordered hospitalized for 120 days to "restore his competency or to determine whether there is a substantial probability that his competency will be restored in the foreseeable future."

Some of the less sophisticated arrestees elicit more pity than fear. Shannon Conley, a Denver teenager recently sentenced to four years in prison after pleading guilty to material support of ISIS, repeatedly told openly identified FBI agents that she was planning to break the law and join ISIS. Her cluelessness mirrors the three Brooklyn men who openly opined about killing President Barack Obama to identified FBI agents.

Others are teenagers, for whom decades in prison may not be humane or wise. Thomas Durkin, a lawyer for Mohammed Hamza Khan, a young man from Bolingbrook, Illinois, attempted to cast his client's behavior not as high treason, but merely a teenager's confusion about his religious obligations. In a pretrial hearing, he praised Denmark's "deprogramming" practice as more progressive than anything in the United States: "I would submit that that's the approach that needs to be taken here."

> An analysis of court documents in more than a dozen cases shows the arrest of three bumbling Brooklyn would-be jihadis in February is only the most recent example of the FBI overhyping a threat that was largely of its own making.

Denmark's approach to extremist disengagement and reintegration into society contrasts with the draconian approach of many Western European countries. "What's easy is to pass tough new laws," Allan Aarslev, a Danish law enforcement official, told the *Guardian*. "Harder is to go through a real process with individuals: a panel of experts, counseling, healthcare, assistance getting back into education, with employment, maybe accommodation. With returning to everyday life and society. We don't do this out of political conviction; we do it because we think it works."

Shah, of Amnesty International, agrees that's the proper approach. "If the U.S. government believes that certain youth in communities are at risk of this behavior, and they want to direct programs at what they believe is a threat, based on scientific evidence, then they ought not to have the FBI taking the lead," she said. "It should be social services–oriented agencies."

Durkin, the defense attorney, also highlighted the discrepancy in treatment between Conley, the Denver teen who the FBI tried to talk out of traveling to Syria, and his client. "But I'd like to know how it is that Shannon Conley gets reported to her parents, and Hamzah Khan gets arrested. I'd like them to justify that," he said in a pre-trial hearing. "And I don't think there is any justification for it other than the obvious."

Beyond questionable investigative tactics, the drumbeat over homegrown extremists obscures, rather than clarifies, the threat they pose. The likelihood of Al Qaeda or ISIS launching a massive attack inside the United States is "infinitesimal," according to the *Washington Post*, yet a recent poll found 86 percent of Americans now see ISIS as a threat to U.S. security.

That perception, however, is based largely on a myth. The Triangle Center's report states that publicly available information does "not indicate widespread recruitment of Muslim-Americans by transnational terrorist organizations to engage in attacks in the United States, or sophisticated planning by the handful of individuals who have self-radicalized."

Despite the hype, there's a good chance that the latest would-be jihadi is more a hapless wannabe than violent terrorist. "As public debate continues over terrorism, it is worth keeping these threats in perspective," the report concludes. "Terrorists aim to instill fear disproportionate to their actual capabilities to generate violence, and to provoke social and policy overreactions that they can use in their recruitment efforts." As the FBI gins up its own disproportionate reactions to these alleged threats, it should heed the warning.

What Guilty Verdict in Silk Road Trial Might Mean for Internet Freedom

By Cristina Maza
Christian Science Monitor, February 5, 2015

On Wednesday, a jury decided that Ross Ulbricht is the "Dread Pirate Roberts," the pseudonym used by the architect of the Silk Road underground drug bazaar.

Before it was shut down by the federal government in 2013, Silk Road was considered the largest marketplace for finding illegal drugs online. The site was also used to sell fake IDs and other illegal goods using bitcoin, an online currency that operates with no central authority or banks. The prosecution said that Mr. Ulbricht was a "kingpin" who received a portion of every transaction that occurred on the site.

Ulbricht will be sentenced in May and faces a minimum of 20 years in prison. He could also be handed a life sentence. The defense has attempted to paint Ulbricht as a naïve kid who was framed after his Frankenstein monster grew out of control. It is expected to appeal the decision.

The case is broadly important, experts say, because it could have implications for Internet freedom. It explores not only the legal question of whether a website operator can be held accountable for how his site is used by others but also how the government ferrets out illegal Internet activity. Along the way, the proceedings have provided an unvarnished look at the Internet's dark side, perhaps for the first time.

"What's most interesting about this case is that it is the first case in its enormity involving the Dark Net and it's going to be a wakeup for anyone using the Dark Net thinking they have anonymity. You cannot remain anonymous on the Internet," Darren Hayes, assistant professor and director of cyber security at Pace University, told CNBC.

Ulbricht was arrested after the Federal Bureau of Investigation discovered a server in Iceland that linked him to Silk Road. But how the FBI discovered the server has been a point of contention. Ulbricht's defenders claim that the government used illegal methods to locate Silk Road, violating his constitutional right to privacy, though a judge denied that line of defense.

The anonymity protections provided by the cryptographic software Tor mean that law enforcement would need to obtain a search warrant to discover the location of Silk Road's servers, Ulbricht's defenders say. The lack of a warrant taints the evidence found in the subsequent investigation, the defense stated in a memo.

The FBI stated that it located the server due to a misconfiguration of Silk Road's CAPTCHA system—the string of letters and numbers that helps protect a site from spam. This error inadvertently revealed the server's IP address, the FBI said.

But experts claim that it would be impossible to use the CAPTCHA to find the server. Some suggest that the National Security Agency might have had a hand in locating the server.

"My guess is that the NSA provided the FBI with this information. We know that the NSA provides surveillance data to the FBI and the DEA, under the condition that they lie about where it came from in court," wrote Bruce Schneier, Chief Technology Officer of Co3 Systems and a fellow at Harvard's Berkman Center, on his blog.

Meanwhile, the idea of charging a website's operator with wrongdoing when a user conducts illegal activity raises interesting questions about Internet freedom, says Hanni Fakhoury, an attorney at the Electronic Frontier Foundation.

"The main issue, the main Internet freedom issue is at what point are website operators accountable for what happens on their site? In Silk Road, it's an easy case because they were catering to illegal activity. But what is interesting is that you start with easy cases and then you start to go towards some of the borderline cases," he said to CNBC.

In Ulbricht's case, the jury decided that, as the mastermind behind a site catering to the sale of nefarious content, he should be held accountable. The evidence against Ulbricht, most of which was located on his laptop, was overwhelming and included digital chat records, traced bitcoin transactions, and a diary he kept detailing the tribulations he faced while running the site.

The jury deliberated for under four hours before it found Ulbricht guilty on seven counts, including money laundering, drug trafficking, and computer hacking, among others.

5
Racial, Ethnic, and Political Profiling

Men participate in Friday prayer at the Omar Mosque on February 24, 2012, in Paterson, New Jersey. The New York Police Department (NYPD) came under criticism following revelations that officers crossed into New Jersey to conduct surveillance on Newark and area Muslims, including students at Rutgers University. The NYPD contended that they informed their counterparts in New Jersey and that the surveillance was part of their post-9/11 security measures. Officials in New Jersey, including the mayor Cory Booker, claimed they were not informed.

Who to Watch?: Racial, Ethnic, and Political Profiling in Surveillance

Profiling is the use of a person's demographic characteristics, such as age, race, ethnicity, religious affiliation, economic or employment status, or political views, to determine whether that person might be involved in criminal activity. Physical and psychological characteristics can be an important component in locating criminals, and both the police and federal agencies, like the FBI, use profiling to determine the most likely characteristics of individuals associated with certain crimes. Profiling becomes controversial when police or other government agencies stop, search, detain, or target an individual solely on the basis of demographic characteristics.

In the wake of 9/11, Muslims living around the world were subjected to increased scrutiny from police and security agencies. Supporters of profiling argue that mass surveillance is ineffective unless strategies are used to narrow the population under observation. Given the links between terrorism and fundamental Islamic groups, government agencies have justified disproportionately watching Islamic and Muslim communities. Critics point out that the U.S. constitution guarantees freedom from persecution due to race, ethnicity, creed, or political affiliation and argue that profiling in surveillance violates the constitutional guarantees. Muslims have been subjected to higher scrutiny since 9/11, but in the United States, African Americans and Hispanic/Latino Americans are routinely targeted by police using controversial profiling methods.

Profiling in America

The Fourteenth Amendment of the U.S. Constitution, ratified in 1868, guarantees equal protection under the law, regardless of creed, race, religion, or gender. The so-called equal protection amendment was a response to state laws that were established or applied in such a way as to facilitate racial persecution. For instance, the "black codes" established in several southern states after the Civil War resulted in legal persecution of African Americans for crimes such as "vagrancy," while African Americans, having recently been freed from slavery, were often poor and unemployed. The Fourteenth Amendment made it illegal for police or other agencies to detain, arrest, or otherwise persecute an individual solely on the basis of race, national background, political affiliation, or religion.

After World War II, political and social profiling became rampant in the United States as intelligence and security agencies attempted to combat the perceived threat of communism. This period—known as the Red Scare or McCarthyism, after its proponent Senator Joseph McCarthy—resulted in widespread persecution of individuals belonging to leftist organizations or organizations with links, even tenuous ones, to communism, the Soviet Union, or other Communist nations. The House Committee on Un-American Activities, a controversial panel that became famous for its investigations of the Hollywood film industry, conducted a highly unethical series of hearings in the 1960s that resulted in the imprisonment of hundreds of Americans on the basis of links to subversive or potentially Communist organizations or individuals. Many of the arrests and detainments conducted as part of communism investigations were later seen by legal analysts as clear violations of constitutional rights and were possible only because of the widespread panic over the danger of communism to national security.

While political subversives were persecuted during the Red Scare, police and security agencies also profiled and targeted African Americans and their supporters during the civil rights movement from the 1950s to the 1960s. Under the auspices of protecting the populace from the imminent threat of civil unrest, the FBI and CIA conducted unwarranted surveillance operations on civil rights and black empowerment organizations during this period. In hundreds of documented cases, African Americans were singled out for scrutiny solely on the basis of their race, and this tendency on behalf of the police and government agencies became a cornerstone of civil rights complaints about the treatment of minorities in America.

After 9/11, state and federal agencies began targeting Middle Eastern Americans and Americans with links to Islamic organizations. Leaked government documents from the NSA and CIA, revealed to the public in 2013 and 2014 by investigative journalists, revealed intentional religious and ethnic profiling used by the NSA and CIA to determine which populations to target in surveillance programs. Critics argue that these actions are a violation of the Fourteenth Amendment protections, while supporters argue that given the Islamic links to known terrorist organizations, it is acceptable for security agencies to concentrate surveillance efforts on Muslims and people with links to Islam or Islamic nations.

Racial Profiling Today

Police profiling of African Americans never abated, despite the broader political successes and gains of the civil rights movement. Department of Justice (DOJ) statistics from 2013 indicate that of 1,516,879 prisoners sentenced to state or federal prison, 454,100 were white and 526,000 were African American. Across the United States, African Americans are arrested at far higher rates than white Americans. For instance, in a 2014 article in *USA Today*, reporters said that in the suburb of Dearborn, Michigan, African Americans make up 4 percent of the population but account for more than half of the arrests made in the suburb each year.

Some analysts have argued that racial profiling can be justified by legitimate correlations between race and crime. For instance, in the book *Please Stop Helping Us*, conservative African American political analyst Jason L. Riley argues that African Americans commit more crimes than white Americans and therefore are justifiably targeted by law enforcement. Statistics from the DOJ and other sources do not support Riley's argument and indicate that, even in cases where white Americans commit a higher percentage of crimes, African Americans are more likely to be arrested and/or convicted. For instance, African Americans make up an estimated 12 percent of the population that use or sell drugs, and yet 59 percent of prisoners convicted of drug charges and 38 percent of those arrested are African American. The disproportionate number of African Americans arrested and convicted for drug offenses has been linked to police policies involving targeting low-income African American communities for drug sting investigations. In this case, profiling of potential offenders leads police toward the population where, statistically, fewer drug crimes are being committed and skews statistics to appear as if African Americans are more likely to use or sell drugs.

The unjust association between African Americans and drug crimes provides an example of how profiling facilitates an "unconscious bias" toward certain groups or races that then encourages further profiling. Media outlets follow and report on police activities and, therefore, if police target and arrest individuals based on racial or other demographic profiling, though offenders may be legitimately captured, the targeting of a specific group creates a wider bias within society, equating that group with illegal activity.

In the United States, media coverage, police behavior, and persistent racial attitudes have contributed to a demonstrable bias against young African American men and women. DOJ studies have shown that young African Americans are disproportionately targeted by police, sentenced to imprisonment by courts, and identified as "potential defenders" by the public. In many cases, statistics do not support this bias. For instance, the Center for Disease Control and Prevention's (CDC) 2013 Youth Risk Survey revealed that 10.7 percent of white students admitted having carried a gun, compared to 9.8 percent of black male students. However, young African Americans are more than twice as likely to be arrested for carrying weapons than white male students.

A 2014 report from The Sentencing Project investigated the issue of bias in public opinion regarding connections between crime and race. In general, survey participants overestimated African American and Hispanic/Latino involvement in crime by 20 to 30 percent. Similarly, the University of Chicago's General Social Survey (GSS) has routinely shown that the American population as a whole views African Americans and Hispanic/Latino Americans as more "prone to violence" than white Americans.

Effectiveness of Profiling

The Immigration and Customs Enforcement (ICE) department is responsible, in the United States, for preventing drug shipments from entering the United States across borders or through airports. A study of the organization between 1998 and 2000 indicated that racial profiling was often used to select individuals who would be stopped, questioned, or searched in airports or at border stations. Specifically, the study found that while African Americans and Hispanics comprised less than 30 percent of the traveling population, 43 percent of all individuals detained or searched were African American or Hispanic. In 2000, ICE adopted a series of reforms, including the principle that searches must be based on behavioral indicators, that supervisors needed to be present during all searches, and that searches should concentrate on travelers coming from nations where drugs were known to originate. As a result, ICE recorded a 75 percent reduction in searches but an 18 percent increase in successful drug seizures.

The ICE reforms indicate that behavioral profiling and limited, targeted surveillance measures can, in some cases, be more effective than utilizing broader racial, ethnic, or social profiling. However, the 2000 ICE reforms came before 9/11, which inspired major changes in immigration policies. After 9/11, the U.S. government openly accepted "national" profiling, subjecting individuals from nations like Afghanistan, Yemen, Saudi Arabia, and Pakistan to targeted screening before individuals from those nations could enter or leave the United States.

Critics argued that national profiling encourages ethnic and racial profiling and is also ineffective in combating terrorism. For instance, in a 2010 *New York Times* article, former FBI Agent Michael German argued that profiling is a "shortcut based on bias rather than evidence" and that there was no reliable way to profile a terrorist. Domestic terrorists like the "shoe bomber" Richard Reid and London subway bomber Germaine Lindsay violate profiles that have been put into place to prevent terrorism and highlight the fact that terrorism often emerges from within a population and can involve individuals of any race or ethnic background.

Profiling in the Internet Age

The mass surveillance of digital communications conducted by the NSA and CIA after 9/11 was guided by racial, ethnic, and religious profiling. For instance, documents revealed in 2014 indicated that the NSA and CIA were targeting and monitoring several high-profile Muslim-Americans working as lawyers, academics, political candidates, and civil rights leaders, none of whom had any demonstrable connection to radical Islamic organizations. An FBI memo revealed in the report used the name "Mohammed Raghead," as the code for the agency exercise.

In the modern era of surveillance, there is a disconnection between those conducting surveillance and their targets. Given the task of collecting and analyzing thousands of digital communications, there is an increased danger that police and intelligence agencies will rely on bias and broad categorical assumptions, rather than on clear evidence linking specific individuals and/or groups to crime or terrorism. In many cases, specific behavioral profiling is a useful and necessary tool, but the use of such tools must be handled carefully, ensuring that police and other agencies can justify each decision with evidence.

Micah L. Issitt

Racial Profiling Reported in NSA, FBI Surveillance

By Tom Risen
U.S. News & World Report, July 9, 2014

The National Security Agency and the FBI have reportedly been overzealous trying to prevent terrorist attacks to the point that anti-Islamic racism in those agencies led to the surveillance of prominent Muslim-Americans, revealing a culture of racial profiling and broad latitude for spying on U.S. citizens.

An NSA document leaked by former agency contractor Edward Snowden to reporter Glenn Greenwald shows 202 Americans targeted among the approximately 7,485 email addresses monitored between 2002 and 2008, Greenwald's news service *The Intercept* reports.

To monitor Americans, government agencies must first make the case to the Foreign Intelligence Surveillance Court that there is probable cause that the targets are terrorist agents, foreign spies or "are or may be" abetting sabotage, espionage or terrorism. Despite this filter *The Intercept* identified five Muslim-Americans with a high public profile including civil rights leaders, academics, lawyers and a political candidate.

Racial profiling of Muslims by security officers has been a controversy since the terrorist attacks of 2001 spiked fears about al-Qaida trainees preparing more attacks. The New York Police Department has disbanded its unit that mapped New York's Muslim communities and that designated surveillance of mosques as "terrorism enterprise investigations" after pressure from the Justice Department about aggressive monitoring by police.

A 2005 FBI memo about surveillance procedures featured in *The Intercept* story uses a fake name "Mohammed Raghead" for the agency staff exercise. This latest report about email surveillance of successful Muslim-Americans is akin to "McCarthyism" that fed paranoia about communist spies during the Cold War, says Reza Aslan, a professor at the University of California, Riverside.

"The notion that these five upstanding American citizens, all of them prominent public individuals, represent a threat to the U.S. for no other reason than their religion is an embarrassment to the FBI and an affront to the Constitution," Aslan says.

There is a risk of radicalization among citizens Americans, evidenced by some who have gone to fight jihads in Syria and Somalia, but mass shootings carried out by U.S. citizens of various racial backgrounds occurs much more often, says Vanda

> **"The notion that these five upstanding American citizens, all of them prominent public individuals, represent a threat to the U.S. for no other reason than their religion is an embarrassment to the FBI and an affront to the constitution,"** [Reza] Aslan says.

Felbab-Brown, a senior fellow on foreign policy at the Brookings Institution. Since 1982, there have been at least 70 mass shootings across the U.S. "We have seen very little domestic terrorism in the U.S.," Felbab-Brown says.

This lack of terrorism is due in part to the willingness of the Islamic community to cooperate with law enforcement to identify possible radical threats, out of gratitude that the U.S. is a stable, secure country compared with the Middle East, she says.

"That could go sour if law enforcement becomes too aggressive, too extreme," she says.

The FBI's ability to spy on U.S. citizens—even government employees and those without criminal records—will expand this summer when its new facial recognition database becomes fully operational. The new database, called Next Generation Identification system, or NGI, will include photos of anybody who sends images as part of an application for a job that requires fingerprinting or a background check.

The Muslim-Americans monitored by the government included Nihad Awad, the executive director and founder of the Council on American-Islamic Relations, a Muslim advocacy and civil rights organization. The group has been represented by the Electronic Frontier Foundation in a case challenging the NSA's mass collection of Americans' call records.

"These disclosures yet again demonstrate the need for ongoing public attention to the government's activities to ensure that its surveillance stays within the bounds of law and the Constitution," said a blog post from EFF Staff Attorney Mark Rumold. "And they once again demonstrate the need for immediate and comprehensive surveillance law reform."

Spying on Occupy Activists: How Cops and Homeland Security Help Wall Street

By Matthew Rothschild
The Progressive, June 2013

Over the last few years, the Department of Homeland Security and local law enforcement officers have engaged in widespread domestic spying on Occupy Wall Street activists, among others, on the shaky premise that these activists pose a terrorist threat. Often, Homeland Security and other law enforcement agencies have coordinated with the private sector, working on behalf of, or in cooperation with, Wall Street firms and other companies the protesters have criticized.

Thousands of public documents recently obtained by DBA Press and the Center for Media and Democracy add new evidence to an increasingly powerful case that law enforcement has been overstepping its bounds. The documents, obtained through state and federal open records searches and Freedom of Information Act requests, demonstrate that law enforcement agencies may be attempting to criminalize thousands of American citizens for simply voicing their disapproval of corporate dominance over our economic and political system.

The anti-terrorist apparatus that the U.S. government established after 9/11 has now been turned against law-abiding citizens exercising their First Amendment rights. This apparatus consists not only of advanced surveillance technologies but also of "fusion centers" in state after state that coordinate the efforts of law enforcement up and down the line and collaborate with leading members of the private sector. Often, the work they do in the name of national security advances the interests of some of the largest corporations in America rather than focusing on protecting the United States from actual threats or attacks, such as the one at the Boston Marathon on April 15.

"The government has built a giant domestic surveillance apparatus in the name of homeland security that has been unleashed on ordinary Americans expressing concern about the undue influence of corporations on our democracy," says Lisa Graves, the executive director of the Center for Media and Democracy and the former senior legislative strategist on national security for the ACLU. "Millions and millions of our tax dollars are being squandered violating the rights of innocent

Americans who dare to dissent about legal policies and who have zero connection to any violent crime intended to cause terror."

The documents reveal many instances of such misdirected work by law enforcement around the country. The picture they paint of law enforcement in the Phoenix area is a case in point. The police departments there, working with a statewide fusion center and heavily financed by the Department of Homeland Security, devoted tremendous resources to tracking and infiltrating Occupy Phoenix and other activist groups.

In October 2011, Jamie Dimon, the president and CEO of JPMorgan Chase, was coming to town. A giant on Wall Street, Dimon heads the largest bank in the country, which played a pivotal and disreputable role in the collapse of the U.S. economy in 2008. Dimon was holding an event with thousands of his employees at Chase Field, home of the Arizona Diamondbacks, in downtown Phoenix. Four days before the meeting, JPMorgan Chase's regional security manager, Dan Grady, called detective Jennifer O'Neill of the Homeland Defense Bureau of the Phoenix Police Department and told her of the impending event. The two of them were primarily concerned that activists who had recently formed the group Occupy Phoenix might try to disrupt the event—or otherwise inconvenience Dimon.

O'Neill made it her job to monitor possible "terrorist" activity by Occupy Phoenix connected with Dimon's visit.

The monitoring of social media for JPMorgan Chase is just a glimpse into the widespread snooping on Occupy activists that Arizona law enforcement engaged in, often on behalf of the private sector. O'Neill serves as the coordinator of the "Community Liaison Program" of the Arizona Counter Terrorism Information Center, which is the state's fusion center. That center consists of representatives from the Phoenix, Mesa, and Tempe police departments' homeland defense units; the Maricopa County Sheriff's Office; the Arizona Department of Public Safety Intelligence Unit; the FBI Arizona Joint Terrorism Task Force; Arizona Infragard, an FBI-business alliance; and Homeland Security. The fusion center received $30,000 in funding from Homeland Security in 2012 for "advertising" its work, and expanding private sector participation in it.

O'Neill often shares intelligence from this center with the security chiefs at banks and other corporations. The stated purpose of the liaison program is to prevent terrorist activity, to identify terrorist threats, protect critical infrastructure, and "create an awareness of localized security issues, challenges, and business interdependencies." But records indicate that it was often used as an advance warning system to alert corporations and banks of impending Occupy Phoenix protests.

O'Neill had good intelligence on Occupy Phoenix, since the police department had sent an undercover cop to attend some of the earliest meetings of the group. The impostor presented himself as a homeless Mexican national named Saul De-Lara, and he attended the Occupy Phoenix planning meeting held on October 2 at a local coffee shop. He delivered a detailed report on the activists' plans to Sergeant Tom Van Dorn of the Phoenix Police Department's Major Offender Bureau Career

Criminal Squad. Meanwhile, the Phoenix Police Department was continually monitoring the group's Facebook page at the urging of Van Dorn.

The Phoenix Police Department held an "Occupy Arizona Event Planning Meeting" in early October 2011, which was attended by two detectives from the department who also worked as Terrorism Liaison Officers for the Arizona Counter Terrorism Information Center. The Phoenix Convention Center's head of security was also invited to the meeting. The department came up with an "incident action plan" to handle protests, which included "mass arrest" teams and the possible formation of a "mobile field force" or "tactical response unit" empowered to use pepper spray and chemical agents.

Detective Christopher "CJ" Wren, one of the Terrorism Liaison Officers, was designated as the "group supervisor" of the incident action plan. He worked with the Phoenix Fire Department as well as the Phoenix Drug Enforcement Bureau, which assigned thirteen undercover vice unit officers to the Occupy Phoenix events.

> **The monitoring of social media for JPMorgan Chase is just a glimpse into the widespread snooping on Occupy activists that Arizona law enforcement engaged in, often on behalf of the private sector.**

The Phoenix Police Department was also working closely with the Downtown Phoenix Partnership. That group "exists to strengthen Downtown Phoenix development and to encourage an environment of activity, energy, and vitality," says its website. Among its board members are executives from such financial institutions as the Alliance Bank of Arizona, the consulting firm Ernst & Young, the huge mining company Freeport-McMoRan, and Republic Media, which owns the state's largest newspaper, *The Arizona Republic*, as well as the Phoenix NBC affiliate.

The Phoenix Police Department called this downtown group a "strategic partner" in preparation for Occupy Phoenix events. The police department briefed downtown banks about planned protests and, according to one document, vowed that it would continue to work with them on this issue.

On October 14, about 300 protesters assembled at Civic Space Park in downtown Phoenix and marched peacefully to Chase Tower, Bank of America, and Wells Fargo Plaza. The police made no arrests that day.

On October 15, some 1,000 protesters gathered in Cesar Chavez Plaza, and several hundred of them marched to a nearby park, where police officers began issuing warnings to protesters to disperse at 11 p.m. The police arrested forty-five protesters for refusing to leave the park, and three more at Cesar Chavez Plaza—one for trespassing and two for "creating an unsafe hazard in the street."

The Phoenix Police Department spent $245,200.08 in taxpayer funds on the policing of Occupy Phoenix between October 14 and October 16, 2011, according to the documents obtained by DBA Press and the Center for Media and Democracy.

But that wasn't the end of the surveillance. In an October 17 e-mail, the Phoenix Police Department assistant chief in charge of the Homeland Security Division, Tracy Montgomery, asked another officer to "gather intel" from "folks monitoring social media, and any other intel streams and give an update on our potential for ongoing 'Occupy' protests this week" and insisted on figuring out a "plan for monitoring these individuals long term."

The long-term monitoring meant police were watching Occupy Phoenix members' Facebook conversations and personal social media use well into 2012.

One member of the Phoenix Police Department seemed to do little else during the fall of 2011 and much of 2012 besides keeping tabs on Occupy Phoenix. Brenda Dowhan is with the department's Homeland Defense Bureau and serves as a Terrorism Liaison All-Hazards intelligence analyst with the Arizona Counter Terrorism Information Center. Much of her work involved the monitoring of social media sites such as Facebook to track individuals connected to Occupy Phoenix. She distributed the information she gathered to other law enforcement agencies, including the FBI.

"Tracking the activities of Occupy Phoenix is one of my daily responsibilities," Dowhan wrote in one e-mail to FBI agent Alan McHugh. "My primary role is to look at the social media, websites, and blogs. I just wanted to put it out there so that if you would like me to share with you or you have something to share, we can collaborate."

During the October 2011 events, she drafted alerts to Downtown Phoenix Partnership Members and advised other business members to contact police if they experienced "problems with demonstrators."

When a Mesa detective told her that a Mesa city council member had said that he had been invited to join a Bank of America protest by members of Occupy Phoenix, Dowhan alerted other officers at the Phoenix Police Department and at the Arizona Counter Terrorism Information Center.

On November 3, 2011, the Mesa Police Department's Intelligence and Counter Terrorism Unit issued a bulletin on "Bank Transfer Day," the nationwide effort by the Occupy movement to get people to withdraw funds from the giant banks. O'Neill contacted Dowhan and asked whether there was "anything downtown banks need to know that would be more beneficial." Dowhan responded: "Occupy Phoenix just updated their page saying that they will be marching to Wells Fargo, B of A [Bank of America], and Chase Tower. They are supposed to hold a 'credit card shredding ceremony,' but we haven't identified which bank they will be doing that at. We will have to monitor their FB [Facebook]."

To facilitate Dowhan's work, other Phoenix police officers regularly fed her logs containing the names, addresses, Social Security numbers, physical descriptions, driver's licenses, and home addresses of citizens arrested, issued citations, or even given warnings by police in connection with Occupy Phoenix.

Dowhan also used facial recognition technology to try to identify individuals believed to be involved with the Occupy group. Dowhan grabbed photographs of activists on Facebook and then ran them through their facial recognition system.

Here is one example of the use of facial recognition. On November 18, 2011, the Arizona Counter Terrorism Information Center got an anonymous tip about an "Occupy nut" who was allegedly making vague violent threats. "Since I'm aware no crime has technically been committed," the tipster wrote, "I've got an actual crime for you as well: illegal possession/use of marijuana. I've seen her smoking it on camera. I will attempt to get a picture in the future." The tipster proceeded to get a photograph of the activist at her computer.

Dowhan tried to take it from there. "We have a Facebook photo and tried to do facial recognition, but she was wearing glasses," wrote Dowhan in a December 23 e-mail.

Dowhan didn't confine herself to Arizona. She compiled a spreadsheet from data supplied by thirty-one fusion centers from around the country of the emerging Occupy movement in fifty cities and twenty-six states. Whatever the excitement this work might generate for a busybody like Dowhan, a summary of that report noted that "the vast majority of the participants have been peaceful, cooperative, and law abiding."

One citizen who complained about the Phoenix Police Department's crackdown on Occupy immediately became a subject of inquiry by the department. On December 14, 2011, a concerned citizen by the name of David Mullin wrote an e-mail to the department.

"Dear Sir or Madam," the e-mail began. "Please consider leaving the Occupy movement alone. They speak for me and I suspect a large portion of America who are upset with corporate greed and the ability to purchase politicians and their votes. We are going to take America back for its citizens, and it would probably be better for your careers not to get in the way. Thanks, David Mullin."

Mullin was apparently reacting to a police raid on Occupy Phoenix's small camp in Cesar Chavez Plaza on December 8, when police arrested six activists on charges of violating the city's "urban camping" ordinance.

Within minutes of sending his e-mail, Mullin caught the attention of the Phoenix Police Department's assistant chief in charge of the Homeland Security Division, Tracy Montgomery, who wrote in an e-mail: "Interesting e-mail threatening our careers. Anyone know the name?"

That very evening, the department's Homeland Defense Bureau commander, Geary Brase, told Lieutenant Lawrence Hein to have someone check out the e-mail. That someone was Dowhan.

At 6:51 the next morning, Dowhan e-mailed a link to Mullin's Facebook page to Hein. One fellow officer sent Dowhan a note of congratulation: "Great work Brenda!"

As she continued her spy work, Dowhan became concerned that she might be detected online and asked her superiors if they could get her a "clean computer," possibly one with an "anonymizer."

Meanwhile, Dowhan's undercover colleague, Saul DeLara, was having a harder time remaining anonymous.

In July 2011, a Phoenix-area activist, Ian Fecke-Stoudt, mentioned that "a creepy guy who looked like he was probably a cop" had been hanging around Conspire, a coffeehouse in downtown Phoenix. (In 2010, it won the title of "Best Hangout for Anarchists, Revolutionaries, and Dreamers" by the *Phoenix New Times* but has since gone out of business.)

According to Fecke-Stoudt, the man was clean-cut and middle-aged. He introduced himself as "Saul DeLara." Despite a fit appearance, he claimed to be homeless—and commented frequently on trouble he had had with police during his life on the street. He said he was a native of Juarez, Mexico, but seldom disclosed any other details of his personal life other than to mention that he had ties to anarchists there.

In an October 3 e-mail, Sergeant Van Dorn of the department's Major Offender Program wrote that "Saul attended the '#OccupyPhoenix' meeting at Conspire on 10/2." Van Dorn circulated DeLara's notes of items from the meeting. One item the activists mentioned was "working with police." They even discussed making "You are one of us signs." In a November 3 e-mail, Van Dorn wrote: "Saul will be spending today and tomorrow hanging out in the Plaza and with the Anarchists to try and gather additional information."

DeLara continued to inform on Phoenix activists until November 9, 2011. In his final month, much of his attention was centered on a pending protest against the American Legislative Exchange Council (ALEC). That protest, which occurred on November 30, took place outside the gates of the Westin Kierland Resort and Spa in Scottsdale, where ALEC was holding its States and Nation Policy Summit.

ALEC claims to have 2,000 state lawmakers as members, who meet with representatives from the nation's leading corporations and conservative think tanks to come up with "model" legislation. It has sparked criticism in recent years for disseminating voter ID bills and especially "Stand Your Ground" legislation, which created a controversy following the 2012 shooting death of Florida teenager Trayvon Martin.

In Arizona, activists denounced ALEC for promoting the "No More Sanctuary Cities for Illegal Immigrants Act." The nation's leading operator of for-profit prisons and immigrant detention facilities—Corrections Corporation of America—was a longstanding member and underwriter of the ALEC Public Safety and Elections Task Force. The second and third largest private prison and detention center operators—the Geo Group and the Management and Training Corporation—also have had ALEC ties.

And so, when law enforcement got wind of the ALEC protest, it sent Saul on a mission.

An e-mail to police higher ups about that meeting stated: "Bosses: Saul attended an organizational meeting for the disrupt ALEC movement last night at [redacted]. The flyers they handed out for upcoming meetings, locations, and planned events can all be found on their website. . . . Members of the Occupy movement are joining in the effort to protest and disrupt at the ALEC conference as well. Information to follow on their FB [Facebook] page soon. . . . Because ALEC helped write/sponsor SB 1070, the Hispanic community is joining in on the efforts as well. . . . In addition to the Kierland Resort several other locations are being targeted for disruption and are listed on the above website."

Members of the Phoenix Police Department met with the head of security for the Westin Kierland at the Arizona fusion center to go over the upcoming ALEC protest. And the Phoenix Police Department came up with a "Face Sheet" about activists involved in the planning for the ALEC protest. Fecke-Stoudt was on it, with his driver's license photo. So too was Jason Ohdner, a Quaker street medic who was present at the November 9 ALEC protest meeting.

But DeLara's time as an infiltrator was up. After the meeting, an immigrants' rights activist approached him and confronted him about his life as a cop. According to the activist, she had worked as a barista at a Phoenix Starbucks years ago that DeLara often patronized. When she confronted him, DeLara denied having ever seen her before and angrily denied being a cop. Nevertheless, word of DeLara's law enforcement background spread, blowing his cover. While he was at it, though, he rubbed elbows not only with members of Occupy Phoenix and the ALEC protesters but also with faith-based organizations and immigrant and indigenous rights groups.

Here is the response the Phoenix Police Department gave me to questions I asked about DeLara and its tracking of the Occupy movement.

"Occupy presented itself with a great deal of civil unrest over a long period of time," wrote Sergeant Trent Crump in an e-mail to me. "We monitored available Intel during that time, as it is used for Intel-driven policing. Intel dictated resources and response tactics to address, mitigate, and manage the ongoing activity, which was fluid and changing day to day. This approach ensured that citizens could exercise their rights, but with our efforts of protecting the community and their property at the same time. I will not confirm any information about a possible plainclothes or undercover officer of this department."

The Arizona fusion centers and the Phoenix Police Department's obsession with the Occupy movement and the ALEC protest led them to monitor a visit by civil rights leader Jesse Jackson. He was scheduled to be the keynote speaker at the "We Are One" conference on December 2, 2011. It was sponsored by the Coalition of Black Trade Unionists, the NAACP, the National Council of La Raza, and numerous other labor and civil rights groups.

Phoenix police officers working with the fusion center noted that Jackson got to town early and met with members of Occupy Phoenix on November 30.

"At approximately 2100 hour, Jessie [sic] Jackson and a few staff members arrived at the protest and spoke with demonstrators," an internal police department e-mail states. "He stayed for a little more than an hour, and a couple of media outlets arrived and filmed the visit."

The police department's counter-terrorism officers were concerned that Jackson was also going to join the ALEC protests and participate in an Occupy Phoenix march to the offices of Freeport-McMoRan. (Freeport-McMoRan served as a sponsor for the ALEC State and Nation Policy Summit.)

> **What emerges is a "disturbing picture of federal law enforcement agencies using their vast power in a systematic effort to surveil and disrupt peaceful demonstrations," said Mara Verheyden-Hilliard, executive director of the Partnership for Civil Justice Fund.**

Jackson did go to those events. When the crowd got to the Freeport-McMoRan building, Jackson said, "We are the people who care about and love this country," according to the *Downtown Devil*, a student newspaper of Arizona State University's Phoenix campus. "March on day after day until there is justice and love and healing in the land." The march headed to Cesar Chavez Plaza, where Jackson added: "Occupy is a spirit—a spirit of patriotism and democracy. That spirit cannot be jailed or pepper-sprayed."

The intrusive and ridiculously wasteful anti-terrorism effort in Phoenix is just one snapshot in a huge album of information that DBA Press and the Center for Media and Democracy have uncovered about law enforcement and counterterrorism resources being used to track peaceful protesters. According to the documents, police departments around the country, along with the FBI, were monitoring the Occupy movement.

They also were coordinating their responses. On October 11, 2011, "representatives from thirteen police agencies took part in a telephone conference to address shared concerns" about "the growing protests," said one e-mail circulating in the Phoenix Police Department. "The conference call ended with the understanding of continued efforts by all agencies involved to work together to come up with effective strategies to address issues that arise from the Occupy Wall Street protests in future days and weeks."

And the documents reveal that law enforcement, from Homeland Security and the U.S. Capitol Police Office of Intelligence Analysis down to the Phoenix Police Department, monitored activists who opposed the National Defense Authorization Act, which gives the president the right to toss any person into jail and deprive that person of due process.

The documents obtained by DBA Press and the Center for Media and Democracy jibe with other evidence about the role of Homeland Security, the FBI, and local law enforcement in tracking the Occupy movement and other left-wing activism.

An early April release of government documents obtained through the Freedom of Information Act by the Partnership for Civil Justice Fund shows that Homeland Security included in its daily intelligence briefing a report on "Peaceful Activist Demonstrations." Their documents note that the FBI treated the Occupy movement as a potential terrorist threat. They show Homeland Security surveillance of protests in Asheville, Boston, Chicago, Dallas, Detroit, Fort Lauderdale, Houston, Jacksonville, Jersey City, Lincoln, Miami, Minneapolis, Phoenix, and Salt Lake City.

What emerges is a "disturbing picture of federal law enforcement agencies using their vast power in a systematic effort to surveil and disrupt peaceful demonstrations," said Mara Verheyden-Hilliard, executive director of the Partnership for Civil Justice Fund.

Other bits of the story have come from various news organizations, including WikiLeaks. In February of 2012, it released a Department of Homeland Security document, dated October 2011, that was entitled "Special Coverage: Occupy Wall Street." The first sentence, in bold, reads: "Mass gatherings associated with public protest movements can have disruptive effects on transportation, commercial, and government services, especially when staged in major metropolitan areas. Large scale demonstrations also carry the potential for violence, presenting a significant challenge for law enforcement."

It noted "the peaceful nature of the protests" but warned that "the growing support for the OWS movement has . . . increased the potential for violence." The document, first reported on by *Rolling Stone,* concluded that "heightened and continuous situational awareness" was required.

The surveillance of the Occupy movement is part of an alarming pattern of infringement of Americans' civil liberties since 9/11. Law enforcement agents from campus police all the way up to the National Guard and the Pentagon have gotten into the act, treating lawful political protest as tantamount to terrorism. The creation of Joint Terrorism Task Forces and fusion centers has spawned the widespread sharing of personal information on perfectly innocent demonstrators. The close relationship between these law enforcement groups and the private sector (as well as the FBI-business association Infragard) has blurred their allegiances.

Fusion centers, in particular, have become founts of faulty information. An October 2012 report by the Senate Committee on Homeland Security and Governmental Affairs concluded that "fusion centers forwarded 'intelligence' of uneven quality—oftentimes shoddy, rarely timely, sometimes endangering citizens' civil liberties and Privacy Act protections, occasionally taken from already published public sources, and more often than not unrelated to terrorism." In fact, in the thirteen-month period that the committee studied fusion centers, it concluded that it "could identify no reporting which uncovered a terrorist threat."

The History of Surveillance and the Black Community

By Nadia Kayyali
Electronic Frontier Foundation, February 13, 2014

February is Black History Month and that history is intimately linked with surveillance by the federal government in the name of "national security."

Indeed, the history of surveillance in the African-American community plays an important role in the debate around spying today and in the calls for a congressional investigation into that surveillance. Days after the first NSA leaks emerged last June, EFF called for a new Church Committee. . . . Dr. Martin Luther King, Jr., was one of the targets of the very surveillance that eventually led to the formation of the first Church Committee. This Black History Month, we should remember the many African-American activists who were targeted by intelligence agencies. Their stories serve as cautionary tales for the expanding surveillance state.

The latest revelations about surveillance are only the most recent in a string of periodic public debates around domestic spying perpetrated by the NSA, FBI, and CIA. This spying has often targeted politically unpopular groups or vulnerable communities, including anarchists, anti-war activists, communists, and civil rights leaders.

Government surveillance programs, most infamously the FBI's "COINTELPRO," targeted Black Americans fighting against segregation and structural racism in the 1950s and 1960s. COINTELPRO, short for Counter Intelligence Program, was started in 1956 by the FBI and continued until 1971. The program was a systemic attempt to infiltrate, spy on, and disrupt activists in the name of "national security." While it initially focused on the Communist Party, in the 1960s its focus expanded to include a wide swathe of activists, with a strong focus on the Black Panther Party and civil rights leaders such as Dr. Martin Luther King, Jr.

FBI papers show that in 1962 "the FBI started and rapidly continued to gravitate toward Dr. King." This was ostensibly because the FBI believed black organizing was being influenced by communism. In 1963 FBI Assistant Director William Sullivan recommended "increased coverage of communist influence on the Negro." However, the FBI's goal in targeting Dr. King was clear: to find "avenues of approach aimed at neutralizing King as an effective Negro leader," because the FBI was concerned that he might become a "messiah."

The FBI subjected Dr. King to a variety of tactics, including bugging his hotel rooms, photographic surveillance, and physical observation of King's movements by FBI agents. The FBI's actions went beyond spying on Dr. King, however. Using information gained from that surveillance, the FBI sent him anonymous letters attempting to "blackmail him into suicide." The agency also attempted to break up his marriage by sending selectively edited "personal moments he shared with friends and women" to his wife.

The FBI also specifically targeted the Black Panther Party with the intention of destroying it. They infiltrated the Party with informants and subjected members to repeated interviews. Agents sent anonymous letters encouraging violence between street gangs and the Panthers in various cities, which resulted in "the killings of four BPP members and numerous beatings and shootings," as well as letters sowing internal dissension in the Panther Party. The agency also worked with police departments to harass local branches of the Party through raids and vehicle stops. In one of the most disturbing examples of this, the FBI provided information to the Chicago Police Department that aided in a raid on BPP leader Fred Hampton's apartment. The raid ended with the Chicago Police shooting Hampton dead.

The FBI was not alone in targeting civil rights leaders. The NSA also engaged in domestic spying that included Dr. King. In an eerily prescient statement, Senator Walter Mondale said he was concerned that the NSA "could be used by President 'A' in the future to spy upon the American people, to chill and interrupt political dissent."

The Church Committee was created in response to these and other public scandals, and was charged with getting to the bottom of the government's surveillance overreach. In response to its findings, Congress passed new laws to provide privacy safeguards, including the Foreign Intelligence Surveillance Act. But ever since these safeguards were put in place, the intelligence community has tried to weaken or operate around them. The NSA revelations show the urgent need to reform the laws governing surveillance and to rein in the intelligence community.

Today we're responding to those domestic surveillance abuses by an unrestrained intelligence branch. The overreach we've seen in the past underscores the need for reform. Especially during Black History Month, let's not forget the speech-stifling history of US government spying that has targeted communities of color.

A Racial "Big Brother" Debacle: Why Is the Government Spying on Black Lives Matter Protests?

By Heather Digby Parton
Salon.com, March 19, 2015

It's comforting that we have the assurance of everyone from the president on down that the government has no interest in intruding on the lives of fellow Americans without cause as they did back in the bad old days. After all, in these days of hyper awareness over the terrorist threat, it doesn't take much imagination to see how that sort of thing could get out of hand, so it's important that they follow the rules. Now there was a time when the cause of anti-communism required that we be extra-vigilant because the Russians were coming and dissent was closely monitored by police and the FBI in order that the government keep tabs on all those potential commie infiltrators such as Martin Luther King and John Lennon.

And even quite recently, it was found that the authorities had peace activists under surveillance in the wake of 9/11. *The Washington Post* reported in 2006:

> A database managed by a secretive Pentagon intelligence agency called Counterintelligence Field Activity, or CIFA, was found last month to contain reports on at least four dozen antiwar meetings or protests, many of them on college campuses. Ten peace activists who handed out peanut butter and jelly sandwiches outside Halliburton's headquarters in Houston in June 2004 were reported as a national security threat. So were people who assembled at a Quaker meeting house in Lake Worth, Fla., or protested military recruiters at sites such as New York University, the State University of New York and campuses of the University of California at Berkeley and at Santa Cruz.

> The protesters were written up under a Pentagon program called Talon, which is supposed to collect raw data on threats to defense facilities in the United States. CIFA, an agency created just under four years ago that now includes nine directorates and more than 1,000 employees, is charged with working to prevent terrorist attacks.

The logic that *peace* activists must be in league with terrorists has never been adequately explained, but it follows along the same line of thought which leads conservatives to assume that decadent left-wing hippies are natural allies of Muslim fundamentalists. The great sage of late twentieth-century conservative philosophy, Ann Coulter, said it best:

> We need to execute people like John Walker [Lindh] in order to physically intimidate liberals, by making them realize that they can be killed, too. Otherwise, they will turn out to be outright traitors.

She later clarified that statement by saying, "When I said we should 'execute' John Walker Lindh, I mis-spoke. What I meant to say was, 'We should burn John Walker Lindh alive and televise it on prime-time network TV.' My apologies for any misunderstanding that might have occurred." Yes, she said we should burn him alive on television.

The Pentagon ended the appropriately dystopian sounding program Talon, although it's hard to know exactly what any of the agencies charged with keeping the terrorist threat at bay are really doing because they are secret. Edward Snowden's revelations only involved the most sophisticated of high-tech government surveillance activities. It was shocking because of the sweeping nature of the programs and the fact that the NSA said outright that the mission was to "collect it all."

But perhaps the more prosaic forms of domestic surveillance activity should concern us as well. For instance, Lee Fang reported at *The Intercept*:

> Members of an FBI Joint Terrorism Task Force tracked the time and location of a Black Lives Matter protest last December at the Mall of America in Bloomington, Minnesota, email obtained by *The Intercept* shows.

> The email from David S. Langfellow, a St. Paul police officer and member of an FBI Joint Terrorism Task Force, informs a fellow task force member from the Bloomington police that "CHS just confirmed the MOA protest I was talking to you about today, for the 20th of DEC @ 1400 hours." CHS is a law enforcement acronym for "confidential human source."

> Jeffrey VanNest, an FBI special agent and Joint Terrorism Task Force supervisor at the FBI's Minneapolis office, was CC'd on the email. The FBI's Joint Terrorism Task Forces are based in 104 U.S. cities and are made up of approximately 4,000 federal, state and local law enforcement officials. The FBI characterizes them as "our nation's front line on terrorism."

It should be noted that this so-called threat happened months before the al-Shabab video vaguely implying a threat to the Mall was released in late February. In this earlier incident, a confidential informant told the police that someone was preparing to vandalize the mall as part of the Black Lives Matter protest. An FBI spokesman told *The Intercept* they have absolutely no interest in that campaign and that they make certain not to interfere with people exercising their rights under the First Amendment. They also noted that vandalism is not a "crime" that the Joint Terrorism Task Force is authorized to track and had no idea why it would have been informed of this information. Unfortunately, considering the federal government's history of illegally spying on Americans for any number of reasons, the burden to explain such activity belongs to them.

One thing to keep in mind is that there is no prohibition against using information of other potential crimes gleaned during terrorism related investigations to pursue non-terrorism investigations. So perhaps it's also useful to recall this exposé from a while back in which it was revealed that the DEA routinely lies about where it got information:

> A secretive U.S. Drug Enforcement Administration unit is funneling information from intelligence intercepts, wiretaps, informants and a massive database of telephone records to authorities across the nation to help them launch criminal investigations of Americans.
>
> Although these cases rarely involve national security issues, documents reviewed by *Reuters* show that law enforcement agents have been directed to conceal how such investigations truly begin—not only from defense lawyers but also sometimes from prosecutors and judges.

One of the ways they do that is by "re-creating" the investigative trail to hide how they got the information. This is routinely done to protect confidential sources from being revealed in open court, but the government has evidently decided that its secret surveillance activities now qualify for that designation as well.

There is no evidence that anything like this happened in this Black Lives Matter surveillance, but those stories illustrate just how incestuous all these police agencies are. It's not difficult to see how easy it is that members of the joint terrorist task force, whether local or federal or both, might be doing what these agencies have always done—monitor the peaceful activities of American citizens protesting their government under the guise of keeping us safe from foreign threats. Whether their information comes from secret wiretaps or secret informants, it's wrong.

All that is part of an old story in American life and one which requires that civil libertarians be constantly vigilant in keeping an eye on them and pushing back wherever possible. But Fang reports that we have gone to a new level of Big Brotherism with the Mall of America:

> As reported by the *Star Tribune*, emails released earlier this week reveal apparent coordination between Sandra Johnson, the Bloomington city attorney, and Kathleen Allen, the Mall of America's corporate counsel. "It's the prosecution's job to be the enforcer and MOA needs to continue to put on a positive, safe face," Johnson wrote to Allen two days after the protest, encouraging the mall company to wait for a criminal charge from the city before pursuing its own lawsuit. "Agree—we would defer any civil action depending on how the criminal charges play out," Allen wrote back.

This means that the city was working hand in hand with a private corporation, using the criminal justice system as "the enforcer" to help the corporation collect money in a civil action. Evidently they felt it would look better in civil court if the protesters who were being asked to pay the costs of policing the mall during the protest had been charged. Eleven of them were hit with misdemeanors, none of them having to do with property damage or theft.

But that's not the most chilling part. In a follow-up article, Fang revealed something even more insidious:

> Documents obtained by *The Intercept* indicate that security staff at the Mall of America in Bloomington, Minnesota, used a fake Facebook account to monitor local Black Lives Matter organizers, befriend them, and obtain their personal information and photographs without their knowledge.
>
> Evidence of the fake Facebook account was found in a cache of files provided by the Mall of America to Bloomington officials after a large Black Lives Matter event at the mall on December 20 protesting police brutality. The files included briefs on individual organizers, with screenshots that suggest that much of the information was captured using a Facebook account for a person named "Nikki Larson."
>
> Metadata from some of the documents lists the software that created them as belonging to "Sam Root" at the "Mall of America." A Facebook account for a Sam Root lists his profession as "Intelligence Analyst at Mall of America."

The Mall of America corporation had been privately collecting dossiers on protesters of many kinds for months. In fact, one of the Facebook accounts used to stalk them online was created all the way back in 2009.

We know that much of our national security surveillance work has been outsourced to private companies. But that's Eisenhower's military industrial complex doing what it's been doing for 50 years.

The Mall is quite proud of its "counter-terrorism" unit called Risk Assessment and Mitigation, or RAM which is known for its aggressive behavior toward patrons, especially those who look as though they just might be terrorists (whatever those patrons look like.) For some strange reason, they seem to have thought the Black Lives Matter campaign was worthy of similar attention.

So what we have here are the national Joint Terrorism Task Force, the local police, the City Attorney and some clandestine corporate "intelligence" operation for the Mall of America all involved in the monitoring of the Black Lives Matter campaign, which is not a matter of terrorism, national security, or criminal behavior. The only known "threat" has to do with an unknown confidential informant who allegedly told police (who then informed the FBI) the protesters planned to vandalize the mall.

We know that much of our national security surveillance work has been outsourced to private companies. But that's Eisenhower's military industrial complex doing what it's been doing for 50 years. Perhaps the domestic police agencies have come up with a more modern "public/private partnership" where the private corporation does the dirty work of stalking peaceful protesters and then "confidentially informs" the police agencies who, as part of a "Joint Task Force" will keep the federal agencies in the loop. After all, it would be an infringement of the corporation's individual freedom to suggest they don't have a right to spy on anyone they choose, especially citizens protesting the police. They're just trying to keep a "positive, safe face" on the USA's single greatest achievement, the shopping mall. What could be more patriotic than that?

Black America's State of Surveillance

By Malkia Amala Cyril
The Progressive, April 2015

Ten years ago, on Martin Luther King Jr.'s birthday, my mother, a former Black Panther, died from complications of sickle cell anemia. Weeks before she died, the FBI came knocking at our door, demanding that my mother testify in a secret trial proceeding against other former Panthers or face arrest. My mother, unable to walk, refused. The detectives told my mother as they left that they would be watching her. They didn't get to do that. My mother died just two weeks later.

My mother was not the only black person to come under the watchful eye of American law enforcement for perceived and actual dissidence. Nor is dissidence always a requirement for being subject to spying. Files obtained during a break-in at an FBI office in 1971 revealed that African Americans, J. Edger Hoover's largest target group, didn't have to be perceived as dissident to warrant surveillance. They just had to be black. As I write this, the same philosophy is driving the increasing adoption and use of surveillance technologies by local law enforcement agencies across the United States.

Today, media reporting on government surveillance is laser-focused on the revelations by Edward Snowden that millions of Americans were being spied on by the NSA. Yet my mother's visit from the FBI reminds me that, from the slave pass system to laws that deputized white civilians as enforcers of Jim Crow, black people and other people of color have lived for centuries with surveillance practices aimed at maintaining a racial hierarchy.

It's time for journalists to tell a new story that does not start the clock when privileged classes learn they are targets of surveillance. We need to understand that data has historically been overused to repress dissidence, monitor perceived criminality, and perpetually maintain an impoverished underclass.

In an era of big data, the Internet has increased the speed and secrecy of data collection. Thanks to new surveillance technologies, law enforcement agencies are now able to collect massive amounts of indiscriminate data. Yet legal protections and policies have not caught up to this technological advance.

Concerned advocates see mass surveillance as the problem and protecting privacy as the goal. Targeted surveillance is an obvious answer—it may be discriminatory, but it helps protect the privacy perceived as an earned privilege of the inherently innocent.

The trouble is, targeted surveillance frequently includes the indiscriminate collection of the private data of people targeted by race but not involved in any crime.

For targeted communities, there is little to no expectation of privacy from government or corporate surveillance. Instead, we are watched, either as criminals or as consumers. We do not expect policies to protect us. Instead, we've birthed a complex and coded culture—from jazz to spoken dialects—in order to navigate a world in which spying, from AT&T and Walmart to public benefits programs and beat cops on the block, is as much a part of our built environment as the streets covered in our blood.

In a recent address, New York City Police Commissioner Bill Bratton made it clear: "2015 will be one of the most significant years in the history of this organization. It will be the year of technology, in which we literally will give to every member of this department technology that would've been unheard of even a few years ago."

> **Without oversight, accountability, transparency, or rights, predictive policing is just high-tech racial profiling—indiscriminate data collection that drives discriminatory policing practices.**

Predictive policing, also known as "Total Information Awareness," is described as using advanced technological tools and data analysis to "pre-empt" crime. It utilizes trends, patterns, sequences, and affinities found in data to make determinations about when and where crimes will occur.

This model is deceptive, however, because it presumes data inputs to be neutral. They aren't. In a racially discriminatory criminal justice system, surveillance technologies reproduce injustice. Instead of reducing discrimination, predictive policing is a face of what author Michelle Alexander calls the "New Jim Crow"—a de facto system of separate and unequal application of laws, police practices, conviction rates, sentencing terms, and conditions of confinement that operate more as a system of social control by racial hierarchy than as crime prevention or punishment.

In New York City, the predictive policing approach in use is "Broken Windows." This approach to policing places an undue focus on quality of life crimes—like selling loose cigarettes, the kind of offense for which Eric Garner was choked to death. Without oversight, accountability, transparency, or rights, predictive policing is just high-tech racial profiling—indiscriminate data collection that drives discriminatory policing practices.

As local law enforcement agencies increasingly adopt surveillance technologies, they use them in three primary ways: to listen in on specific conversations on- and offline, to observe daily movements of individuals and groups, and to observe data trends. Police departments like Bratton's aim to use sophisticated technologies to do all three.

They will use technologies like license plate readers, which the Electronic Frontier Foundation found to be disproportionately used in communities of color and communities in the process of being gentrified.

They will use facial recognition, biometric scanning software, which the FBI has now rolled out as a national system, to be adopted by local police departments for any criminal justice purpose.

They intend to use body and dashboard cameras, which have been touted as an effective step toward accountability based on the results of one study, yet storage and archiving procedures, among many other issues, remain unclear.

They will use Stingray cellphone interceptors. According to the ACLU, Stingray technology is an invasive cellphone surveillance device that mimics cellphone towers and sends out signals to trick cellphones in the area into transmitting their locations and identifying information. When used to track a suspect's cellphone, they also gather information about the phones of countless bystanders who happen to be nearby.

The same is true of domestic drones, which are in increasing use by U.S. law enforcement to conduct routine aerial surveillance. While drones are currently unarmed, drone manufacturers are considering arming these remote-controlled aircraft with weapons like rubber bullets, tasers, and tear gas.

They will use fusion centers. Originally designed to increase interagency collaboration for the purposes of counterterrorism, these have instead become the local arm of the intelligence community. According to Electronic Frontier Foundation, there are currently seventy-eight on record. They are the clearinghouse for increasingly used "suspicious activity reports"—described as "official documentation of observed behavior reasonably indicative of pre-operational planning related to terrorism or other criminal activity." These reports and other collected data are often stored in massive databases like e-Verify and Prism. As anybody who's ever dealt with gang databases knows, it's almost impossible to get off a federal or state database, even when the data collected is incorrect or no longer true.

Predictive policing doesn't just lead to racial and religious profiling—it relies on it. Just as stop and frisk legitimized an initial, unwarranted contact between police and people of color, almost 90 percent of whom turn out to be innocent of any crime, suspicious activities reporting and the dragnet approach of fusion centers target communities of color. One review of such reports collected in Los Angeles shows approximately 75 percent were of people of color.

This is the future of policing in America, and it should terrify you as much as it terrifies me. Unfortunately, it probably doesn't, because my life is at far greater risk than the lives of white Americans, especially those reporting on the issue in the media or advocating in the halls of power.

One of the most terrifying aspects of high-tech surveillance is the invisibility of those it disproportionately impacts.

The NSA and FBI have engaged local law enforcement agencies and electronic surveillance technologies to spy on Muslims living in the United States. According to FBI training materials uncovered by *Wired* in 2011, the bureau taught agents to treat "mainstream" Muslims as supporters of terrorism, to view charitable donations by Muslims as "a funding mechanism for combat," and to view Islam itself as a "Death Star" that must be destroyed if terrorism is to be contained. From New York

City to Chicago and beyond, local law enforcement agencies have expanded unlawful and covert racial and religious profiling against Muslims not suspected of any crime. There is no national security reason to profile all Muslims.

At the same time, almost 450,000 migrants are in detention facilities throughout the United States, including survivors of torture, asylum seekers, families with small children, and the elderly. Undocumented migrant communities enjoy few legal protections and are therefore subject to brutal policing practices, including illegal surveillance practices. According to the Sentencing Project, of the more than 3 million people incarcerated in the United States, more than 60 percent are racial and ethnic minorities.

But by far, the widest net is cast over black communities. Black people alone represent 40 percent of those incarcerated. More black men are incarcerated than were held in slavery in 1850, on the eve of the Civil War. Lest some misinterpret that statistic as evidence of greater criminality, a 2012 study confirms that black defendants are at least 30 percent more likely to be imprisoned than whites for the same crime.

This is not a broken system, it is a system working perfectly as intended, to the detriment of all. The NSA could not have spied on millions of cellphones if it were not already spying on black people, Muslims, and migrants.

As surveillance technologies are increasingly adopted and integrated by law enforcement agencies today, racial disparities are being made invisible by a media environment that has failed to tell the story of surveillance in the context of structural racism.

Reporters love to tell the technology story. For some, it's a sexier read. To me, freedom from repression and racism is far sexier than the newest gadget used to reinforce racial hierarchy. As civil rights protections catch up with the technological terrain, reporting needs to catch up, too. Many journalists still focus their reporting on the technological trends and not the racial hierarchies that these trends are enforcing.

Martin Luther King Jr. once said, "Everything we see is a shadow cast by that which we do not see." Journalists have an obligation to tell the stories that are hidden from view.

We are living in an incredible time, when migrant activists have blocked deportation buses, and a movement for black lives has emerged, and when women, queer, and trans experiences have been placed right at the center. The de-centralized power of the Internet makes that possible.

But the Internet also makes possible the high-tech surveillance that threatens to drive structural racism in the twenty-first century.

We can help black lives matter by ensuring that technology is not used to cement a racial hierarchy that leaves too many people like me dead or in jail. Our communities need partners, not gatekeepers.

Together, we can change the cultural terrain that makes killing black people routine. We can counter inequality by ensuring that both the technology and the police departments that use it are democratized. We can change the story on surveillance to raise the voices of those who have been left out.

There are no voiceless people, only those that ain't been heard yet. Let's birth a new norm in which the technological tools of the twenty-first century create equity and justice for all—so all bodies enjoy full and equal protection, and the Jim Crow surveillance state exists no more.

Bibliography

Ackerman, Evan. "Poll Shows Concern About Drones and Domestic Surveillance." *IEEE Spectrum*. Institute of Electrical and Electronics Engineers, June 25, 2012; http://spectrum.ieee.org/automaton/robotics/military-robots/poll-shows-concern-about-drones-and-domestic-surveillance.

"Automated License Plate Readers—State Legislation." *NCSL*. National Conference of State Legislatures, April 13, 2015, http://www.ncsl.org/research/tele-communications-and-information-technology/2014-state-legislation-related-to-automated-license-plate-recognition-information.aspx.

Ball, James. "NSA Collects Millions of Text Messages Daily in 'Untargeted' Global Sweep." *The Guardian*, January 16, 2015, http://www.theguardian.com/world/2014/jan/16/nsa-collects-millions-text-messages-daily-untargeted-global-sweep.

Bamford, James. "The Most Wanted Man in the World." *Wired*, August 2014, http://www.wired.com/2014/08/edward-snowden/.

Bankston, Kevin. "Breaking News on EFF Victory: Appeals Court Holds That Email Privacy Protected by Fourth Amendment." *Electronic Frontier Foundation*. December 14, 2010, https://www.eff.org/deeplinks/2010/12/breaking-news-eff-victory-appeals-court-holds.

Bergen, Peter, et al., *Do NSA's Bulk Surveillance Programs Stop Terrorists?* New America Foundation, January 13, 2014, http://newamerica.net/publications/policy/do_nsas_bulk_surveillance_programs_stop_terrorists.

Berry, Michael, and Nabiha Syed. "State Legislation Governing Private Drone Use." *The Washington Post*. Nash Holdings, September 25, 2014, http://www.washingtonpost.com/news/volokh-conspiracy/wp/2014/09/25/state-legislation-governing-private-drone-use/.

"Bush Lets U.S. Spy on Callers Without Courts." *The New York Times*, December 16, 2005, http://www.nytimes.com/2005/12/16/politics/16program.html?pagewanted=all.

Byman, Daniel, and Benjamin Wittes, "Reforming the NSA," *Foreign Affairs*, May–June 2014, http://www.foreignaffairs.com/articles/141215/daniel-byman-and-benjamin-wittes/reforming-the-nsa

Carson, E. Ann. "Prisoners in 2013." *BJS*. U.S. Department of Justice, September 2014, http://www.bjs.gov/content/pub/pdf/p13.pdf.

Cotrupe, Jeff. "Stratecast Confidential: The Impact of the NSA on the Big Data Market and Global Communications." Frost & Sullivan, April 2014; http://images.discover.frost.com/Web/FrostSullivan/NA%20PR_Clarissa_NSA-BDA_6Aug14_9689.pdf

"Criminal Justice Fact Sheet." *NAACP.* National Association for the Advancement of Colored People, 2015, http://www.naacp.org/pages/criminal-justice-fact-sheet.

Dahl, Erik J. *Intelligence and Surprise Attack: Failure and Success from Pearl Harbor to 9/11 and Beyond.* Washington, DC: Georgetown University Press, 2013.

Foreign Intelligence Surveillance Act of 1978.

"Global Opposition to USA Big Brother Mass Surveillance." *Amnesty.* Amnesty International, Mar. 18 2015; https://www.amnesty.org/en/articles/news/2015/03/global-opposition-to-usa-big-brother-mass-surveillance/.

"Global Opposition to U.S. Surveillance and Drones, but Limited Harm to America's Image." *Pew Global.* Pew Research Center, July 14, 2014, http://www.pewglobal.org/2014/07/14/global-opposition-to-u-s-surveillance-and-drones-but-limited-harm-to-americas-image/.

Goldfarb, Ronald. *After Snowden: Privacy, Secrecy, and Security in the Information Age.* New York: Thomas Dunne Books, 2015.

Greenwald, Glenn. "NSA Collecting Phone Records of Millions of Verizon Customers Daily." *The Guardian.* Guardian News and Media, June 6, 2013, http://www.theguardian.com/world/2013/jun/06/nsa-phone-records-verizon-court-order.

Harris, Shane, *The Watchers: The Rise of America's Surveillance State.* New York: Penguin Press, 2010.

Heath, Brad. "Racial Gap in U.S. Arrest Rates: 'Staggering Disparity.'" *USA Today.* Gannett Media, November 19, 2014, http://www.usatoday.com/story/news/nation/2014/11/18/ferguson-black-arrest-rates/19043207/.

"H.R. 2048—The USA Freedom Act." *Congress.* United States Congress, 2015, https://www.congress.gov/114/bills/hr2048/BILLS-114hr2048rh.pdf.

"H.R. 4681—Intelligence Authorization Act for Fiscal Year 2015." *Congress.* United States Congress, 2015, Web. May 1, 2015; https://www.congress.gov/bill/113th-congress/house-bill/4681

"H.R. 6304—FISA Amendments Act of 2008." *Congress.* United States Library of Congress, 2015; https://www.congress.gov/bill/110th-congress/house-bill/6304.

Jackman, Tom. "Experts say law enforcement's use of cellphone records can be inaccurate." *Washington Post*, June 27, 2014, http://www.washingtonpost.com/local/experts-say-law-enforcements-use-of-cellphone-records-can-be-inaccurate/2014/06/27/028be93c-faf3-11e3-932c-0a55b81f48ce_story.html.

Jennings, Angel, Richard Winton, and James Rainey. "L.A. County Sheriff's Dept. Used Spy Plane to Watch Compton." *Los Angeles Times*, April 23, 2014, http://www.latimes.com/local/la-me-compton-surveillance-20140424-story.html#page=1

Juul, Peter. "Adapting to the Future of Intelligence Gathering," Center for American Progress, July 23, 2013, https://cdn.americanprogress.org/wp-content/uploads/2013/07/IntelligenceGathering.pdf

Khazan, Olga. "Gentlemen Reading Each Others' Mail: A Brief History of Diplomatic Spying." *The Atlantic*, June 17, 2013, http://www.theatlantic.com/international/archive/2013/06/gentlemen-reading-each-others-mail-a-brief-history-of-diplomatic-spying/276940/.

Koebler, Jason. "North Dakota Man Sentenced to Jail in Controversial Drone-Arrest Case." *U.S. News and World Report,* January 15, 2014, http://www.usnews.com/news/articles/2014/01/15/north-dakota-man-sentenced-to-jail-in-controversial-drone-arrest-case.

Linder, Doug. "The Right to Privacy." *UMKC.* University of Missouri, Kansas City Law. Exploring Constitutional Conflicts, 2011, http://law2.umkc.edu/faculty/projects/ftrials/conlaw/rightofprivacy.html

Liu, Edward C., Andrew Nolan, and Richard M. Thompson II. "Overview of Constitutional Challenges to NSA Collection Activities and Recent Developments." *CRS.* Congressional Research Service, April 1, 2014, https://www.fas.org/sgp/crs/intel/R43459.pdf.

Lye, Linda. "Documents Reveal Unregulated Use of Stingrays in California." *ACLU.* American Civil Liberties Union, March 13, 2014, https://www.aclu.org/blog/documents-reveal-unregulated-use-stingrays-california.

Madden, Mary. "Public Perceptions of Privacy and Security in the Post-Snowden Era." *Pew Internet.* Pew Research Center, November 12, 2014, http://www.pewinternet.org/2014/11/12/public-privacy-perceptions/.

Marcos, Cristina. "In Surprise Vote, House Backs NSA Limits." *The Hill,* June 19, 2014, http://thehill.com/blogs/floor-action/house/210027-house-votes-to-limit-nsa-spying.

McNeal, Gregory. "Drones and Aerial Surveillance: Considerations for Legislators." Brookings, November 2014, http://www.brookings.edu/~/media/Research/Files/Reports/2014/10/drones-aerial-surveillance-legislators/Drones_Aerial_Surveillance_McNeal_FINAL.pdf?la=en.

"Module One – Overview and History of Racial Profiling." *MASS Gov.* Massachusetts State Government Executive Office of Public Safety and Security, 2015, http://www.mass.gov/eopss/law-enforce-and-cj/law-enforce/faip/trng-modules/module-one-overview.html.

"National Security Agency Inspector General Draft Report." *Washington Post*, June 27, 2013, http://apps.washingtonpost.com/g/page/world/national-security-agency-inspector-general-draft-report/277/.

Neuman, Scott. "Sen. Rand Paul Stages 'Filibuster' To Protest Patriot Act." *NPR News.* May 20, 2015, http://www.npr.org/sections/thetwo-way/2015/05/21/408417139/sen-rand-paul-stages-filibuster-to-protest-patriot-act.

Newton, Huey P. *War against the Panthers: A Study of Repression in America.* New York: Harlem River Press, 1998.

Offices of the Inspectors General of Department of Defense, Department of Justice, Central Intelligence Agency, National Security Agency, Office of the Director of National Intelligence. *Report on the President's Surveillance Program,* July

10, 2009, http://www.nytimes.com/interactive/2015/04/25/us/25stellarwind-ig-report.html.

Poulsen, Kevin. "Visit the Wrong Website, and the FBI Could End Up in Your Computer." *Wired*, Aug. 5 2014, http://www.wired.com/2014/08/operation_torpedo/.

"Race and Punishment: Racial Perceptions of Crime and Support for Punitive Policies." *Sentencing Project*. The Sentencing Project, September 3, 2014, http://www.sentencingproject.org/detail/news.cfm?news_id=1870.

Rainie, Lee and Mary Madden. "Americans' Views on Government Surveillance Programs." *Pew Internet*. Pew Research Center, March 16, 2015, http://www.pewinternet.org/2015/03/16/americans-views-on-government-surveillance-programs/.

"Regulations Will Facilitate Integration of Small UAS into U.S. Aviation System." *FAA*. Federal Aviation Administration, February 15, 2015, http://www.faa.gov/news/press_releases/news_story.cfm?newsId=18295&cid=TW299.

Riley, Jason L. *Please Stop Helping Up*. New York: Encounter Books, 2014.

Risen, James. *State of War: The Secret History of the CIA and the Bush Administration*. New York: Free Press, 2006.

Risen, James, and Laura Poitras. "N.S.A. Collecting Millions of Faces from Web Images." *New York Times*. New York Times Company, May 31, 2014, http://www.nytimes.com/2014/06/01/us/nsa-collecting-millions-of-faces-from-web-images.html?_r=0.

Risen, Tom. "Racial Profiling Reported in NSA, FBI Surveillance." *U.S. News and World Report,* July 9, 2014, http://www.usnews.com/news/articles/2014/07/09/racial-profiling-reported-in-nsa-fbi-surveillance.

Sakiyama, Mari, et al. "Nevada vs. U.S. Residents' Attitudes Towards Surveillance Using Aerial Drones." *UNLV*. University of Nevada Las Vegas. Center for Crime and Justice Policy, December 2014, http://www.unlv.edu/sites/default/files/page_files/27/NevadaU.S.Residents%27Attitudes.pdf.

Sanchez, Julian. "Leashing the Surveillance State: How to Reform Patriot Act Surveillance Authorities." Cato Institute, May 16, 2011, http://www.cato.org/publications/policy-analysis/leashing-surveillance-state-how-reform-patriot-act-surveillance-authorities.

Savage, Charlie. "Declassified Report Shows Doubts about Value of N.S.A.'s Warrantless Spying," *New York Times,* April 25, 2015, http://www.nytimes.com/2015/04/25/us/politics/value-of-nsa-warrantless-spying-is-doubted-in-declassified-reports.html

Savage, Charlie. "Judge Questions Legality of N.S.A. Phone Records." *New York Times,* December 16, 2013, http://www.nytimes.com/2013/12/17/us/politics/federal-judge-rules-against-nsa-phone-data-program.html.

Schneier, Bruce. "Let the NSA Keep Hold of the Data." *Slate.com*, February 14, 2014, http://www.slate.com/articles/technology/future_tense/2014/02/nsa_surveillance_metadata_the_government_not_private_companies_should_store.html.

Shipler, David K. "It's Time for a 21st Century Debate on Privacy and Surveillance." *The Nation,* June 17, 2013, http://www.thenation.com/article/174839/its-time-21st-century-debate-privacy-and-surveillance.

"The Southern 'Black Codes' of 1865–66." *CRF-USA.* Constitutional Rights Foundation, 2015; http://www.crf-usa.org/brown-v-board-50th-anniversary/southern-black-codes.html.

Steinhauer, Jennifer. "House Votes to End N.S.A.'s Bulk Phone Data Collection." *The New York Times*, May 13, 2015; http://www.nytimes.com/2015/05/14/us/house-votes-to-end-nsas-bulk-phone-data-collection.html?_r=0.

Steinhauer, Jennifer and Jonathan Weisman. "U.S. Surveillance in Place Since 9/11 Is Sharply Limited." *The New York Times*, June 2, 2015, http://www.nytimes.com/2015/06/03/us/politics/senate-surveillance-bill-passes-hurdle-but-showdown-looms.html?_r=0.

Timberg, Craig. "New Surveillance Technology Can Track Everyone in an Area for Several Hours at a Time." *The Washington Post*, February 5, 2014, http://www.washingtonpost.com/business/technology/new-surveillance-technology-can-track-everyone-in-an-area-for-several-hours-at-a-time/2014/02/05/82f1556e-87 6f-11e3-a5bd-844629433ba3_story.html.

"Transcript of Erik Dahl," interviewed by Mike German, June 2, 2014, http://www.brennancenter.org/transcript-erik-dahl

Treverton, Gregory, "Intelligence Test," *Democracy* 11 (Winter 2009), http://www.democracyjournal.org/11/6667.php?page=1

"Will Profiling Make a Difference?" *New York Times*, January 4, 2010, http://roomfordebate.blogs.nytimes.com/2010/01/04/will-profiling-make-a-difference/.

Wingfield, Nick, and Somini Sengupta. "Drones Set Sights on U.S. Skies." *New York Times,* February 17, 2012, http://www.nytimes.com/2012/02/18/technology/drones-with-an-eye-on-the-public-cleared-to-fly.html?_r=0.

Wohlstetter, Roberta. *Pearl Harbor: Warning and Decision.* Stanford, CA: Stanford University Press, 1962.

"Youth Risk Behavior Surveillance—United States, 2013." *CDC.* Centers for Disease Control and Prevention. Morbidity and Mortality Weekly Report, June 13, 2014, http://www.cdc.gov/mmwr/pdf/ss/ss6304.pdf?utm_source=rss&utm_medium=rss&utm_campaign=youth-risk-behavior-surveillance-united-states-2013-pdf.

Zetter, Kim. "The Senate Fails to Reform NSA Spying, Votes Against USA Freedom Act." *Wired*, May 23, 2015, http://www.wired.com/2015/05/senate-fails-end-nsa-bulk-spying-votes-usa-freedom-act/.

Zetter, Kim. "Tor Torches Online Tracking." *Wired*, May 17, 2005, http://archive.wired.com/politics/security/news/2005/05/67542?currentPage=all.

Websites

American Civil Liberties Union

https://www.aclu.org/

The ACLU works in courts, legislatures, and communities to fight for the individual rights and liberties guaranteed by the Constitution and the laws of the United States. In recent years, it has worked to establish new privacy protections for the digital age and in light of widespread government surveillance.

Bill of Rights Defense Committee

http://bordc.org/

This nonprofit and nonpartisan organization works with grassroots groups to educate Americans about their rights and fundamental freedoms and to encourage civic participation and convert concern and outrage over the erosion of freedom and privacy rights into political action.

Center for Democracy and Technology

https://cdt.org/

This nonprofit organization works to support laws, corporate policies, and technology tools that protect the privacy of Internet users and advocates for stronger legal controls on government surveillance.

Electronic Frontier Foundation

https://www.eff.org/

This leading nonprofit organization is devoted to defending civil liberties in the digital world "through impact litigation, policy analysis, grassroots activism, and technology development." It leads the fight against the National Security Agency's mass surveillance program.

Electronic Privacy Information Center (EPIC)

https://www.epic.org/

EPIC is an independent nonprofit research center that works to protect privacy, freedom of expression, and democratic values. The organization works with experts in law, technology, and public policy and regularly "speaks before Congress and judicial organizations about emerging privacy and civil liberties issues," especially in the light of increasing government surveillance.

National Security Agency/ Central Security Service

https://www.nsa.gov/

NSA is a major intelligence-gathering organization of the United States government. Its mission is to collect, process, and disseminate information for intelligence and counterintelligence purposes and to support military operations.

Open Technology Institute

https://www.newamerica.org/oti/

The Open Technology Institute at New America is committed to freedom and social justice in the digital age. The organization conducts data-driven research, intervenes in traditional policy debates, and builds technology designed for privacy and security. It studies the impacts of technology and policy on people, commerce, and communities, with a key focus on surveillance.

Index